COMMENTARIES

ON

THE PUNJAB CAMPAIGN, 1848-49

COMMENTARIES

ON

THE PUNJAB CAMPAIGN, 1848-49

INCLUDING

SOME ADDITIONS TO THE HISTORY OF THE SECOND SIKH WAR FROM ORIGINAL SOURCES

J. H. LAWRENCE-ARCHER, CAPT. H. P.

GYAN

Published by

GYAN

Gyan Publishing House
5, Ansari Road
Daryaganj, New Delhi-110002
Phone: 011-47034999, 9811692060
E-mail: books@gyanbooks.com

Distribution Network
gyanbooks.com
India, USA, Canada, UK, Australia, France

ISBN: 978-81-212-9402-7 (PB)
First Published, 1878

2nd Impression 2023

Printed at: Gyan Press, Delhi.

COMMENTARIES ON THE PUNJAB CAMPAIGN, 1848-49

AUTHOR: J. H. LAWRENCE-ARCHER

COMMENTARIES

ON

THE PUNJAB CAMPAIGN,

1848–49.

COMMENTARIES

ON

THE PUNJAB CAMPAIGN, 1848–49.

INCLUDING

SOME ADDITIONS TO
THE HISTORY OF THE SECOND SIKH WAR,
FROM ORIGINAL SOURCES.

BY

J. H. LAWRENCE-ARCHER, CAPT. H. P.
AUTHOR OF "THE ORDERS OF CHIVALRY," ETC.

LONDON:
WM. H. ALLEN & CO., 13 WATERLOO PLACE, S.W.

1878.

CONTENTS.

PREFATORY REMARKS.

The object of the following pages is to supply from original and official sources, information on some points of interest, which have not been fully explained either in the Despatches relating to the Punjab Campaign, or in other publications on the subject. But in order to give unity to the design, it has been deemed advisable, as succinctly as possible, to review the preceding current of events from the death of Runjeet Singh to the period in question.

The Punjab Campaign, although perhaps not one of the most brilliant, was nevertheless, as is well known, of the greatest importance in its results, while even in its temporary failures it afforded many lessons, eminently instructive, occurring, as it did, at what may be assumed to have been a period of transition, as regards our military system.

Besides the acquisition of an important and extensive territory, this campaign influenced the subsequent annexation of Oude, and, through the administrative abilities of certain eminent men, it afforded at a later period, an admirable recruiting field for our auxiliary forces, as became fully apparent, on the revolt of the Bengal army; and it is not unworthy of note, that, at the present moment, when so much uneasiness has been expressed about the Mahomedans of India, probably, the best native troops that we have—Sikhs, Goorkhas and Rajpoots—are of the Brahmanical and Buddhist creeds and their offshoots.

During this campaign, moreover, the true value of our relations with the Affghans was tested, and the lesson may again be useful.

The movements of the army proved the disadvantage of a divided command, and the dangers attending the absence of topographical knowledge and of an intelligence department. It proved the inestimable value of the Irregular Cavalry, commanded, as it was, by officers of remarkable ability. It taught us the folly of undervaluing one's enemy—of neglecting in the earlier actions the proper use of artillery—the error of placing too great a reliance on the power of the bayonet in what may be called jungle warfare—and of the disadvantages of close formations in an attenuated line which, in consequence, was further weakened by wide gaps. It also suggested salutary changes in the uniform of the troops, and the uselessness of regimental standards since arms of precision have been introduced.

With regard to the General's Despatches, a striking innovation was permitted after the battle of Googerat;

and that relating to Sadoolapore was, for so long a period suppressed, for reasons which will be apparent, that a confusion occurred in the chronology of the campaign.

There were at that time no representatives of the press with our armies, and, in consequence, while many striking incidents were overlooked, some remarkable errors—especially topographical—finding their way through private correspondents into the public papers, have ever since remained uncorrected, as a reference to the Ordnance Survey of the Punjab will satisfy the public.

It only remains to be said that, as a result of the crowning victory of Googerat, the celebrated *Koh-i-noor*, was transferred to the Imperial diadem of England.

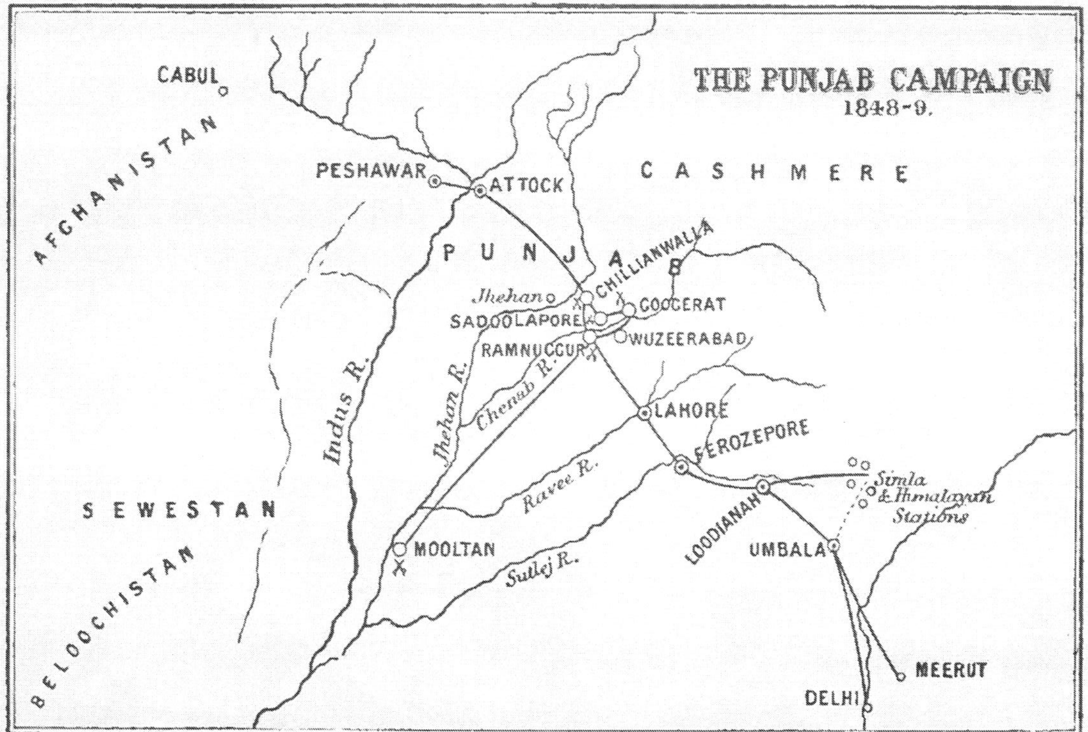
THE PUNJAB CAMPAIGN
1848-9.
CABUL
AFGHANISTAN
PESHAWAR
ATTOCK
CASHMERE
PUNJAB
CHILLIANWALLA
Jhehan
GOOGERAT
SADOOLAPORE
WUZEERABAD
RAMNUGGUR
Indus R.
Jhehan R.
Chenab R.
LAHORE
FEROZEPORE
Simla
& Himalayan
Stations
Ravee R.
SEWESTAN
MOOLTAN
Sutlej R.
LOODIANAH
UMBALA
BELOOCHISTAN
MEERUT
DELHI

THE COMBAT OF RAMNUGGUR.

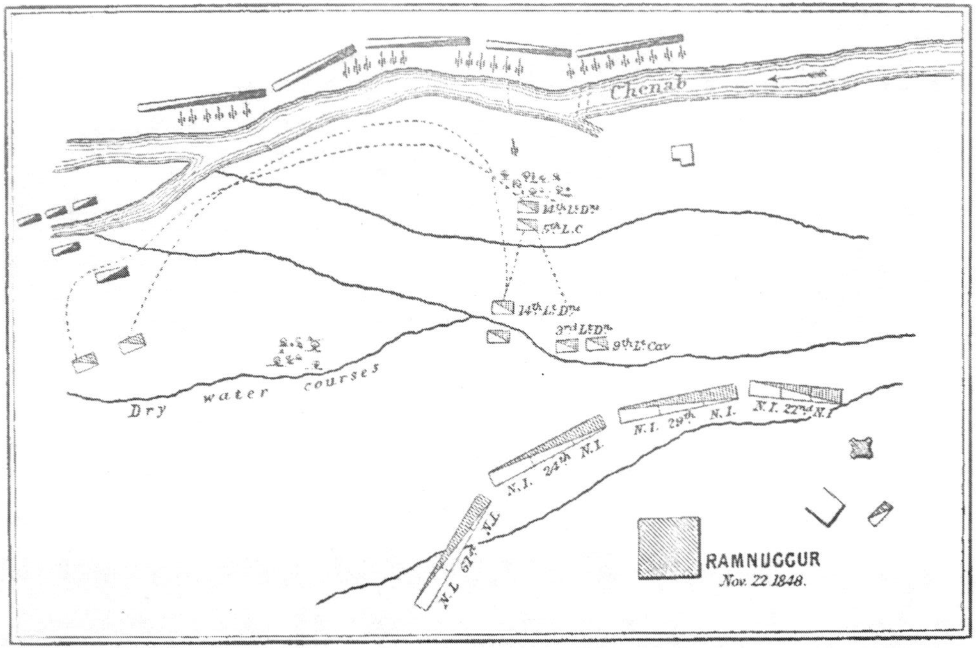

REFERENCES.

Troops of Horse Artillery accompanied the Cavalry. The remainder of the Artillery was massed in front of the Second Brigade from the right. The position of the abandoned gun is marked in front of the grove.

N.B.—For "22nd" read "2nd Europeans."

THE ACTION OF SADOOLAPORE.

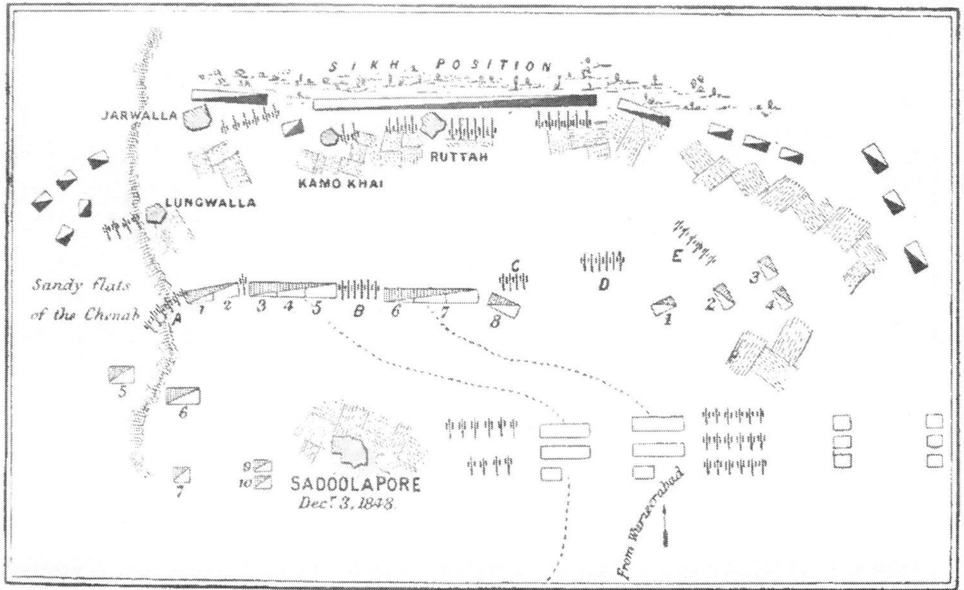

ARTILLERY, commanded by
A Warner.*
B Kinleside.†
C Austin.
D Huish.
E Christie.

* Also at Lungwalla.

CAVALRY.
1. 8th B. L. C.
2, 3, 4. 3rd Light Dragoons.
5. Tait's Horse.
6. 5th B. L. C.
7, 9, 10. Detachments.

INFANTRY.
1. 31st N.I. } Eckford's Brigade.
2. 56th N.I. }
3. 46th N.I. }
4. 36th N.I. } Hoggan's Brigade.
5. H.M. 61st }
6. H.M. 24th }
7. 25th W.I. } Pennicuick's Brigade.
8. Wing of 22nd N.I. }

THE BATTLE OF CHILLIANWALLA.

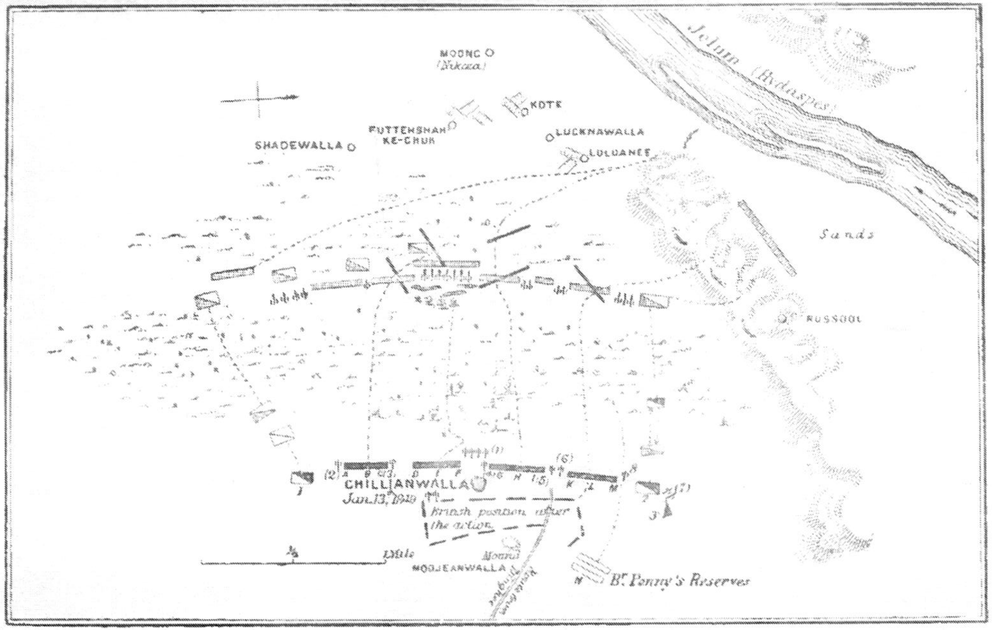

CAVALRY.

1. White's Brigade (3rd Lt. Drags., 5th and 8th Light Cavalry).
2. Pope's Brigade (14th Dragoons, squadron of 9th Lancers, &c.)

ARTILLERY.

1. Heavy guns.
2, 3, 4, 5, 6, 7, 8. Field Bat. & H.A.

INFANTRY.

A 36th N.I., B H.M. 61st, C 46th N.I. — Hoggan's Brigade.

D 45th N.I., E H.M. 24th, F 25th N.I. — Pennicuick's Brigade.

G 30th N.I., H H.M. 24th, I 56th N.I. — Mountain's Brigade.

K 31st N.I., L 2nd Europeans, M 70th N.I. — Godby's Brigade.

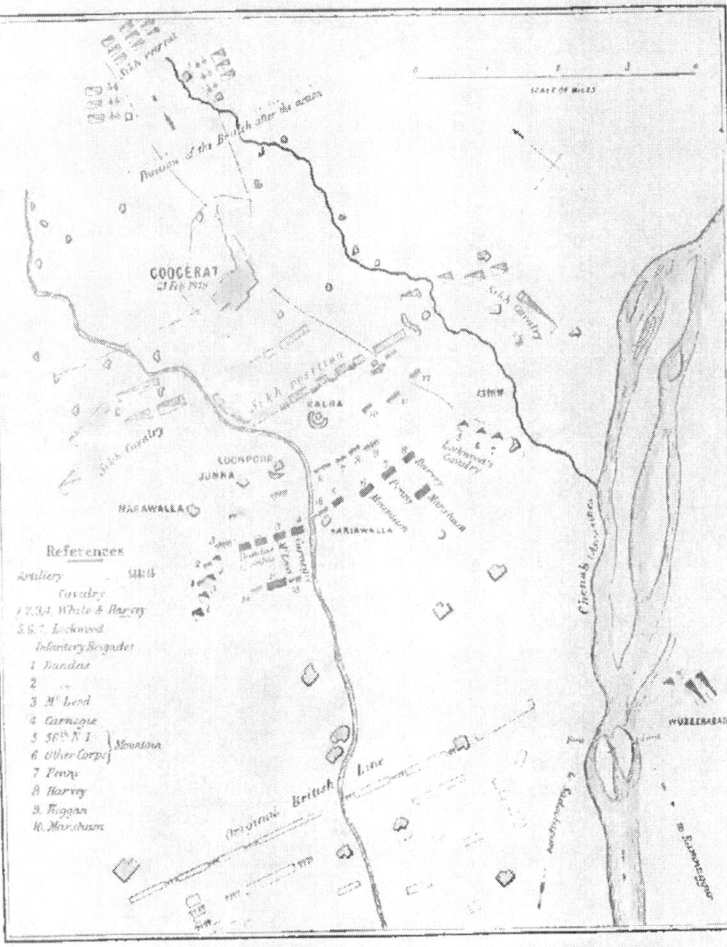

THE BATTLE OF GOOGERAT.

The troops and batteries of Artillery in the above Plan were commanded by the following officers:-

1. Huish.
2 Duncan.
3. Dlood.
4. Ludlow.
5. Robertson.
6. Lane (previously 11)
7. Day
8 Dawes.
9. Hersford.
10. Fordyce.
11. Anderson.
12. Mackenzie.
13. Warner
14. See No. 8.
15. Kinleside
16. Shakespeare.

COMMENTARIES

ON THE

PUNJAB CAMPAIGN.

CHAPTER I.

ON the death of Runjeet Singh, the celebrated sovereign of the Punjab, in 1844, and the accession of his son, the youthful Duleep Singh, powerless in the tutelage of the Regent-mother at Lahore, the Khalsa, or Sikh army, mutinied. The British frontier was threatened, and, in the summer of the following year, the Sikhs boldly crossed the boundary river Sutlej, and invaded the British territory.

The Governor-General pressed by Lord Gough, the Commander-in-Chief, who fully realised the danger, hastily assembled, by forced marches, a small army, which was immediately encountered by the enemy; and the first battle, "Midnight Moodkhee," was lost by the invaders. In rapid succession followed the victories of Aliwal, Ferozeshuhr, and Sobraon; at the last of which the Khalsa, utterly routed, was driven in disorder across the Sutlej.

But the Sikhs thus conquered were not subdued, and although the result of this, the first Sikh war, was the establishment of a British Resident at the Court of Lahore, it remained for Lord Dalhousie, his successor, to follow up the temporising policy of Lord Hardinge, by the annexation of the Punjab.

Two years after these events, Lord Dalhousie arrived in India (12th Jan. 1848), and a few days later his predecessor embarked (18th Jan.) for England.

"In the Punjab everything seemed to betoken a long continuance of peace," so far as peace can ever be of long duration in India; and throughout the country of the Five Rivers, "English officers, civil and military, were quietly drilling" their late enemies, and "giving lessons in good government" to respectful Sikh officials.

About that time the Dewan or Governor of Mooltan was treating with the Council of Regency at Lahore about the surrender of his post; for, disgusted with the unaccustomed checks placed by his nominal masters on his once unbounded sway, he sought to be released from his thankless post.

On the 18th of April, while the change of governors was being effected at Mooltan, under the superintendance of two British officers, Mr. Vans Agnew and Lieut. Anderson, the latter were suddenly attacked and wounded, and, on the 20th, their place of retreat having been taken by assault, they were slain, under circumstances of great barbarity.

What part the ex-Dewan Moolraj really took in this tragedy has never been clearly shown; but it seemed now to be incumbent on him to head the movement to expel the British from his country, and to stir up Sikhs, Hindus, and Mussulmans alike to defend their nationality, under the name of a Holy War.

While the British Resident at Lahore, justly apprehensive, was urging the Commander-in-Chief to move up troops from Ferozepore, in order to crush the insurrection before it should become general, Col. Cortlandt and Lieut. Herbert Edwardes, afterwards so much distinguished, were already marching with a few thousand Sikhs (still well affected), and Pathans, towards the scene of the coming struggle. On the 18th June was fought between them and the Mooltanees, the combat of Kineyrie, followed on the 1st July by that of Suddosam, when Moolraj fled to the security of Mooltan, which he prepared to defend.

A plot was now discovered to massacre the British officers at Lahore. The principals were executed, while the Queen-mother was arrested and sent a prisoner to Benares. Several others were in custody, and the palace itself was guarded by an English regiment.

About the end of July, Gen. Whish moved, at length, with a field force over six thousand strong, including two English regiments (10th and 32nd) on Mooltan, and summoned Moolraj to surrender, but without effect; and, on the 5th September, the British guns opened fire. Thus began the siege of the great Sikh stronghold; but in consequence of the defection of Rajah Shere Singh and about five thousand of his contingent, who deserted to the enemy on the 13th, on the 15th the siege was raised, and the British force fell back. On the 24th September, however, Gen. Whish resumed the siege; and early the following month, Shere Singh, distrusted by Moolraj himself, retired with his whole force from Mooltan, and while he proceeded to raise the south of the Punjab, his father, the old Chutter Singh, was negociating with Dost Mahomed to render back to the Afghans, Peshawur, for his aid against the British.

Flying from this stronghold, Major Lawrence and his family were captured; and then only remained Herbert in Attock, and Abbot, Nicholson, and Taylor, to uphold the last shreds of the British influence outside Lahore, and the camp of Whish.

Several minor affairs took place between our late allies and our irregular auxiliaries; while Golab Singh, a domestic tyrant, but faithful, or wily ally, looked down from his mountain kingdom of Cashmere.

Through perhaps the erroneous fear of a hot-weather campaign, and the neglect to reinforce the gallant Cortlandt and Edwardes, with their ally, the Bhawulpore Rajah, or, possibly, to avoid the contingency of a protracted guerilla warfare, the danger which, at the outset, might have been averted or entirely dissipated, had now been allowed to reach a crisis.

A certain vacillation seemed to prevail in the counsels of the British; or defective intelligence may have given rise to a suspicion, by which the enemy largely profited.

Orders and counter-orders for the movement of the troops at Ferozepore, on the frontier, were frequent, and afforded an instructive lesson on the relative effect of mental influences on the health of the European soldiers, who crowded the hospital with fever cases when their hopes of relief from the wearisome cantonment life of India seemed lost, as rapidly as a sudden rumour of immediate operations at once had the opposite effect.

At length, early in October (1848), it was announced in general orders, that a force would be assembled, and designated "the Army of the Punjab," under the personal command of Lord Gough.

This force consisted of three infantry divisions: the *first*, under Maj.-Gen. Whish; the *second*, under Maj.-Gen. Sir W. R. Gilbert; and the *third*, under Maj.-Gen. Sir Joseph Thackwell, subsequently transferred (on the appointment of this distinguished veteran to the command of the Cavalry) to Brig.-Gen. Colin Campbell.

The Cavalry Division was at first assigned to the command of Col. Cureton, then Adjt.-Gen. of Queen's Troops, a post subsequently held by Col. Lugard.

Several changes of brigades and regiments took place during the campaign that followed, but these need not now be noticed.

The Bunnoo troops, the chief strength of the army under Shere Singh, were raised out of the remnant of the old Khalsa * army. As was to have been expected, these stern veterans could ill brook the domination of a foreign power, and eagerly availed themselves of the first opportunity of joining their countrymen in the field, under Chutter Singh, Governor of the Peshawur district. They were disciplined and equipped after the European manner, and were accompanied by Artillery and Cavalry.

It was believed that the intention of the enemy was to advance on Lahore, and the suspicion was aggravated by the circumstance that a party of the Sikh Cavalry made an attempt to destroy the bridge of boats over the Ravee, on the northern side of that capital, which, however, was frustrated by the prompt appearance of Havelock at the head of the 14th King's Light Dragoons.

The close proximity of the enemy, and the disaffection of the population of Lahore, rendered the position of Sir Frederick Currie, the British Resident there, perilous in the extreme.

In the meantime, a brigade of Cavalry had assembled

---

* Commonwealth.

at Ferozepore; and Col. Charles Cureton, Adjt.-Gen. of Queen's Troops, was despatched to take command. Brigadier Wheeler with a small force was already in advance, while Brigadier Godby, with another, moved northward towards the Ravee, about the 3rd November.

It was expected that the enemy would oppose the advance of the British at Goojranwallah,* a small town or rather fort, about three days march from Lahore; but Cureton found the position abandoned, and when his force was united to that of Brig.-Gen. Colin Campbell, who had likewise advanced in the same direction, an impression prevailed, that these officers might, by a decisive blow, terminate the incipient struggle, and thus frustrate the ambition of those who yet hoped to share in the glories of a campaign on a larger scale. The idea is not unworthy of a passing remark as an indication of the confidence of the troops, and their contempt of the enemy.

The following table of commands in the army of the Punjab will facilitate future references in the course of the ensuing narrative, although several changes subsequently occurred:—

1st Div. Maj.-Gen. Whish.	1st Brig. (Markham).	32nd Foot	Staff	Asst. Adjt.-Gen. Capt. Whish.
		49th N. I.		Asst. Qr.-Mr. Gen. Lieut.-Col. Becher.
		51st N. I.		A.D.C. Lieut. Need.
	2nd Brig. (Harvey).	10th Foot		
		8th N. I.		
		72nd N. I.		

* Said to be the birth-place of Runjeet Singh.

2ND DIV. Maj.-Gen. Sir W. R. Gilbert.	1st Brig. (Mountain).	29th Foot, 30th N. I., 52nd N. I.	Staff	Asst. Adjt.-Gen. Major Chester. Asst. Qr.-Mr. Gen. Lieut. Galloway. A.D.C. Lieut. Colt.
	2nd Brig. (Godby).	2d Europeans, 31st N. I., 70th N. I.		
3RD DIV. Maj.-Gen. Sir Joseph Thackwell.	1st Brig. (Pennywick).	24th Foot, 25th N. I., 45th N. I.	Staff	Asst. Adjt.-Gen. Major Ponsonby. Asst. Qr.-Mr. Gen. Ensign Garden. A.D.C. Lieut. Thackwell.
	2nd Brig. (Penny).	15th N. I., 20th N. I., 69th N. I.		
	3rd Brig. (Hoggan).	61st Foot, 36th N. I., 46th N. I.		
CAV. DIV. Brig.-Gen. Cureton.	1st Brig. (White).	3rd Dragoons, 14th Dragoons, 5th Lt. Cav., 6th Lt. Cav.	Staff	Dep. Asst. Adjt.-Gen. Capt. Pratt. Asst. Qr.-Mr. Gen. Lieut. Tucker. A.D.C. Lt. Cureton.
	2nd Brig. (Pope).	9th Lancers, 1st Lt. Cav., 6th Lt. Cav.		
	3rd Brig. (Hearsey).	Irregular Cavalry.		
	4th Brig. (Salter).	11th Lt. Cav., Irregular Cavalry.		

(*See* Plan of Action of Goozerat and Despatch.)

On the General Staff were—

Bt. Lieut.-Col. Lugard, Act. Adjt.-Gen. Queen's Troops.
Lieut.-Col. Gough, Qr.-Mr. Gen.
Capt. Ramsay, Commissariat.
Med. Dept.: Insp.-Gen. of Hosp. Franklin, Drs. Renny and MacLeod.

ARTILLERY.
Brigadier Tennant.

ENGINEERS.
Brigadier Cheape.

General Staff of the Army.

Lord Gough, Com.-in-Chief.
Lieut.-Col. Gough, C.B., Qr.-Mr. Gen.
Major Lugard, Act. Adjt.-Gen.
Capt. Ottor, Act. Asst. Adjt.-Gen., Queen's Troops.
Lieut.-Col. Grant, Adjt.-Gen. of the Army.
Major E. Kins, Dep. Adjt.-Gen. of the Army.
Major Tucker, Asst. Adjt.-Gen. of the Army.
Lieut.-Col. Garden, C.B., Qr.-Mr. Gen. of the Army.
Lieut. Tytter, Asst. Qr.-Mr. Gen. of the Army.
Lieut. Paton, Dep. Asst. Qr.-Mr. Gen. of the Army.
Lieut.-Col. Birch, Judge Adv. Gen.
Lieut. Johnson, Dep. Judge Adv. Gen.
Capt. Ramsay, Dep. Com. Gen.
Major Thomson, Asst. Com. Gen.
Lieut.-Col. Curtis, Asst. Com. Gen.
Capt. Campbell, Paymaster to the Army.
Capt. Lacy, Postmaster.
H. Franklin, Esq., Ins. Gen. of H.M's Hospitals.
Capt. P. Haines, Military Secretary.
Major Bates, Lieut. Bagot, Capt. Gubbett, Lieut. Hardinge, A.D.C.
Lieut. - Prenderghast, Persian Interpreter.
Dr. Renny, Sup. Surg., Dr. MacRae, Field Surg.
Rev. Whiting, Chaplain.

Present with Com.-in-Chief—
Sir H. Lawrence, Maj. Mackeson, Mr. Cocks, C.S., Capt. Nicholson, Major Anstruther, Lieut. Mayne.

On the 9th of November, 1848, the force under the personal command of Lord Gough, breaking up camp at Ferozepore, crossed the boundary river Sutlej and entered the territory of the nominal ruler of the Punjab, who, under the tutelage of Sir Frederick Currie, the British Resident, was received by the Commander-in-Chief at his head-quarters, when, some days later the latter lay encamped before his capital, Lahore.

After a halt of two days, although the heavy guns had not arrived from Delhi, Lord Gough, moved by the representations of Sir Frederick Currie, ordered the division of Sir Joseph Thackwell to advance across the Ravee. Four days later, a junction with the main body under the Commander-in-Chief, which followed, was effected at the small village of Noewallah, distant about ten miles from the enemy's position at Ramnuggur, a walled town on the left bank of the Chenab, and distant about three miles from that river—an extensive open plain covered for a considerable distance with a low scrub or jungle intervening, with a small tope or grove of trees in the mid distance.

On the morning of the 22nd November, about 3 o'clock, the Commander-in-Chief, unknown to the majority of his personal staff, placed himself at the head of the advanced force, consisting of the 3rd and 14th Light Dragoons, 5th and 8th Light Cavalry, 12th Irregular Cavalry, and the Horse Artillery of Lane and

Warner,—followed by the Infantry Brigade of Godby, with Austen and Dawes' batteries,—the remainder of the force being encamped in rear of Ramnuggur, and unconscious of the movement, until the morning had considerably advanced.

Although the ostensible object of this movement was simply to reconnoitre the position of the enemy, it was conjectured that an engagement would be precipitated; for it was correctly rumoured that a large portion of the Sikh army had encamped on the left bank of the river, while the main body occupied an entrenched position on the right bank.

While the advanced force was moving upon the former, the remainder of the army, some hours later, followed it up, and as the combat that ensued was progressing, took up a position in front of Ramnuggur as spectators of the distant fight, albeit obscured by clouds of dust and smoke.

"As the British force advanced, the Sikh army fell back, retiring to the river. The bones of dead camels and horses, and embers of recent fires, strewing the road . . . the report that the enemy had been in great force on the left bank."

CHAPTER II.

At this season of the year, the Chenab contracts to a comparatively narrow channel, exposing several dry water-courses and sandy flats. On the opposite side, however, the bank of the river is high.

In the middle of these flats appeared an islet, called, for convenience, "the Green Island"; but the retreating waters had left it high and dry, although there were still some stagnant pools around it.

While the Sikhs, withdrawing from the fire of the British guns, were endeavouring to cross the ford, our cavalry came up with them, and were inflicting some loss, when, from a rising ground in front, the enemy's artillery opened so heavy a fire, that Lane's and Warner's troops of Horse Artillery found their position untenable and prepared to retire; but it was found that one of the guns was inextricably sunk in the heavy sand. The enemy perceiving the futile attempts made to save it, increased their fire, and renewed the combat.

To cover the retreat of the Artillery, a squadron of the 3rd Light Dragoons, under the command of Capt. Ouvry, charged the enemy near the island already mentioned. "This squadron," says Thackwell, "swept the sandy plain with extraordinary rapidity, and cleared aside all obstacles with such irresistible impetuosity that the enemy neither opened fire on them, nor offered any formidable opposition."

"The supposition was that the enemy were paralyzed"; but it is much more probable that their guns had not as yet taken up their subsequent advanced position.

Some other charges were executed, but to no purpose; for the Sikh infantry lining the nullahs, by their galling fire proved the inutility of further attacks, and as the troopers were falling a retreat was effected, whereupon the enemy once more advanced towards the abandoned gun.

Irritated at the defiant attitude of the Sikhs, Lieut.-Col. Havelock of the 14th Light Dragoons, obtained permission to charge with his own corps, supported by the 5th Light Cavalry. At the daring onset, the enemy took to flight, hotly pursued by Havelock, who now exceeding his orders, dashed down to the spot where the abandoned gun lay in the sand. The horses of the pursuers soon, however, became exhausted in the heavy sand and mud, and, at the same time, the Sikh guns opened their fire, while their infantry making another stand, offered a stout resistance. "Follow me!" cried the gallant Havelock, as he plunged into the masses of the foe, never to return. His mutilated body was discovered some days later.

Col. Cureton, commanding the Cavalry, observing the rash valour of the 14th Dragoons, hastened to withdraw them from the combat, when the bullet of a matchlock man concealed in a nullah pierced his heart.

Shortly afterwards his naked body was brought to the rear, but not before Capt. Holmes had made a desperate and futile attempt to rescue it.

Thus fell Brig.-Gen. Cureton, an officer held in the highest respect for his soldier-like qualities.

In this disastrous but glorious charge, the loss was considerable in proportion to the numbers engaged.

In consequence of the death of Cureton, Sir Joseph Thackwell was appointed Commandant of Cavalry, and his vacated division (3rd Infantry) was bestowed upon Brigadier Colin Campbell, since better known as the late gallant Lord Clyde.

During this combat Col. Alexander, commanding the 5th Light Cavalry, while leading on his sowars, was struck in his uplifted sword-arm by a round shot, and fell from his horse, when he would certainly have been despatched by the enemy, but for the gallantry of Sergt.-Maj. Mallet, who, single-handed, kept them at bay until succour came.

Amongst the officers distinguished on this occasion may be mentioned Capts. Fitzgerald and MacMahon, Capt. Holmes (of the 12th Irregular Cavalry), Malcolm, Tait, Christie, and Chamberlain, the present Sir Neville, Commander-in-Chief of the Madras Army.

The army was now occupied in erecting batteries in advance of the camp, and these were gradually pushed forward; but they were scarcely within range, in any part, of the enemy's guns, although spent shot came close to the more advanced.

The Sikh cavalry hovered about the British position, and a sharp encounter took place with some foragers near the ford of *Ghurree-ke-Puttun*, where some of the enemy's small field-pieces opened fire.

Meantime, Col. Penny, who was in charge of the heavy train in rear, was delayed two or three days by the *discovery* that the fort of Jubbur, midway on the British line of communication between Ramnuggur and Lahore, was, strange to relate, garrisoned by a considerable force of the enemy, although the British army had passed in ignorance within a few miles of it. Col. Penny proceeding to demolish the fort, had fired only a few rounds when the adventurous garrison surrendered at discretion.

On the 28th November, Cheyt Singh, brother of Uttur Singh, made his submission, and delivered himself up to the Commander-in-Chief.

Immediately afterwards (30th), the heavy guns and Engineer's park, under the command of Col. Penny, arrived in camp.

A council of war was now held, at which it was proposed to strike a decisive blow, by detaching a force to turn the enemy's left flank, while the main body of the army made a grand attack in front. In order, however, to carry out this plan, the possession of one of the fords of the Chenab was necessary; but in the then state of the intelligence department this was not so easily to be found.

The three fords between Ramnuggur and Wuzeerabad were Ghuree-ke-Puttun, about eight miles distant; and up the stream, Runeekhan-ke-Puttun, and Allee Shere-ke-Chuck five miles further on. There was also a ford at Wuzeerabad, nearly thirty miles from the camp. "That these fords," says Thackwell, "were not subjected to a minute scrutiny, in which the highest authorities should have actively participated, was afterwards deeply lamented."

The command of the force destined to cross this rapid and dark river (as its name signifies), was given to Maj.-Gen. Sir Joseph Thackwell (a Peninsular and Waterloo veteran, who had lost his left arm at the latter battle).

The force itself consisted of three troops of Horse Artillery, two Native light field batteries, two 18-pounders, the 3rd Light Dragoons, 5th and 8th Light Cavalry, 3rd and 12th Irregulars, H.M.'s 24th and 61st regiments, and the 25th, 31st, 36th, 46th, 56th, and four companies of the 22nd Native Infantry.

The pontoon train also accompanied the force; but, as often has happened, proved unserviceable.

Accordingly, the force got under arms at 1 a.m. on the 1st December (1849), in order to reach the ford of Runeekhan-ke-Puttun at an early hour, and march down on the Sikh position; but to provide against unforeseen obstacles, a small detachment was despatched to the ford near Wuzeerabad, for the purpose of securing it, and any native boats that might be found there.

The objection to the nearer ford of Ghuree-ke-Puttun was, its close proximity to the enemy, and the probability of a disputed passage.

The force, in light marching order, accordingly assembled, on the right flank of the camp, close to the Wuzeerabad road. Absolute secrecy, silence, and despatch were the essential conditions of success; but, unfortunately, the camp followers raised an astounding clamour, while the infantry division of Brig.-Gen. Colin Campbell, unprovided with a guide, became entangled and confused in the intricacies of so large a camp, and did not, in the thick darkness, reach the place of rendezvous before 3 a.m., and, under the circumstances, it is a question whether it would not have been wiser to defer the diversionary movement. However, once in motion, the force managed to feel its way slowly over broken ground, in the intense darkness, while its advance was still further impeded by the long halts necessitated by the remarkably slow progress of the pontoon train. At the same time, the preliminary chaos of noisy sounds must have apprised the least vigilant of the enemy of some unusual proceeding in the British camp.

It was now 11 a.m., when the force reached its destination, the ford of Runeekhan-ke-Puttun, but the head of the column being out of sight of the river, Thackwell with his staff, rode down to its bank, to make a reconnaissance.

The Chenab, at this point was found divided into four separate channels, with sandbanks, and, as was said, also dangerous quicksands. So broad was the bed of the river, that the opposite bank was out of range, while, to add to the difficulty, parties of the enemy were descried guarding the ford.

These proceedings occupied about three hours, and as all the conditions of success had evidently failed, Brig.-Gen. Campbell counselled an immediate return to camp, but Sir Joseph Thackwell, unwilling to do so, preferred the alternative of trying the ford at Wuzeerabad, and the march was accordingly resumed.

On reaching the latter ford, it was found that a party of Nicholson's Irregular Pathan Horse, held seventeen large boats for the transport of the force across the river. Thackwell, in his narrative, says, that the troops "had taken advantage of the time devoted to the examination of the fords, to enjoy a meal, rendered all the more welcome by the fact, that they had not tasted any food since the preceding night." But this cannot apply to the whole force, for the writer, who was present with it, tasted nothing until long after the arrival of the troops, about 6 p.m., at the ford of Wuzeerabad, when a piece of unleavened bread (chuppattie) was all that he, or his companions, could manage to procure, after a protracted march of twenty-five miles.

It was now a very dark night; and, in the mazes of small channels and pools of water, which chequered the loose sands, many a regiment lost its way, while the increasing darkness added to the general confusion, and the knowledge of abounding quicksands, produced a sense of insecurity.

It is hard to say what might not have befallen the force, had the enemy only taken the trouble to guard this ford, or to form an ambuscade.

The boats were, however, capacious, and the transportation of a portion of the guns was rapidly effected, in reliance on the assurance of the Pathans, that there was no appearance of the enemy on the farther bank.

The 6th Brigade of Infantry (Pennicuick's) which included H.M.'s 24th Foot, crossed in the boats, while the 3rd Brigade, under Brigadier Eckford, having waded through the first and second branches of the stream, was unable to proceed farther, and had to bivouac on a sandbank, between the second and third.

Tait's Horse (3rd Irregulars), crossed the ford, which was indicated by stakes; but, nevertheless, three sowars were drowned in the attempt.

Sir Joseph Thackwell, with the remainder of the force, continued that night, on the left bank of the river, and was enabled to mitigate the severity of the weather by lighting fires, and having recourse to the provisions which had followed. But the 3rd and 6th Brigades, on the opposite bank, after so long and fatiguing a march under a hot sun, were obliged to pass that bitterly cold and dark night without food or fuel, and, in order to escape the piercing wind, some, with their hands scooped out hollows in the sand, in which they found a slight protection. Here a few shots assured the vigilance of the sentries, but their alarm was groundless.

Next morning the remainder of the force crossed,—the Infantry and guns by boat, and the Cavalry and Artillery horses, by fording the river, which, in some places rose above the men's knees, the latter having divested themselves of their overalls.

The pontoon train, two light field guns, the 12th Irregulars, and two companies of the 22nd Native Infantry, as pre-arranged, returned to the camp at Ramnuggur.

It will probably be suspected, that the security of the British detached force, depended entirely on the negligence of the enemy, and the fidelity of Nicholson's Pathans.

The commissariat arrangements were, to a certain extent, defective; and, with one exception, the Quarter-master General's Department failed to discharge its functions with its usual intelligence.

The pontoon train proved a useless encumbrance; while the providential discovery of ferry boats, at Wuzeerabad, was an accident.

The two general officers were divided in opinion; and their topographical knowledge could not be said to have extended beyond the immediate vicinity of the locality which the troops occupied.

Every one seemed reliant on another, and nobody appeared to know anything with certainty.

Considering how well acquainted, even at the very outset, the Sikhs must have been with the scope of the British strategy, and that their vigilance throughout the day was untiring, it does seem remarkable, that they should, in the long run, have shown so much supineness.

Preparatory to resuming the march, at the request of the second in command, the Sepoys were permitted to take their dinner, a circumstance which caused much delay, and it was 2 p.m. before the force was again in movement.

In passing over fields of turnips, and by sugar-cane *khets*, the European soldiery snatching at these esculents continued, as they went, to supplement their previous frugal meal.

The order of battle was thus formed:—Three Brigades in brigade columns of companies, half distance, left in front, at deploying intervals. White's Cavalry Brigade on the right, and the Irregular Cavalry on the left. Each Infantry Corps was covered by its own skirmishers, while patrols connected the movement with the river.

After a march of twelve miles, the force reached the mud village of Doorewal at dusk, but as the men's quilts had not arrived, they were compelled, once more, to lie on the bare ground.

During the night, a messenger, mounted on a camel, brought a despatch from the Commander-in-Chief, desiring Sir Joseph Thackwell to attack the enemy the following morning, and that he would be prepared to make a simultaneous attack in front,—that he was in secret treaty with the Sikh boatmen for their boats then moored under the enemy's batteries, and that, moreover, he expected to secure the defection of certain Sikh regiments, by *diplomatic* means. It is much more probable that, as the event proved, the Commander-in-Chief had been duped.

The useful *mirzais*, or quilts, with which the army in India is supplied, had, by this time, been brought up from the rear, and, in consequence, the repose of the troops, secured against a searching cold, was undisturbed; therefore, on the following morning, Sunday the 3rd of December, they had entirely recovered from their fatigue combined with want of sufficient food and rest, and advanced in the same order as on the preceding day.

But, ere the force had progressed a distance of six miles, another communication from Lord Gough was received by the Commander, who was now prohibited from courting collision with the enemy, until reinforced by Godby's Brigade, which would effect a junction by crossing at the intermediate ford of Ghurree-ke-Puttun.

In consequence, Sir Joseph Thackwell directed the march of his force on some villages, almost in a line with the ferry in question; and, with the view of securing his communications with this important point, he despatched a wing of the 56th Native Infantry and a portion of Tait's Irregular Horse (3rd I. C.) to protect it, as it appeared to be threatened by a body of the enemy.

CHAPTER III.

The sky was bright and unclouded, and the warmth of sunshine was welcome, when, on the level grassy plain in front of the village of Sadoolapore, with the three hamlets already referred to before them, the troops piled arms, and fell out,—some to partake of a scanty breakfast from their havresacks, or to smoke, while others, under the genial influence of the atmosphere, surrendered themselves to sleep, soon forgetting the proximity of an enemy, and in ignorance of his immediate presence,—when, suddenly, a peculiar sound was heard overhead, and on looking up, a shell was discovered bursting in mid-air, between the British line and the villages in front,—a distance of about half a mile of level turf. After this came round shot.

" It was difficult to believe," says Thackwell, that " this shot was fired by the enemy, for the scouts and patrols had raised no alarm of their approach"; but, " the shots rapidly increased, and no doubt could any longer exist," that an action had commenced, in which, instead of being the assailants, we were the assailed.

The force * now stood to their arms; Infantry deployed; while the skirmishers, too far advanced to receive support, were ordered by the General in Command, to fall back, and resume their place in the line. Whether or no this retrogression were judicious, has been questioned, for the skirmishers were equi-distant, or about four hundred yards away from either force, and, by a sudden dash, it is not altogether improbable, that the enemy's masked position,—occupying the three mud villages, Tarwalla, Ruttee, and Kamokhail, connected with each other by dense sugar-cane khets (like a bracelet of alternate lava and malachite),—might have been carried. On the other hand, however, the General Commanding had been taken somewhat by surprise, and was in entire ignorance of the numbers arrayed against his small force.

"In order to gain a respectable distance from this dangerous covert, the General ordered the line to retire about two hundred yards. The advantage of a (wide and) clear front, which was secured in some measure by this movement, may be easily conceived; but the enemy who were rapidly advancing, interpreted this retrograde manœuvre, into a retreat." At any rate, their boldness implied as much.

The silken standards, now uncased, were floating proudly along the line, and the whole force seemed inspired with ardour for a closer conflict, when Sir Joseph

---

* About 7,000 of all arms.

Thackwell, counselled by Brig.-Gen. Campbell, who rode beside him, "ordered the Infantry to throw themselves down upon the ground,—a precaution which saved the life of many a man"; for, even in this position, cannonaded for some hours, without a gun on the British side replying, several lives were sacrificed to the excellent ricochet practice of the enemy.

Thus holding its ground in the open plain, with the right flank thrown slightly back, *en potence*, the British force patiently received the fire of the enemy, from about 11 o'clock until nearly 4 in the afternoon, when, at last, the British Artillery opened fire.

In the meantime, while the enemy maintained his heavy cannonade, and volumes of smoke were rising from his guns,—partially concealed by the green sugar-cane khets,—into the pure atmosphere, the British line, without the advantage of the slightest cover, received his ricochet shots as it lay on the grass.

On the left, "where the high bank of the Chenab," says Thackwell, "and a nullah, or dry watercourse afforded some advantage to the enemy, a plantation of sugar-cane was occupied by the latter, whereupon, a British Brigadier was observed to be forming contiguous close column," —a dangerous movement, at once checked by the General in Command.

The same writer describes the "beating of tom-toms, discordant horns, and wild yells of defiance," which proceeded from the Sikh position, but they were, certainly, not audible to the Infantry.

From one of his masked batteries, the enemy opened fire on a patrol of the 5th Light Cavalry, and, about the same time, attempted to turn both flanks of the small British force, which, not exceeding, all told, 7,000, in a weak and exposed position, was a task that seemed by no means impracticable. But Warner's Horse Artillery, supported by the 5th Light Cavalry, having been promptly moved to the left, to reinforce Biddulph's Irregular Cavalry, the enemy recoiled.

On the right, a similar attempt was frustrated by Christie's Horse Artillery, the 3rd Light Dragoons, and 8th Light Cavalry; and, after losing a few sowars in a skirmish, the enemy's horse retired on his Infantry.

The British Cavalry on the right, was now ordered to charge, and, if possible, capture the enemy's guns; but, as no opportunity presented for them to do so, and as the day was already on the wane, the order was cancelled,—this being deemed advisable, as the exact position of the latter was imperfectly understood, although it was known that his centre and right were strongly posted.

By sunset, a profound silence reigned on both sides; and, as darkness was rapidly approaching, and the sleeping quilts of the men had arrived, the latter rolled up singly in the absence of any better cover, were formed into a frail breastwork, as it were, in front of the line, and behind it, the Infantry, having partaken of a scanty meal, lay down to rest.

Some incidents, not altogether unworthy of a passing remark, occurred during this engagement, as, for example, the following:—

Major Harris, of the 24th Foot, had his horse shot under him by a ricochet shot; and, at the close of the day, some men of the 61st Foot were sufficiently unprejudiced against equine food, to make broth of portions of the poor animal.

One of the earliest casualties occurred in this wise:— One of the sergeants with the colours, rising from his recumbent posture on his elbows, was instantly struck full in the face by a round shot and killed on the spot, his brains bespattering one of the standards.

Then, there is Thackwell's graphic description of a Brigadier taking his frugal breakfast, quietly, and reflecting, seriously, on the profanity of doing battle on the *seventh* day,—a thought admirable, but ill-timed.

Nothing farther occurred, until about midnight, when the loud barking of dogs in the villages ahead, indicated some movement on the part of the enemy; and, next morning, instead of a renewal of the action, as the General had anticipated, it was discovered, that the Sikhs had retreated.

There can be little doubt that the advance of Thackwell compelled the Sikhs to retire; and it is surprising that, with all the latter's advantages, they did not venture a combat at close quarters, considering the extremely weak position occupied by the British, and for which, in his despatch, the General apologises. The latter could scarcely say, like the Athenian, "With this Fortune had nothing to do!"

Matters, as they often do, righted themselves; and the pious mind acknowledges that, whatever happens is for the best.

But sufficient to counterbalance all the errors of generalship, was the lively spirit of the troops, with whom novelty in the toils of war, seemed sufficient to dissipate all other reflections.

During this action, the enemy did not bring up his masses to the front; "and," says the General in his despatch, "my brave, steady, and ardent Infantry, whom I had caused to lie down to avoid the heavy fire, had no chance of firing a shot, except a few companies of the left of the line."

The enemy's loss was probably not so severe as the General was led to suppose; while that of the British amounted to only seventy-three men, and forty-eight horses killed and wounded.

The Commander-in-Chief appears to have been under the impression that, during the night after this engagement, the Sikhs had "*precipitately* fled, *concealing* or carrying with them their artillery, and *exploding* their magazines," and had, in their disorderly retreat, "subsided into *three* divisions," which, as Sir Joseph Thackwell says,—relying on the reports brought to him, "have become more a flight than a retreat; and, I understand a great number of them, not belonging to the revolted Khalsa, have dispersed and returned to their homes."

In truth, no one at the time knew what had become of the enemy; and, in order to ascertain, as was supposed, that they had taken the direction of Dinghee, towards the Jhelum, Lord Gough despatched next morning, from Ramnuggur, the 9th Lancers and 14th Dragoons in "pursuit."

Meantime, the Commander-in-Chief having ascertained that the force under Sir Joseph Thackwell had crossed the Chenab and was in movement, on the 2nd December, opened a heavy cannonade on the Sikh position opposite Ramnuggur, which was returned by only a few guns that guarded effectually the ford, and were so placed, that, although the practice of our Artillery was admirable, we could not, from the width of the river, silence them.

But the enemy's fire gradually slackened, and then altogether ceased; when, as was afterwards * ascertained, the Sikhs had fallen back about two miles.

The Commander-in-Chief, however, continued to push forward his breast works as well as batteries, the same night, to the left bank of the river, and having thus secured the ford, by daylight on the 3rd, he detached Godby's

* By Capt. Robbins, who, on the night of the 3rd, subjected the ford and opposite bank to minute inspection.

Brigade of Infantry, six miles up the river, to effect a junction with Thackwell's force. But this design failed through various causes.

It appears that Godby encountered greater difficulties than the Commander-in-Chief had anticipated, in his attempts to cross the ford. The water was found too deep to admit of the troops wading through it. The pontoon train could not be fixed; and, as before, boats again formed the last resource. Thus, about 5 p.m., the work of embarkation commenced, just as the action at Sadoolapore was closing, and, by 8 p.m., only one corps, the 2nd Europeans, had actually crossed the ferry of Runneekhan-ke-Puttun, which, it may be remembered, Thackwell had found impracticable on the 1st December. This corps bivouacked during the night, and it was not until 9 a.m. on the 4th, that Godby effected the desirable junction.

In the meantime, besides the detachment sent to Runeekhan-ke-Puttun to cover the passage of Godby's reinforcements, a considerable guard was withdrawn from the field, to protect the baggage in rear of Sadoolapore, and, in consequence, the force that remained to engage the enemy, "was thoroughly inadequate to the task imposed upon it."

But it is questionable, whether the efforts of the enemy against Thackwell were at any time serious. The Sikhs opposed to the latter, were estimated by Sir Henry Lawrence, whose knowledge of the Punjab was accurate, not to have exceeded 10,000, whereas, it was suppose that the whole of the enemy's force was present.

The object of Shere Singh appears merely to have been diversionary, in order to cover the strategical movement of the main body in rear; and, therefore, had the British Commander at first occupied the three villages in his front, when they were not as yet in the enemy's hands, —considering how close his skirmishers were to them,— a better position might have been secured, if not a decided advantage. But, on the other hand, with notoriously defective information, and unsupported by Godby's Brigade, such a movement might have been hazardous; and yet, what position could well be imagined weaker and more dangerous than that which was preferred?

In his despatch of the 5th December, Lord Gough says, "Having communicated to Sir Joseph Thackwell my views and intentions, and although giving discretionary powers to attack any portion of the Sikh force sent to oppose him, I expressed a wish that, when he covered the crossing of Brigadier Godby's Brigade, he should *await their junction*, except the enemy attempted to retreat. This induced him to halt when within *three or four miles of the left of their position.*"

The confusion in the official chronology of the Punjab campaign, is thus explained by the author of "The Second Sikh War."

"General Thackwell's despatch descriptive of his action (Sadoolapore), was not published till after the battle of

Chillianwalla. The document was transmitted to Lord Gough three or four days after the fight; it contained, however (so the authorities declared), a serious informality," inasmuch as he had thanked Mr. John Angels, a volunteer, who although deemed by the General worthy of honorable mention, being a civilian, had been described as an *extra aide-de-camp.*

This was certainly an error, but as it might at once have been corrected, the true cause of the suppression of the despatch must be looked for elsewhere, nor is it difficult to find.

Thus was effected "the Passage of the Chenab."

CHAPTER IV.

On the 4th December, the Infantry of Thackwell's force, having been allowed to take a hurried breakfast, received orders to follow the Cavalry, which had previously, under the personal command of the General himself, proceeded in advance, with the ostensible object of harassing the enemy's retreat by the Jhelum, Jullalpore, and Pind Dadan Khan roads; and at length the force, reinforced by the 9th Lancers and 14th Light Dragoons, encamped, about sunset, at a village on the road to Jullalpore, and distant about eleven miles from the Chenab.

During the march, which was necessarily slow, the troops had subsisted on coarse chuppatties, and raw turnips pulled up while traversing the cultivated fields.

Nothing had been seen of the enemy, and next morning (5th December), Thackwell moved forward to Heylah, one of those numerous mud villages, which, in the Punjab, have arisen on the accumulated *débris* of others which had probably occupied the same sites from time immemorial. Some of these, in the flat scenery of the Doabs, present rather an imposing aspect.

On the confines of this wild and gloomy expanse, bounded by the rugged peaks of the "Salt Range," Thackwell sent two corps of Cavalry to reconnoitre the road to *Dinghee*, and three others, including the 14th Light Dragoons, with a troop of Horse Artillery, towards Jullalpore; the latter observed two bodies of the enemy, apparently 400, and 800 strong, which, at the distance, suggested the idea that they were the rear-guard of the Sikh army. But it was found impossible to obtain reliable information of the enemy's real movements, while the villagers asserted that Shere Singh had already crossed the Jhelum.

As, at Sadoolapore, Sir Joseph Thackwell expressed regret * at not having overtaken any of the enemy's troops or guns; nor is such a regret surprising, when it is considered what the real state of the matter proved to be. At that time, all relating to the enemy's designs and movements seemed to be wrapped in the most profound obscurity, so much so, indeed, that it is scarcely an exaggeration to say, that all the operations of the British were marked by hesitation and inaccuracy, tending to shake the confidence of troops less attached to their leader. But the faith of the army was profound in the personal gallantry and ultimate success of the brave Lord Gough, so that, although victory came by surprise, as well

* *See* his Despatch.

as the loss of opportunities, the men were satisfied to attribute this uncertainty to the cause assigned by the Author of "The Second Sikh War," namely, that every movement of the army was directed by a supreme *civil* authority, some hundreds of miles from the scene of operations, and that the veteran Commander was, in truth, under the tutelage of a young officer who, as representative of the Governor-General, controlled all his movements, and allowed him only a discretionary power when a crisis had been, against his own judgment, precipitated, or the occasion for striking a blow allowed to pass, in view of some political scheme which, as might have been seen, never could have come to maturity.

The British camp at Heylah was, in truth, only distant about ten miles from that of the Sikhs, and during the long period of inaction in this position, the latter's guns were often heard in the distance.

Gradually, as the dense belt of jungle in front yielded to the advances of the wood-cutters, several desultory skirmishes occurred between the patrols and the enemy's Ghorchurhas; and, one day, a body of about two hundred Sikhs attacked a small convoy, which sought safety in flight. But the outlying picquets were never attacked, and the British camp itself, presented an aspect almost of repose, if not of monotony.

In the meantime, Lieut. Young of the Engineers, having constructed an excellent bridge of boats over the Chenab, at Ramnuggur, the direct line of communication with

Lahore, the British base of operations, was completed, and the Commander-in-Chief crossed the river on the 18th December, and encamped within a distance of three miles of Heylah. The same day, Shere Singh advanced a force of about 10,000 men to Dinghee, and seemed to threaten a movement on the Wuzeerabad ford, which would seriously have compromised the British position. Lord Gough, therefore, purposed to march on Googerat, and transmitted to Sir Joseph Thackwell his orders to conform to the movement. But this design was almost immediately abandoned, and instead, Brigadier Pope, with three guns and two Light Cavalry corps, was despatched to occupy the town and adjacent fords of Wuzeerabad, in order to secure that line of communication with Lahore, and, at the same time, to prevent reinforcements reaching the enemy from the capital, which was filled with insurgents.

On the 19th December, a salute of forty or fifty guns in the Sikh camp was supposed to announce the fall of Attock, and the adhesion of the Ameer of Cabul to the cause of the Sikhs.

About this period, Brigadier White, with his Cavalry, was ordered to intercept Narain Singh, a Sikh chieftain, reported to be on his way from Mooltan, with men and guns to join Shere Singh, but the movement proved abortive.

A rumour was now spread, that great scarcity both of food and money prevailed in the enemy's camp, and that reinforcements from Peshawur had refused to cross the Jhelum until they should receive pay. But neither report seems to have had any real foundation,—for much less suffices for the support of a Native army in the field than for a European; and it seems improbable that, at such a conjuncture, a question of money was uppermost in the thoughts of the auxiliary force, in the face of a struggle for empire.

At the same time, two troops of Horse Artillery, which Chutter Singh had received as a gift from the British Government (and which were thoroughly disciplined and efficient), at an earlier period, for the purpose of checking any aggression on the part of the Afghans,—were now brought by his father to Shere Singh, and afterwards did severe execution on the troops of the donors,—the Sikhs serving them with admirable skill, and almost religious veneration.

Moreover, many Sepoys disbanded on the reduction * of Bengal Infantry Corps, still in the prime of life, and seeking for service anywhere, flocked to the hostile standard.

* Short service, without pension, tends now (1876) to the same results. We discipline a Sepoy, and, when he is most serviceable, we relegate him to the Nizam or the Nepaul rulers.

CHAPTER V.

MAJOR MACKESON, the Governor-General's political agent, on the 10th of January, having communicated to the Commander-in-Chief, the fall of Attock, and the advance of Sirdar Chutter Singh with reinforcements for his son Shere Singh, whose force was estimated at from 30,000 to 40,000 men, with sixty-two guns, thus concluded his letter:—"I would urge, in the event of your Lordship's finding yourself strong enough, with the army under your command, to strike an effectual blow at the enemy in our front, and that the blow should be struck with the least possible delay."

In consequence of this suggestion, Lord Gough advanced from Loah Tibbah,* at daylight on the 12th, to Dinghee, a distance of about twelve miles. Here, learning from spies and other sources of information, that Shere Singh still held, with his right, the village of Lukhneewalla and Futtehshah-ke-Chuck, the main body of his force being at Woolianwalla, and the left resting

---

* A village in the position at Heylah.

on the strong position of Russool, on the Jhelum, his Lordship, who had some time previously been informed of the impracticable nature of the country, for all arms, proceeded to reconnoitre.

The following morning, the British force again advanced.

Here it was ascertained that the Sikh army, under Shere Singh, had taken up a position between the village of Futtehshah-ke-Chuck, and the low hills of Russool, on which its left flank rested.

This range of hills presents a sloping aspect to the plains; but, as was afterwards discovered, on the side towards the Jhelum, it forms innumerable ravines and fissures, and is abruptly terminated by precipitous bluffs along the sandy flats and channels of the river. The spurs of these hills were crowned by extensive earthworks, which, however, were not, during the action which subsequently took place, approached.

A broad, and, in some parts, extremely dense jungle, principally of thorny bushes, occasionally attaining to the height of seven or eight feet, stretches in a south-easterly direction, but does not preserve the same density in the direction of Dinghee, its wildest character ceasing at the village of Chillianwalla.

About this time, the presence of a large body of Cashmere troops, under Colonel Steinbach, at Meerpore, on the right bank of the Jhelum, was a source of uneasiness, and although it was said that Golab Singh had directed that they should create a diversion in favour of the British, their attitude was sufficiently doubtful, to justify Lord Gough's protest against their approaching the scene of operations.

It was one of those pleasant mornings peculiar to the cold season in Upper India, that ushered in the eventful 13th of January. The air was still and bracing, and the increasing warmth of sunshine, in an almost unclouded atmosphere, produced the glow so welcome, after the cold of the early dawn.

Bugles and trumpets were sounding their familiar regimental calls, tents were rapidly struck, and the troops seemed thoroughly aware of the object of the approaching movement; and, in justice to that portion of them, described by the author of a "Narrative of the Second Sikh War," as having, the night before, been "re-iterating prognostications in a tone of vaunting superiority, that the sun would not set twice on the concentrated forces of the proud Khalsa,"—it ought to be said, by one who had a better opportunity of knowing the corps more particularly referred to,† that no such tone existed in it, either on the day of battle, or that preceding it.

The British force now advanced in contiguous columns of brigades, with artillery in the intervals, and made a considerable *detour* to the right, in the direction of Moong, "partly," says the subsequent despatch, "in order to distract the enemy's attention, but principally to get . . . clear of the jungle, on which it would appear the enemy mainly relied." How far these reasons were justified, under the circumstances, may be discovered in the sequence of events.

CHAPTER VI.

The British were now approaching that dense, and, to them, unknown jungle tract stretching to the left bank of the Jhelum or Hydaspes, memorable as the battle-field where, upwards of 2,000 years before, coming from the north-west, Alexander the Great had vanquished the host of Porus, in a combat, which, on the authority and showing of Arrian, must avouch to all posterity, the genius of the Macedonian hero.

It was about noon when the force reached the mound close to the village of Chillianwalla, where a strong outpost of the enemy's Cavalry and Infantry was observed. The 24th Foot immediately proceeded to dislodge them, but they avoided collision, and rapidly retired. It was on this occasion, and *not* afterwards, that Colonel Brookes cried out, waving his sword, "Follow me, my men, and with God's help we'll gain a glorious victory!" This incident is of importance, as it has been recorded as one of the causes of confusion in the subsequent advance, with which, however, it had no connection.

From the mound now occupied by Lord Gough and his staff, and, likewise, from some lofty trees near the village of Chillianwalla, an extensive view of the country in front was obtained, and the army of Shere Singh, amounting to, it is said, between 30,000 and 40,000 men, with about sixty (sixty-two) guns, drawn out in battle array, and occupying an advanced position, which had been taken up that morning, seemed like a line of white surf on the farther confines of the dark jungle which separated the two armies by the distance of about a mile.

Shere Singh appears, on discovering the object of Lord Gough's flank march towards Russool, at once to have anticipated it, and by throwing forward his right, to have compelled him to accept battle on ground of his own choosing. The importance of this manœuvre, however, does not appear to have been immediately recognised, and the British Commander, having abandoned his intention of awaiting the morrow nearer Dinghee, where water was found to be scarce, now judged it expedient boldly to pitch his camp in line with the small mud village of Chillianwalla, where, at any rate, there were several wells.

The regiments had piled arms, while the Engineers were examining the country in front, and the Quarter-Master General was in the act of taking up ground for the encampment, when the enemy advanced some guns and opened fire. A round shot fell close to the Commander-in-Chief, who at once ordered the heavy guns, from their position in front of the village of Chillianwalla, to return the enemy's fire. But, instead of silencing the latter, as had been expected, the enemy replied with nearly the whole of his field artillery, and thus revealed his true position, which the jungle had partially concealed.

It has been said that the Sikh leader had determined to allow the British to encamp in such dangerous proximity, but that the impatience or indiscretion of his Artillery officers had frustrated this design. Now, however, when the heavy guns of the British promptly replied, this stratagem being foiled, Shere Singh lost no time in bringing every available gun into action, thus exposing his position, which had been, hitherto, to some extent masked by the jungle.

It was now about 3 o'clock; the day was far advanced, and the exposure to a night attack on ground imperfectly known, seemed so hazardous, that order of battle was at once formed.

Sir Walter Raleigh Gilbert's division occupied the right, flanked by Brigadier Pope's brigade of Cavalry, strengthened by the 14th Dragoons, and three troops of Horse Artillery under Lieut.-Col. Grant.

The heavy guns were in the centre, under Major Horsford, with whom were Bt. Major Ludlow and Sir R. Shakspear. Brig.-Gen. Campbell's division formed the left, flanked by Brigadier White's brigade of Cavalry, and three troops of Horse Artillery under Lieut.-Col. Brind.

The field batteries were with the Infantry divisions, between the intervals of brigades.

The reserve was under Brigadier Penny, and Brigadier Hearsey protected the baggage.

While these arrangements were being carried out, a heavy, but as afterwards appeared, ineffectual fire, was opened by the heavy guns, directed, but under the circumstances, with uncertainty, against the enemy's centre, where his guns appeared to be principally massed, and this fire was supported, on the flanks, by the field batteries of the Infantry divisions.

This cannonade having been maintained for about half an hour,—probably without effect on either side,—Lord Gough determined to advance.

Brig.-Gen. Campbell's division now received orders to attack, and a Staff Officer, according to the narrative of Thackwell, "in breathless haste," rode up to that gallant veteran and "ordered him to carry the guns in his front, at the point of the bayonet." Considering that an unknown jungle had to be traversed for a mile, before actual contact with the enemy could be effected, the propriety of such an order, delivered by one whose name has never transpired, may be questioned, as well as the incident itself. Be that, however, as it may, the Brigadier-General rode up in front of the 24th Foot, and addressed the men in these words,—"There must be no firing, the bayonet must do the work!" &c. He then rode away to the left, where he personally superintended the advance of Hoggan's brigade.

In the meantime, Maj.-Gen. Gilbert and Brigadier Pope

had, almost simultaneously, received orders to advance on the right.

Immediately after Brig.-Gen. Campbell had addressed the 24th, that regiment was put in motion, and when the right had cleared the village of Chillianwalla, just where the jungle began to increase in density, ground was taken more than once to the right flank by echellon of companies, and in consequence, under the circumstances, as each company was of unusual strength, in re-forming line, overlapping occurred by the loss of distance, while the long rows of loose thorny hedges clinging to the men's legs and dragging after them, increased the unsteadiness, primarily caused by the impossibility to hear, at the extremities of the line, the words of command, as they were given from the centre of the corps. Moreover, the men of the 24th, unlike those of other European corps, went into action in full dress, and with the old-fashioned and inconvenient tall chaco, scores of which were subsequently lost in the advance, and particularly at the moment of impact with the enemy.

At length, the jungle became denser at every step, and the keekur and kureel bushes higher. The advance was continued at a rapid pace, and in such an alignment as the various companies, now broken into sections or files, could manage to preserve, acting on the independent judgment of individuals, and the habit of previous training.

After this advance, almost at random, had been continued for about 1,800 paces, the jungle suddenly ceased; and when the regiment, pounded incessantly with round shot by an unseen enemy, emerged from it, rapid discharges of grape and canister, swept away whole sections.

In front, the enemy's position was protected by a natural glacis, a gentle grassy incline, forming a gradient of about six feet in fifty yards, rising from a net-work of pools of water with abrupt margins, and between these were many trees with pendant branches, almost entirely denuded of foliage.

There was no time to pause, and take breath, even had that been necessary, and the line now dispersed and broken in the advance,—in consequence of the men having been unable to pass *through* or over the numerous and high clumps of impervious thorns,—made a rush for the guns. Many fell at this moment, under discharges of grape, and, but for the rapidity of the onset, many more must have fallen. The pools of water in front of the enemy's battery obliged some to make a detour, and in doing so, a few began to load and fire,—the pendant branches of the trees swept off the tall chacos of others,—the air soughed like the wind with the flight of bullets. All order in the wild *mêlée* was gone amongst the confused and scattered groups, as they rushed upon the enemy, and, in a short fierce struggle, enveloped in the gloom of the smoke, which, from some atmospheric cause, still clung about the guns, captured the latter, at the point of the bayonet.

So impetuous was the assault, that the enemy at once gave way, while the men of the 24th, instead of following up their success, committed the error of staying to spike the guns. The delay was fatal to the victors, for the vanquished, now realising the paucity of their numbers, quickly rallied, and reinforced by infantry from behind, recovered possession of the battery in a short and violent hand to hand conflict, in which the gleam of bayonets and flashing of tulwars were conspicuous.

The *coup d'œil* of the field of Chillianwalla, from the point of view of a spectator standing on the mound in rear of the village, or in the village itself, may be thus described:—

As the extended red line of Pennicuick's Brigade plunged into the depths of the dark jungle, it was for a time lost to the eye. Here and there, the gleam of a bayonet, or a red coat struggling onwards, appeared for a moment, and again disappeared. A death-like silence reigned, broken only by the booming of guns.

Rising as it were on the farther limits of this dark ocean of verdure, the white clouds of smoke from the enemy's guns might have been taken for the foam of breakers on the far-off shore, but for the rush overhead of round shot, and the dull thud, as each successively struck the ground.

Then, as nearer and nearer the gleam of bayonets, and the red coats approached the guns in front, the welkin sighed with the storm of missiles passing through it.

At last, the extremity of that part of the jungle was reached, and innumerable scattered groups emerged from it, to find themselves in an open space immediately in front of the enemy's guns, from which many were separated by long and intricate pools of water. Amongst these a few trees, denuded of foliage by the fire, arose here and there.

For a moment, there was a pause to consider these obstacles,—and then a rush. Sections fell prostrate under a storm of grape, but the survivors pressed forward, and at the moment of impact with the enemy, the artillery fire ceased; and, in the apparent lull of the storm, hoarse murmurs arose in that smoky atmosphere which told of the death-struggle, hand to hand.

This was soon over; and the Sikhs, scattered and in disorder, fell back in the gloom, like dusky shadows, and the red uniforms of the British alone were conspicuous in the work of spiking the guns; when, suddenly, a shout arose,—the dusky forms again dashed at their decimated assailants, now surprised in the moment of victory. A short struggle ensued; and the wreck of that gallant corps, the 24th, might have been seen hurled back into the jungle, and retreating on the village from which it had advanced, pursued, a short distance, by the Ghorchurhas, who, however, warned of the approach of a new danger, reined in their horses, and galloped back to meet the assault of another brigade, now emerging in the same manner from the jungle on the left.

It is an error to say, that "a fearful massacre was enacted" on the retreating brigade. The enemy can scarcely be said to have pursued it, for he was almost immediately diverted from doing so, by the onslaught of Hoggan's and Mountain's brigades. The wounded were doubtless despatched in many instances; but the Sikhs had no time allowed them to follow up the butchery.

Pennicuick and his son, both officers of the 24th, fell just as they reached the guns. A stalwart Sikh was inflicting gashes on the body of the former, who had been prostrated by a shot, when the son, a boy of seventeen, who had that morning come off the sick list, rushed forward, and bestriding the lifeless body of his heroic father, dealt an avenging blow. But, overpowered, he too fell dead. This episode is given on Thackwell's authority.

Colonel Brookes, who had recently exchanged from the 69th Foot, and had been on furlough in consequence of his marriage, arrived only a few days prior to the action, and assumed command. He was an officer of martial spirit and chivalric bearing, and fell nobly at the head of his corps.

Major Paynter, shot through the lungs, was carried out of danger by his horse; but subsequently died of the wound.

Major Harris,—he whose horse was shot under him at Sadoolapore, was again unhorsed, and as he was retiring with the remnant of his corps, a single Sikh sowar cut him down from behind in presence of the writer.

Captain Williams, a young officer of robust constitution, fell wounded by a musket-shot, and as he lay insensible on the ground was hacked by the enemy's tulwars; but was carried to the rear with twenty-three wounds, one of his hands being lopped off, and, to the surprise of everyone, he recovered. He received no recompense for his gallantry and sufferings, beyond the usual small pension for the loss of his hand.

There were several other, more or less, interesting incidents during the battle of Chillianwalla, which have not been mentioned in the many desultory narratives of that eventful day, and, amongst others, the following:—

Lieut. Thelwall, distinguished by high courage and quick intelligence, who was acting as a mounted orderly officer of Pennicuick's brigade, had his horse shot under him, and was, at the same time, himself severely wounded in the thigh.

As he lay on the ground (where, had he remained, the enemy would have despatched him, as they did all those who were unable to follow the retreat of the unfortunate brigade), he was surprised by his favourite horse—which he had recently sold to the Brigade Major (Harris) who had just been killed—trotting up to him riderless. Recognising his old master, he appeared to offer his services in a friendly manner. The providential opportunity was not to be lost; and the wounded officer mounting the poor animal, which seemed to understand the necessity for his standing as still as possible, rode to the rear.*

As Pennicuick's shattered brigade rapidly made for the village of Chillianwalla, pursued for a very short distance by a few horsemen, Hoggan's brigade, on the left, came upon the scene of the disaster, and charging up to the batteries in their front, drove the Sikhs before them with heavy slaughter, and then changing direction to the right, speedily recovered the ground won and lost by their less fortunate and unsupported comrades of the Right Brigade, a portion of which,† however, succeeded in joining the victorious battalions.

In the meantime, the enemy's horsemen arrested in their pursuit by the sudden attack of Hoggan's brigade on the position from which they had issued, the defeated brigade might have been seen from a slight elevation of the ground, making its way in a mass, to the village in rear, after which it seemed to disappear.

Immediately afterwards, an officer of another corps,‡ who happened to be serving with the 24th, and who had been delayed by one of the enemy's sowars (who for a few minutes made a feint of attacking him, but, suddenly, for some inexplicable reason, changed his purpose),§

* An obelisk in the gardens of Chelsea Hospital commemorates the slain of the 24th, and a monument on the field has been erected to the memory of all who fell.

† Some Sepoys of the 45th N. I.

‡ This corps was not present.

§ The same conduct on the part of the enemy's horsemen on another part of the field has been attributed to bewilderment produced by *bhung*, but this seems improbable.

reached the village, but seeing no one outside, entered it, when he found a considerable number of the 24th, who, with alacrity, obeyed, when he ordered them to follow him to the open space outside. There, having recognised a colour-sergeant, he called upon the latter to stand about twenty paces off, and shout to his company (naming its number), to "fall in," while he did the same. The result was, that the survivors of the company quickly filled up the space between the officer and the sergeant. The former then "told them off," and awaited further results. In a few moments more, the Light Company, under Ensign Hinde, fell in gradually on the left of the nucleus thus formed, while the remnant of other companies came in on the right, and thus order was restored, and the line reformed.

This formation had barely been completed, when Lieut.-Col. Lugard, Adjutant-General of Queen's Troops, rode up to the corps, now rallied, and inquiring of the officer referred to, who was standing alone in front of the line, what had occurred, the circumstances were briefly explained by the latter, who was thereupon ordered by the Adjutant-General to follow, while he gave "the direction." Accordingly, the officer gave the necessary word of command to the company of which he had assumed charge, (that which he had first rallied having, in the meantime, been taken over by its own subaltern Lieutenant Clark, who had come up), and the others conformed to the movement directed by the gallant Adjutant-General

Queen's Troops, who soon rode out of sight, the corps following with its seven officers.

As this advance was proceeding towards the left front, Capt. Blachford, who had been appointed Acting Field Officer for the day, but had not accompanied the corps in its previous disastrous attack upon the enemy, or been present when it was rallied, now rode up, and having made inquiries of the same officer whom Lieut.-Col. Lugard had addressed, took over the latter's orders from *him*, assumed command, and continued the advance, in the course of which, he was met by the *Assistant* Adjutant-General, who gave him further orders.

But the action was already over; and, on arriving at the enemy's evacuated position, the task was assigned to the regiment of blowing up several of the tumbrils which the Sikhs had just abandoned; and, while doing so, as darkness was approaching, the two last artillery shots of the day, on the left, were fired by the retreating foe, and must have fallen close to the spot, as indicated by the sound.

It may here be observed, that the annals of British warfare present few such losses by a single corps as were sustained by the 24th Foot, in this action.

Penny's reserve brigade, consisting of the 15th and 69th Native Infantry, was, meantime, ordered to retrieve the disaster of Pennicuick's brigade; but, owing to the nature of the ground, where the *point d'appui* was to a certain extent obscure, it inclined too much to the right, and after some sharp fighting, in which its loss was 123, including five European officers, it eventually succeeded in reaching Godby's brigade, with which, during the remainder of the day, it co-operated.

Many and conflicting accounts have appeared in various publications, of these events. But, in estimating the true extent of a danger, it is well to test, by the actual return of casualties, descriptions which may understate the circumstances,—as in the dry despatches, for example, of the General of the Mooltan force—and those in which the graphic power of the writer may, quite unintentionally, give a disproportionate importance to an event, as, for instance, while describing the advance of Pennicuick's brigade, even so gifted a narrator as *Arnold*, has spoken of "the ascent, long and *steep*," of "the *hill* crowned by a Sikh battery," which was stormed by the 24th.

After an action, it sometimes, but, fortunately rarely, happens, that the command of a regiment devolves on an officer who may not have been under fire with it, and who, consequently, is incompetent to describe, of his own knowledge, its conduct. Yet, owing to his position, such an officer has absolute control of the regimental record, and may, as has happened, enter in its pages, an account of battles shaped to an official convenience; and, thus, a scarcely reliable statement, drafted according to the exigencies of the moment, becomes, in the course of time, authoritative, and supplies data and incidents in some instances, while omitting them in others, on which future historians may,—and can scarcely avoid, relying.

In its advance, Pennicuick's brigade was the only one that had not the assistance of flanking batteries of artillery,—an oversight which Brig.-Gen. Campbell discovering, promptly despatched Lieut. Sweton Grant, one of his orderly officers, to repair. But it was too late. "The light field-pieces which ought to have covered the advance, had unaccountably been left behind. Standing there alone,—the Brigadier, Colonel, and Major, already fallen," —without an Adjutant, for that officer, owing to an early wound in one of his hands, had not advanced far with the corps,—and without a single mounted officer,—for although the senior Captain (Blachford) was mounted for the day, as acting field-officer, he had, unfortunately, been prevented from proceeding farther than a little way beyond the village,—with thirteen officers killed on the spot, and ten wounded, out of a total of twenty-nine; while of about 960 which followed them an hour before, scarce one half remained untouched by the "showers of grape and musketry poured in from battery and thicket,"—it was scarcely surprising, that "the brave, but raw yeung soldiers of the 24th, should have been driven headlong from the position which they had captured."

Had the other brigades suffered under such a disadvantage as the absence of supporting artillery, a "Subaltern of the 2nd European regiment" has shown, that the day would probably have been lost.

A comparison between the circumstances of Pennicuick's brigade, and those of the 56th Native Infantry, so highly eulogized in Thackwell's account of the battle, indicates an inconsistency in that narrative that, to the impartial mind, must appear quite unaccountable,—and the more so, as Lord Gough's Despatch, and the statistics of the losses sustained, in a great measure neutralize the value of the writer's opinion on this point.

The 25th and 45th Native Infantry, advancing on the right and left of the 24th Foot, although they did not succeed in keeping up with the latter corps, in time to support it, when it had reached the enemy's guns, nevertheless, sustained heavy loss. Of the 25th, three officers and 201 men; and of the 45th, four officers and 75 men were placed *hors de combat*, while the two regiments lost all their standards.*

In consequence, not only of the comparatively rapid advance of the 24th,—which, however, never *doubled*, as has been asserted, until it had emerged from the jungle, but also of the density and intricacy of the latter,—the Native Infantry corps on its flanks, were unable to support its charge; and, says Thackwell, "it fell to the lot of this gallant regiment to experience an atmosphere solely compounded of fire, grape, and round shot," to counteract

* They lost five colours, one being an honorary standard.

which, "there was no artillery and no fire of musketry —for the men were unloaded."

But there was no unwillingness on the part of the Native corps of this brigade; and many men of *that* which was on the left, joined Hoggan's brigade, which was nearest, and thus participated in its gallant attack on the flank of the same position.

It has been said that the 24th lost its colours, but the fact is, it lost only one, namely, the Queen's colour, and this was a pure accident, arising from the circumstances of the battle. The centre of the regiment, where the standards are always carried, was nearly annihilated by the enemy, whose fire was, for a considerable time, concentrated upon it; and, instead of its being surprising that either was lost, when their bearers were killed, it is rather a matter of wonder how, the colour that was saved should have been accidentally recognized in the confusion, amongst the slain, and recovered by a sergeant.

"Amidst the jungle, it was tantamount to an impossibility for many men of a regiment to keep their eyes on the colours at the same time." The colours and their bearers were often levelled to the earth at the same moment, their falling was apt to be unnoticed, and, in consequence, eight stand of colours were lost in this way, in the jungle of Chillianwalla. On the other hand, unlike the other corps of the army, the 29th Foot took the sensible precaution of casing their standards, as we shall see.

Whether through an oversight, or a mistaken interpretation of the Brigadier-General's order, that there "must be no *firing*," the 24th Foot, covered by its Grenadier company in skirmishing order, certainly advanced *unloaded*. But the Colonel, it must be obvious, could not, as has been said, have caused the men to move at the double, by waving his sword; for, in the intricacies of the jungle, he could have been seen, at most, only by a few of the men immediately behind him, and these could not have directed the movements of their comrades further off, with whom they soon became unconnected.

One of the principal causes of the irregularity of this advance may be attributed, perhaps, to the difficulty of sufficient supervision on the part of the other mounted officers. While the fatal result, was partly due, to the Native còrps on either flank of the 24th Foot, not having reached the enemy's position in time to support the attack of the latter. But the absence of the usual batteries of artillery, as before observed, covering the advance of other brigades, must be regarded as the principal cause of the disaster in this instance.*

"Why the batteries attached to this brigade," says Thackwell, "were left in the background, is a question which must be left to Sir Colin Campbell and Lord Gough. In this matter, for reprehension, Pennicuick was not pro-

* Lieut. Sweton Grant of the 24th, who was orderly officer to Brig.-Gen. Campbell, told the writer that the latter perceiving when, however, too late, this oversight, sent him scouring the field to find the batteries, but that he failed to discover them.

minently implicated. One party declared the Chief ordered that the batteries should be immediately stormed with the bayonet, thereby implying the absence of all necessity for the use of the guns. The other retorts, that the only order given was to advance, and that no General of Division, furnished with artillery, ever went into action without it. We do not undertake to state what the exact nature of the order was; but, it is very manifest, that neither the Brigadier-General, nor his brigadiers, regarded the artillery as necessary; in other words, the contempt of the enemy was not confined to poor Pennicuick."

Most of the officers of the 24th were, comparatively, strangers to their men. The corps had recently arrived in India, with a loss of many old officers, and an influx of new; while, at the same time, the rank, and file composed for the most part of young recruits, had scarcely acquired, as was said, comradeship with the older soldiers.

The exchanges so common amongst officers, under the old system, and the augmentation of officers from other corps, tended to weaken that *habit* which gives unity to a body of men. The 24th was led into action by its Colonel,—a stranger who had arrived in camp barely in time to participate in the anticipated victory, and was personally scarcely known to his men.*

* It may not be out of place to mention that while the 24th was rallying, a strange officer, mounted on a conspicuous *iron grey* charger, galloped past to the rear, shouting—"Save yourselves! Their Cavalry are upon you!"—It was a mistake. His name appears in the Despatch. He was thanked, promoted, &c. (*See* p. 53.)

CHAPTER VII.

Turning to other parts of the field, it was observable, that the interval between the Brigade of Pennicuick, and that of Hoggan, owing to the excessive attenuation of the line, was very considerable. Brig.-Gen. Campbell placed himself at the head of the latter brigade, and was distinguished by his personal daring and imperturbable coolness.

The 61st Foot was frequently surrounded, but by the rapid wheeling of companies,—a circumstance so characteristic of the whole action,—in almost every direction, it gloriously repelled the several attacks made upon it.

On nearing the Sikh position, Campbell poured in volleys of musketry; and the 61st, bringing its left shoulders forward, retook the guns which the 24th had just been obliged to abandon. So resolute, however, were the Sikhs, that, profiting by the numerical inferiority of this brigade, they turned against the 61st, those guns, which, but a few minutes before, the latter had captured, but had failed effectually to spike.

"The contest here," says Thackwell, "was more *equal*, and better maintained than in any other quarter. The

Brigadier-General himself, was wounded in the act of cutting down a Khalsa gunner. The 30th and 46th Native Infantry supported the 61st Foot with steadiness and courage. Conolly, the junior Ensign of the 46th, is described as having encountered extraordinary dangers; while Godby, of the 36th, son of the Brigadier, was cut down by a Ghorchurha, but not killed."

It ought not to be left unnoticed, that, while this brigade was changing its direction to the right, a Khalsa chieftain rode gallantly up to the front of the 61st, and reconnoitered with so cool a demeanour, that he was mistaken for one of the British irregular sowars. Having satisfied himself, he rode away, and in doing so, the 61st corrected their error, by opening fire, but ineffectually, upon him.

Under the eye of the Brigadier-General himself, and led by the gallant McLeod, it is but just to observe, that the 61st, and its faithful comrades of the 36th and 46th, mainly contributed, on the left, to re-adjust the trembling scale of victory.

Gilbert's left brigade, supported by artillery, and commanded by Brigadier Mountain,—who afforded a good example in leading on his men,—had reached the rear of that part of the enemy's position, which had just been unsuccessfully attacked by the 24th, and which the 61st was now simultaneously assailing, when the gallant 29th Foot—judiciously advancing with their standards *cased*, and prepared for hard work,—encountered the most resolute resistance; but with that determined valour, raised to heroism by the proud sentiment of *esprit de corps*, for which this regiment has always been distinguished, these experienced soldiers carried all before them, and spiked several guns, only five of which, however, were secured.

Amongst the casualties, was Lieut. Metge, a gallant officer, who, falling mortally wounded, expired some days after; while Mowbray (of a family renowned in English history), as he carried one of the standards, with imperturbability, was shot through the forage cap, but, happily, escaped being wounded.

This brigade, like all the others, was received with an incessant shower of grape and musketry. But, as often happens, the best services, modestly performed, often escape the general notice, while others, comparatively useless, are eulogized.

The 56th Native Infantry boldly advanced up to the hostile batteries, with undaunted courage, under its leader, the gallant Bamfield, who, however, fell, mortally struck by a bullet, and sunk bleeding into the arms of his son.

Eight officers, and 322 men of this corps, were here killed and wounded,—the colours were lost, and, in the confusion of a combat in which each regiment seemed to fight its own distinct battle, this gallant corps yielded to superior numbers, and was driven back by its brave adversaries, who, however, paid dearly for their momentary success.

The other regiment of this brigade,—the 30th Native Infantry, encouraged by the noble example of the 29th Foot, went well to the front, as its roll of killed and wounded,—eleven officers, and 285 men,—fully attests. It, too, lost one of its colours, not, however, by capture, but by reason of the jungle, where the slain fell unnoticed in the general *mêlée*.

At the same time, the right brigade of Gilbert's Infantry division, under Godby, had not penetrated far into the jungle, when it was assailed on both flanks, in front, and also in rear, in consequence of which, the 2nd Bengal European regiment was compelled to meet the enemy at every point, and, at last, to charge, rear rank in front, while Dawes' Battery was clearing the way for their further advance, and the 31st and 70th Native Infantry ably maintained their ground.

The gallant Sir Walter Gilbert now put himself at the head of this brigade, and directed its brilliant attack on the enemy's guns, four of which were captured.

"The Journal of a Subaltern" of the 2nd European regiment (now 104th Foot), supplies interesting details of a combat, which so greatly added to the renown of that corps; and, as these details have a bearing on the conduct of other brigades, the following extracts acquire an additional value.

"The word came for the Infantry to advance, 'Fix bayonets! *Load!* Deploy into line! Quick march!' And into the jungle we plunged with a deafening cheer, the roll of musketry increasing every moment. On we went at a *rapid double*, dashing through the bushes,* and bounding *over* every impediment; faster rolled the musketry,—crash upon crash the cannon poured forth its deadly contents. On swept our brigade, and gaining *an open space* in the jungle, the whole of the enemy's line burst on our view. "Charge!" ran the word through our ranks, and the men bounded forward like angry bull-dogs pouring in a murderous fire. The enemy's bullets whizzed above our heads. The very air seemed teeming with them. Man after man was struck down. . . . . Onward we went with a steadiness which nothing could resist. (The enemy) fired a last volley, wavered, and then turned and fled. Pursuit in a jungle like that, where we could not see twenty yards before us, was useless; so we halted, and began to collect our wounded,—when all of a sudden a fire was opened upon us in our *rear*. A large body of the enemy had *turned our flank* in the jungle, and got *between* us and the rest of the troops. Another party was on our *left*, and we found ourselves with our light field battery, *completely surrounded*, and *alone* in the field.

"The word was given,—'Right about face,' and we advanced steadily *loading and firing as we went.*

"Captain Dawes' *battery was the saving* of us. As the

---

* The jungle was not so dense on the right as in the centre, for such an advance would have been impossible in front of the village of Chillianwalla.

Cavalry was bearing down, the Brigadier shouted,—'A shower of grape in there' . . . and a salvo was poured in, that sent horse and man head over heels in heaps . . . The fire was fearful; the atmosphere seemed alive with balls. I can only compare it to a storm of hail . . . All this time the enemy were dodging about the bushes, banging away at us, and then disappearing.

"At last General Gilbert rode up and said to Steel,— 'Well, Major, how are you? Do you think you are near enough to charge?' 'By all means,' said Steel. 'Well, then, let's see how you can do it.'

"'Men of the 2nd Europeans, prepare to charge,— Charge!' and on we went with a stunning cheer. Poor Nightingale was shot, and fell at my feet. The Sikhs fought like devils, singly, sword in hand, and strove to break through our line. . . . After a short struggle, we swept them before us, and remained masters of the field.

"We were on the *extreme right*, and the *thickness of the jungle prevented our seeing what was going on* elsewhere.

"We took *three* of their guns in our *second* charge, and spiked them on the ground. . . . Several of our wounded were cut to pieces in the rear. . . . Surrounded, as we were, it could'nt be avoided. . . . The colours were gallantly carried by De Mole and Toogood, —and are shot through and through." *

* The gallant writer describes several of his own hair-breadth escapes.

Sir Joseph Thackwell, second in command, and General of the Cavalry, was on the extreme left. With White's Cavalry brigade, and three troops of Horse Artillery, under Brind, he advanced some distance, and opened fire on that portion of the enemy, which was under the command of Outar Singh, who appeared to be seeking an opportunity to turn the left flank of the British.

The cannonade had not been of long duration, when a body of Ghorchurhas made a demonstration to their right, with the evident intention of penetrating to the rear. To prevent this being carried out, Unett's squadron of the 3rd Light Dragoons, and three squadrons of the 5th Light Cavalry, were ordered to charge, which they did in line. The Sikhs opened a desultory matchlock fire.

The 3rd Light Dragoons forcing their way through the hostile ranks, never pulled rein until they had gone some distance beyond the enemy. Unett, severely wounded, with his men dispersed, resolved with the few near him, to cut his way back, while Stisted and Macqueen returned as they could.

The 5th Cavalry, despite the earnest exhortations of their gallant officers, avoiding collision with the foe, retired with precipitation.

The fate of Unett, and his squadron, seemed inevitable, when at length they were seen to emerge from their perilous position with honour to themselves.

Unett and Stisted were wounded, and many of their

men were killed and wounded.* No mention, however, was made of the devotion of these brave officers, in the body of Lord Gough's despatch, although some days after the action, his Lordship visited the former, and promised to recommend him for promotion.

The enemy's fire had now slackened; when Brind received an order from the Commander-in-Chief to move his guns to the right flank; and shortly after, White's brigade was directed to conform to that movement. But no sooner had the 3rd Light Dragoons been put in motion, than the enemy's fire was redoubled.

In the perplexing intricacies of the jungle, Brigadier Pope's Cavalry brigade, which included a portion of the 9th Lancers, as well as the 14th Light Dragoons, not only overlapped the troops of Horse Artillery, on the right of Sir W. R. Gilbert's division, but even got in front of the latter, so that when the former found it necessary to open fire, the Cavalry proved an unexpected obstruction.

During his advance, Brigadier Pope, who was at the time in bad health, received a severe wound from a tulwar on the head; and it appears that a temporary halt was ordered in consequence, when the Sikh Cavalry skirmishing in front, were emboldened by what they mistook for hesitation.

* This regiment lost during the day, in killed and wounded, twenty-four men killed, and two officers and fourteen men wounded.

Meanwhile, Major Christie, commanding the Horse Artillery, on the right of Gilbert's division, had scarcely expressed astonishment at the movement of Pope's brigade, when, suddenly, the latter was observed to be in full retreat on his guns.

In an instant, guns, gunners, and wagons, were everywhere upset by the rush of the British Cavalry, when the 14th Light Dragoons happened to be pushed against Christie's troop by the other regiments; and to crown the whole, the enemy's Ghorchurhas in close pursuit, entered the ranks of the Artillery.

Major Christie, with many of his gunners, was cut down on horseback, before he had time to draw his sword. Huish would have shared the same fate, had not Major Stewart, of the 14th Dragoons, despatched his assailant with a pistol shot. Many were trampled by the horses. Lieut. Cureton, son of the gallant officer who had so recently fallen at Ramnuggur, met his fate by his horse becoming unmanageable, and carrying him into the hostile ranks.

The few Ghorchurhas who pursued, had been mistaken for a larger body, and would have penetrated still farther, had not one or two squadrons of the 9th Lancers rallied behind the guns, and opposed their progress. Some of the former advanced to within a short distance of Lord Gough and his staff, and his escort of Cavalry was preparing to charge, whereupon the Ghorchurhas retired.

Meanwhile, Major Ekins, Deputy Adjutant-General of the Indian Army, seeking to deliver an order to the retreating brigade, received a wound. His friend, Major Chester, hastened to his assistance; the enemy was close at hand. Ekins, however, begged him to leave him to his fate, and the enemy presently coming up, hacked him to pieces.

This disaster occasioned the loss of all the guns in Christie's troop, and two in Huish's; but two of the former were afterwards recovered,* at the battle of Googerat.

While these events were in progress, Col. Lane, of the Horse Artillery, with his guns, two squadrons of the 9th Lancers, and two of the 6th Light Cavalry, was engaged, repelling an attack of the enemy's horse, on the extreme right.

---

* The day after the action, a court for inquiry into the conduct of the 14th Dragoons was held, with a result satisfactory to that much injured but gallant corps.

CHAPTER VIII.

It was now 5 o'clock, and night was at hand. The enemy were recovering and removing those guns on the left of their line, which although spiked, the British had been unable to carry off. Several points of the attack had failed, and it was even doubtful whether the Sikhs, under cover of the jungle, or of the darkness, might not make a last and supreme effort to snatch the victory, which had scarcely been secured. Had the latter been more enterprising, and perceived their advantage, they might possibly have done so. But they seemed to have forgotten in the rough handling which they had received, accurately to calculate their chances of success in a jungle, when darkness neutralized their superior local knowledge.

Lord Gough proposed to hold the ground occupied by the successful brigades, in order to secure any guns which might be found in the morning, and also to succour the wounded, when Brig.-Gen. Campbell pointed out the necessity of falling back on the village of Chillianwalla, where alone water could be procured, and where the baggage would be ensured protection.

The British army bivouacked on the field, while the surgeons in rear were incessantly engaged throughout the night, in ameliorating the sufferings of the wounded, and in performing the usual difficult surgical operations. During these painful scenes, the chaplain of the army was untiring in his ministrations.

About 8 o'clock, a drizzling rain began to fall, and those who were fortunate enough to secure some of the men's quilts, which were scattered about near the baggage, may have found a little protection from the inclemency of the weather; but the majority of the Europeans were without cover of any kind, while the Sepoys, as many as could be accommodated, sought shelter in the mud hovels of the village of Chillianwalla.

It is by no means so probable, as has been asserted, that the enemy employed the night in massacring the wounded. That was done before; but it is not unlikely that the country-people of the adjacent villages, plundered and stripped the dead.

The loss of the British in this brief action was very severe, and amounted in killed (586), wounded (1641), and missing* (104)—to 2331, of all ranks (518† of these casualties having occurred in the 24th Foot), and 176 horses. The aggregate calibre of the six guns lost, was

* In Indian battles the missing may generally be taken as killed.

† The regimental returns show 520; of the twenty-two European officers killed, thirteen were of the 24th Foot.

54 (pounder); and 76¼ of the twelve captured from the enemy.

Thus ended one of the most severely contested of battles, in which, within the space of two hours and a half, eighty-nine British officers, and two thousand three hundred and fifty-seven fighting men either lost their lives, or were wounded; while an unusual number of standards were lost—not *captured*—and six guns fell into the hands of the enemy, against the twelve small pieces which remained as trophies with the British.

Although the honour of victory remained with the latter, who held the enemy's position at the close of the action, the Sikhs lost no *prestige* by their obstinate struggle. Their strength was nearly double that of their opponents, but their real fighting power was, apparently, confined to only a portion of their force.

Instances of heroic courage on the part of individual Sikhs were frequent, although the excitement of *bhung*, is said to have stimulated many others.

Single combats were not of rare occurrence; and, as the Sikh swordsman had the better weapon, their issue was always doubtful.

Lastly, it is an undeniable fact, that the enemy ended the combat on the left of the line, with their artillery, while Brind, now on the right flank, fired the last shot of the day in that quarter.

Nothing could exceed the ferocity of the Sikhs, and, although quarter was neither given nor taken on either side, they were so determined to inflict death, that they often showered blows on the fallen, after they were disabled by their wounds.

"In front of the village of Chillianwalla," says Thackwell, "lay a wounded Sikh, who had been abandoned by his comrades. He was attired in the usual Khalsa infantry uniform,—a red coat of an old European pattern, with white stripes of braid across the breast, and facings of a different colour; a white turban, and loose blue trousers, completed his costume. His handsome features were adorned with the usual thick black beard, whiskers, and moustache. A cannon-ball had shattered his thigh-bone, and to *alleviate his pain*, he was seeking relief, by taking bhung, a quantity of which seemed to be in his pockets." On the approach of the officer, who has described him in another work, he made a desperate effort to collect his dormant energies, and convulsively grasped at a tulwar, lying within reach; but his strength failed.

Many such incidents are recorded; and it is melancholy to reflect, how often brave men in such a plight, refusing to ask for quarter, have met death with unflinching courage.

It has been truly remarked that, as:—"The ground was covered with thick high brushwood . . . it did not seem improbable that the most carefully arranged combinations might miscarry—that regiments would lose their distance, take a wrong direction, and even mistake friends for foes—as, indeed, happened on more than one occasion during the day, and notably when, towards the close of the action, the 3rd Light Dragoons on approaching Huish's troop of Horse Artillery, being mistaken for the enemy's Ghorchurhas, narrowly escaped being fired into."

The British army was scarcely half the strength of that commanded by Shere Singh; and its advantage of superior discipline, was to a great extent neutralised by an impervious jungle, in which regiments could not preserve their proper formation, while the enemy's knowledge of the ground gave him a decided superiority. Moreover, finding himself considerably outflanked, Lord Gough was obliged to extend his line so considerably, with large vacant spaces between brigades, that, so attenuated, it occupied almost as great a space of ground as that of the British army at Waterloo. On the other hand, it is difficult to excuse the General's neglect sufficiently to employ his artillery—especially his heavy ordnance—in consequence of which, the brunt of the action fell upon the troops and batteries of Huish, Christie, Brind, Dawes, and Lane.

Where so much depends upon Providence, as the result of a battle, it is not always the most glorious victory, that is most instructive to the victor; and the disasters of an action may afford lessons of the highest value.

Chillianwalla was undoubtedly a British victory, although so often questioned; for Lord Gough, on the cessation of the fight, was in full possession of the field;

while the enemy fell back under cover of the darkness and the jungle.

In this action, the victor experienced the consequences of:—1st, undervaluing the enemy; 2nd, imperfect topographical information; 3rd,—executing a flank movement in the presence of an enemy in position; 4th,—disregarding the primary importance of artillery; 5th,—relying on the bayonet, rather than on his superiority in fire-arms, in difficult ground where skirmishing order was appropriate; 6th,—displaying standards in a jungle fight, and thus drawing the fire of the enemy on the leaders of battalions, and exposing, in consequence, the wings to sunderance; 7th,—allowing, on the plea of equalization, additional companies to be made up for the occasion, which, in the *mélée*, lost their cohesion.

It has been said, that Lord Gough, instead of giving orders for an "immediate and headlong attack," should have moved, "for the night, to a less exposed position." But this was simply impossible under the circumstances. There was no option but to fight, and, owing to the enemy's strategy, which precluded any movement to either flank or to the rear, to have done otherwise, under the circumstances of darkness, and an unknown country, would almost certainly have resulted, entangled as it would have been in the mazes of its camp, in at least seriously compromising the British force.

Many things happen on the battle-field, that might afford interesting studies for the metaphysician; but these are, not improperly, excluded from the domain of military history.

Some receive honours, as due to rank and position, which would be denied to the individual. But the influence of the press, has, within the last twenty-four years, extended to the operations of war, and the creditable actions of the subordinate officers, and the rank and file, are now no longer allowed to be consigned to oblivion.

But the salutary reaction, has not been without the effect of producing some singular anomalies, in that combination of incongruous systems, under which, the most useful services and deserts, are liable to be measured by a standard, sometimes reliable, but purely arbitrary in its application, unless influenced by adventitious circumstances.

CHAPTER IX.

On the following morning, Brigadier White, with his Cavalry, scoured the battle-field, in hope of discovering abandoned guns, in which, however, he was disappointed; while the Commander-in-Chief, with Major Mackeson, the political agent, ascended the mound, before described, to reconnoitre the enemy, if not already retreated across the Jhelum. They were, however, perhaps not altogether surprised to discover the defeated, but not subdued foe, nearly three miles off, still occupying their formidable entrenched position on the heights of Russool, on which their left flank had originally rested.

The scene of the retreat of Pennicuick's brigade, presented a melancholy spectacle on the morrow. Rain had fallen during the night, and the mutilated corpses stripped entirely naked, by those who lurk about battle-fields in the darkness, presented a ghastly spectacle; those of the British, pallid and blood-stained, were of the hue of white marble, and formed a striking contrast to the dusky slain of the native soldiery. The attitudes of death were sometimes singularly significant. Many were rigid, in the position of ported arms, and bore a placid expression. They had evidently been instantaneously struck dead. Others, with their mouths slit from ear to ear when on the ground, displayed the whole of their teeth, and were often thus made to bear evidence of the most atrocious mutilation. Some appeared to have expired in the act of protecting their heads from the blows of their assailants; and one, struck down on his knees, had stiffened in that posture with upraised hands, the fingers of which had been sliced off with the blow of a tulwar; the countenance was expressive of horror and agony, and the body was pierced with wounds. In another instance, the wounded man, while still alive, had, with ingenious malignity, been forcibly drawn through a bush, whose crooked thorns, like talons, had torn the skin into ribbons, giving the unhappy sufferer a striped appearance.

The remains of all the officers were recovered; and camels were sent out to bring in the bodies of the private soldiers, piled on their backs, to which they were fastened with ropes, and sometimes hanging suspended from the animals' sides. But so horrid was the sight of these bleached and mutilated corpses, so irreverently conveyed to the camp, that parties were sent forward to bury the remainder, chiefly about the pools of water, already described. On the 15th January, many were interred in the same grave; but, owing to unavoidable circumstances, so hastily, that, afterwards, as the writer passed by these slight tumuli, one evening in the gloamin, the villagers' dogs, and vultures, were seen fighting and gorging themselves on such fragments of humanity as they could drag from these shallow graves.

Mr. Whiting, the chaplain of the army, interred with Christian rites the bodies of the Europeans, including those of all the officers, that had been brought into camp. The latter were placed in one trench, the men in another. But there was one exception. Major Christie's body, at the request of the gallant survivors of his ill-fated troop of Horse Artillery, was buried in the same grave with his fallen comrades.

For the first few days after this sanguinary action, the Engineers were engaged in protecting the camp with earthworks. Official reports were being prepared ; while the chaplain, the medical officers, and burying parties, found incessant occupation.

Some days later, Elihu Bux, the Peshawur artillery officer,—a handsome man, with small beard, and dressed in the Afghan choga,—rode into camp, and surrendered to Lord Gough.

Shortly after this battle, the Commander-in-Chief contemplatd a retreat on Dinghee, in order to keep open his communications with Ramnuggur, where there was a *tête de pont*, occupied by two native infantry regiments and some guns—for the enemy had more than once made menacing movements with large bodies of troops in this direction.

There was, however, another line of communication open

by Heylah, where Thackwell's force had encamped after Sadoolapore; but this was no better protected.

Eventually, Lord Gough decided on maintaining his position, until reinforced by General Whish from Mooltan.

Orders were now despatched to the 53rd Foot, in garrison at Lahore, to march immediately to Ramnuggur, when relieved by the 98th Foot from Umballa; and at the same time, Sir Dudley Hill's reserves were held in readiness to move on Lahore at an hour's notice.

Chutter Singh, who had arrived in the Sikh camp two or three days after "Chillianwalla," was received with a royal salute. He brought large reinforcements, and also his prisoners, Major Lawrence, and Lieuts. Herbert and Bowie, taken on the fall of the forts of Attock and Peshawur.

These officers were treated with much consideration by the Sikh chieftains; but it was found necessary to guard them against the fanaticism of the Akalees. They were subsequently employed as the bearers (on their parole of honour to return) of overtures for peace; but on terms that were unacceptable.

The interchange of negociations served the purpose of keeping the enemy quiet, pending the anticipated fall of Mooltan.

On the 21st January, that stronghold fell; and in consequence, General Whish's troops became available to reinforce the army, under the Commander-in-Chief.

Shere Singh was soon made aware of the surrender of Moolraj; but is supposed to have withheld his knowledge of the fact from his troops, as long as possible.

The following day, the Sikhs were observed to throw back their left flank, which was also on the low hills of Russool; and, suspicious of some hostile design on their part, at dusk a large party was sent to construct a redoubt on the British right flank. This was done with the utmost caution and despatch, and by daylight the work was finished.*

One day, a patrol of the 3rd Light Dragoons suddenly found himself confronted by two of the enemy, and, after a well maintained fight, succeeded in despatching both.

Men were daily employed clearing away the brushwood in front of the camp. But the camp itself was concentrated in far too small a square, while in the centre there were crowded, elephants, camels, the camp-followers, and the enormous quantity of baggage which an Indian army carries with it; an error commented upon by the Roman historian, in his Jugurthine War, who describes Metellus as having dispensed with the encumbrance altogether.

The British patrolling parties occasionally exchanged blows with the Ghorchurhas, who were prowling about

---

* A trivial incident is often highly suggestive. During the night a young officer, who had been indefatigable in filling the sand bags, had just sat down for a moment, about 3 a.m., to rest, when his senior, who had merely been looking on all the while, suddenly and authoritatively addressed him—"How is this, you ought to be doing something!"

everywhere, in quest of food, or plunder; and the 9th Lancers, who were on the right, and consequently nearest to the enemy, were daily disturbed by false alarms; and indeed, so unremitting were the outpost duties, that few ever undressed, except for a hasty ablution.

On the 25th of January, an alarm was raised that the enemy was turning out in battle array; but this proved to be a mistake.

On the 30th, Lieut. Chamberlain, with a party of the 9th Irregulars, intercepted a body of Ghorchurhas, who were endeavouring to seize our camels, which had been sent out to graze. Sixteen were slain, and the rest put to flight. In this affair, the brave leader of the Irregulars received a wound.

It has been thought, that English Cavalry in India, although admirable for any special occasion, and useful in giving solidarity, and setting an example to the Native Horse, has rarely played a prominent part in the more useful, and less stately duties of that arm.

During the campaigns in India, within the present generation, outpost duties, and gathering intelligence, have been chiefly performed by the Irregular Cavalry, the troopers, or sowars, of which as the owners of their own horses, &c., have a stake in the corps, and being more independent, take a real pleasure in the performance of the most harassing duties.

The uniform of the Irregular sowar, is, moreover, better suited to the discharge of the duties imposed upon Light

Cavalry in the field; while, on the other hand, the British Dragoon, and his horse, are subject to such incessant surveillance, that his efficiency is, although it may appear paradoxical, thereby somewhat impaired, when continuous hard work has to be done.

During this campaign, the Irregular Cavalry were, in truth, to use a familiar phrase, *the eyes and ears of the army.**

Celerity of movement, and readiness for an emergency, are the characteristics of the latter. British Cavalry was then, except in pursuit, comparatively of secondary consideration to an army in the field; and, in action, their valour was to a great extent wasted, on those who yielded to the charge, only to inflict heavier loss as the squadron passed by them. These results were notorious during the Punjab campaign, and still more so in that of the Sutlej, when, as at Aliwal, the Khalsa Infantry, allowed the Lancers to break their squares,† and then surrounded them separately, so that victory was dearly purchased.

The reason which induced the Sikhs to abandon their strong position at Russool, has been variously stated. Scarcity of supplies—the discovery that it afforded no line of retreat in the event of defeat—the traditions of past Khalsa victories at Googerat—the interception of the

---

* In the Memoirs of Count Pajol, an excellent idea is given of the uses of Cavalry in a campaign.

† Or "wedges."

force advancing from Mooltan; and, lastly, the treacherous design of their own leaders, to decoy them to their destruction.

When, on the 5th February, it appeared, from the absence of the usual signs of occupation, that the Sikhs had retired from their position at Russool, two officers at once mounted their horses secretly, and set out to explore. Having ridden about two miles through the intervening jungle, they ascended the natural glacis, and entered cautiously the earthworks, which were admirably constructed. The embrasures were strengthened by forked trunks of trees, like the letter Y, beneath which the ground was excavated for the reception of ammunition, and for protection. Beyond this, the ground was deeply rent, in every direction, forming precipitous ravines; while on an isolated little plateau stood the mud village of Russool, connected with the adjacent parts by an extremely narrow neck of land, slightly protected with wood; while, on the opposite side, a deep escarpment was presented to the river Jhelum.

The place was entirely deserted, but swarming with flies.

The two officers, who were the first to enter this singular natural fortification, anticipating no interruption, picqueted their horses, descended to the river, where they bathed, and were returning leisurely through the jungle, when they suddenly came upon two of the enemy's spies—to all appearance, by their long twisted hair, Akalees.

Being quite unarmed,* the officers were obliged to adopt the first idea of self-preservation that presented itself, and, accordingly, plunging the spurs into his horses' sides, one of them dashed past one of the Sikhs, and seizing him as he did so, by the hair, carried him off his feet helpless for a considerable distance, and then dropped him. Both now rode to camp, as rapidly as possible, through the more open jungle, while three musket-shots in their rear, told them that their amateur reconnoitring had been successfully accomplished, without any unpleasant consequences.

The outpost duties, at this period, were, as already remarked, severe. Few were unprepared for any sudden emergency, as the custom was to sleep in one's clothes, —and on dark, bitterly cold, and often wet nights,—on outlying picquet, generally on the bare ground.†

On the 5th February, it was discovered that the Sikhs, during the night, had abandoned their position at Russool; but owing to the state of intelligence, it was some time before the direction which they had taken was ascertained.

The following day, on a false alarm, three signal guns were fired—the camp was struck, and the troops remained

* Their reconnoitring on their own account being contrary to orders, they had dispensed with arms to avoid notice.

† The writer commanded the outlying picquet of his corps, when his company was detailed for that duty, from the battle of Chillianwalla until the close of the campaign.

under arms from noon until sunset, within the entrenchments.* The confidence of several, seemed, in many regiments, by the evidence of doubt as to the enemy's movements, not unshaken.

A good deal is said in "A History of the Second Sikh War," of "the Koree Pass," where a slight affair of outposts occurred, on the 11th February, when "the Sikhs made great demonstrations," and "drove in the patrolling party."

Hand to hand encounters were frequent in the earlier part of the day, and in these, Chamberlain, of the Irregular Cavalry, greatly distinguished himself.

At length, it was discovered that the enemy was marching on Googerat, with the design, probably, of destroying the communications of the British with Lahore.

On the 13th, Brigadier Cheape arrived in camp, from Mooltan, with some squadrons of Irregular Cavalry; and, next day, intelligence was received that Shere Singh had occupied *Googerat.*

On the 15th February, the camp was broken up, and the army pursuing the direction taken by the enemy, marched to Lussoorea.

The next day, it proceeded to Puckha Musjid.

On the 17th, it was at Kunjah, and encamped near a large brick fort, close to which appeared a small, but well built bazaar.

---

* The camp at Chillianwalla is said to have been the first that a British army in India had ever entrenched.

The enemy was now descried in the distance, in the direction of Googerat.

Next morning, the British force moved to Truckhur, in rear of the position which the Sikhs had occupied at the affair of Sadoolapore.

Here there was a halt;* and, on the 20th, the army advanced to Shadawalla, where its picquets were in sight of those of the enemy.

On the previous night, at a late hour, Brig.-Gen. Dundas had arrived; and, during this day, Brigadier Markham followed by forced marches from Mooltan.

---

* In a well near the camp, were discovered a few much decayed bodies of Sikhs who had fallen at Sadoolapore on the 3rd December 1848.

CHAPTER X.

WHILE, and before these operations of the army of the Punjab were in progress, under Lord Gough's personal command, as before stated, so early as October 1848, Brigadier Wheeler was employed in the reduction of the country north of Lahore; and, in the following month, he was engaged in clearing the jungle, in the Doab between the Ravee and the Chenab, of armed marauders; while, in the Julunder Doab, across the river Beeas, a fresh rebellion, which had broken out, was ably repressed by Lawrence.

Reinforced by troops from Bombay, to the number of about 3,000 men, of whom 1,600 were British, with upwards of sixty siege guns, General Whish (who had been obliged to retire a short distance from Mooltan, the stronghold of the rebel Moolraj), on the 26th of November, renewed the siege; on the 27th of December following, he delivered his attack, and, on the 29th, commenced the bombardment.

At noon on the 30th, the enemy's principal magazine blew up with a roar that seemed to shake the earth for miles; and, the following day, the city was stormed. On the 31st, the citadel was invested; and on the 21st of January 1849, it was unconditionally surrendered by Moolraj.

During the period of this siege, as before mentioned, many slight skirmishes occurred, and one action on a larger scale, on the 7th November 1848, when a force, under Herbert Edwardes, defeated an attempt of the enemy, at Soorujkhoond, to raise the siege.

The Mooltan column shortly afterwards arrived at Ramnuggur, under Maj.-Gen. Whish. The menacing disposition of the enemy's force, indicated a design on Lahore, and, amidst conflicting reports, the Commander-in-Chief determined, in the first instance, while at Lussoorea, almost equi-distant between Ramnuggur and Wuzeerabad, to secure the fords of the Chenab near the latter town.

Accordingly, after a counsel of war had been held, an order was despatched to Maj.-Gen. Whish to detach a force from Ramnuggur to these fords. But the order had been ably anticipated; and Col. Byron, with the 53rd Foot, 13th Native Infantry, Holmes' Irregulars, and some guns, already held the ferry and ford, so that when a body of the enemy, numbering about 6,000, made a demonstration of crossing the Soodra ford, that officer prepared to dispute the passage; whereupon, the Sikhs abandoning their design, returned to Googerat.

About this time, Lord Gough resolved to reduce the astounding baggage of the army, by sending all superfluous tents, and camp-followers, to Ramnuggur, with the records of the various departments, and the officers attached to them, who were "dispensed with for a time." In consequence, the army was relieved, to say the least, of the inconvenience of nearly eight thousand camels, and its leader, seems deserving of the commendation bestowed upon him, for so judicious, although tardy a measure.

CHAPTER XI.

The strength of the Sikh army was about 60,000 men of all arms, and fifty-nine pieces of artillery, under the command of Sirdar Chutter Singh, and his son Rajah Shere Singh, with a body of 1,500 Afghan horse, led by Akram Khan, son of the Ameer Dost Mahomed Khan. It, therefore, was a matter of urgency, that the Mooltan reinforcements, as we have seen, should effect a junction with the force under the Commander-in-Chief.

Brigadier Markham had crossed the Chenab at Kanokee by forty-seven boats. Brig.-Gen. Dundas, who had been repeatedly urged to join by forced marches, in consequence of not having at first paid sufficient attention to his orders, during the last *two days*, relieved the anxiety of Lord Gough, by a march of forty-five miles,—harassing to troops on the eve of battle, and which might have been avoided by less compromising procrastination.

On the 20th February, a reconnoissance was made of the enemy's position, and it was ascertained that their camp nearly encircled the finely situated town of Googerat, their regular troops being placed immediately fronting the British advance, and in the open space between the town and a deep watercourse, the tortuous dry bed of the river Dwara.

This nullah, passing round nearly two sides of the town, diverges to a considerable distance on its northern and western faces, and then taking a southerly direction, runs through the centre of the encampment previously occupied by the British, at Shadawalla.

Thus, the enemy's position on the right, owed its chief strength to this nullah affording cover to the Infantry, in front of his guns; while another deep, though narrow wet nullah—an affluent of the Chenab—running from the east of the town, covered his left.

The ground between these nullahs, for a space of nearly three miles, was a dead level, without obstructions of any kind—some three isolated villages rising considerably above it,—and was well calculated for the transit of the heavy guns, as well as the operations of other arms.

Accordingly, the Commander-in-Chief, with the design of penetrating the centre of the enemy's line, so as to turn the position of his force in rear of the nullah, and thus enable the British left wing to cross it, in co-operation with the movement of the right wing, and so double upon the centre of the enemy's wing opposed to it—gave the word, and, at half-past 7 a.m. the army advanced, with the precision of a parade, in the following order:—

On the left, the Bombay column, under Brigadier the Hon. H. Dundas, supported by Sir Joseph Thackwell (second in command), with White's Cavalry brigade, the Scinde Horse, and Duncan's, and Huish's troops of Horse Artillery; while the Infantry was covered by the Bombay Horse Artillery, under Blood.

On the right of the Bombay column, with its right resting on the nullah, Brig.-Gen. Campbell's division of Infantry, covered by Ludlow's and Robertson's Light Field batteries.

In reserve, Brigadier Hoggan's Infantry Brigade.

On the right of the nullah, and in alignment with the force on the left of it,—the Infantry division of Sir Walter R. Gilbert, on the left flank of which, and nearest the nullah, were the heavy guns, eighteen in number, drawn by elephants, under Majors Day and Horsford, and Captain Sir Richmond Shakespear.

The line was farther prolonged by Whish's division of Infantry, with Markham's brigade in support, covered by the three troops of Horse Artillery of Fordyce, Mackenzie, and Anderson, with Dawes' Light Field Battery,—Lane and Kenleside's troops of Horse Artillery in a second line being in reserve, under Col. Brind.

The right flank was protected by Brigadier Hearsey's and Lockwood's Cavalry, and Warner's troop of Horse Artillery.

The baggage was protected by Lieut.-Col. Mercer, with the 5th and 6th Light Cavalry, 45th and 69th Native Infantry, and the Bombay Light Field Battery.

The village of Burra Kalra, the centre of the three

mid-way in the plain, and that of Chota Kalra on the right, were almost simultaneously attacked; the former by Penny's brigade, and the latter by that of Harvey, while the third village, on the left, was taken without resistance by the skirmishers of the 24th Foot.*

The enemy had been observed to fall back in considerable numbers on Burra Kalra, which was flanked by two Sikh batteries. Sir Walter Gilbert ordered Penny's brigade to storm it, when at about 200 yards distance, in consequence of the galling fire of the retreating Sikhs from it. The 2nd Europeans, supported by the 31st and 70th Native Infantry, and led on by their gallant Brigadier himself, advanced to the attack. The resistance was most obstinate on the part of a portion of the enemy, who covered the retreat of their comrades from the other side of the village, as the British entered it. No quarter was given. Those who shut themselves up in the small mud huts and houses, found there no protection. The doors were burst open, volley after volley was poured in, and the defenders perished, fighting bravely to the last, with a rare courage, as the casualties of the victors proved—172 in the Native Infantry alone, exclusive of the Europeans. Three standards were captured during the combat. While the left wing of the Europeans held the village, the right debouched on the plain, and found themselves

* The enemy directed a heavy cannonade, but it was ineffective, the shot passing at least thirty paces to the left of this village.

under a hot fire of grape and canister, which was concentrated upon them, in consequence of the supporting troop of Horse Artillery having been disabled in the attack.

In the meantime, the village of Chota Kalra was carried in brilliant style by Harvey's brigade, composed of the 10th Foot, under Col. Franks, and the 52nd and 8th Native Infantry, supported by Fordyce's troop of Horse Artillery. The assailants effected an entrance under a galling fire from loop holes. The 10th Foot in a few minutes had sixty, the 52nd, thirty-five, and the 8th, fifty-nine, put *hors de combat*. During this affair, Anderson's Horse Artillery was exposed to a heavy fire, under which their leader fell mortally wounded; while Fordyce's troop was nearly annihilated.

The Sikh Cavalry made several attempts to turn the British right, but were out-manœuvred by Brigadier Hearsey. "The enemy," says Thackwell, "poured a heavy fire into the 14th Dragoons,* whose skirmishers often resolutely repulsed the daring foe."

Warner's troop of Horse Artillery arrested the advance of the Ghorchurhas, a large party of whom, however, penetrated to the rear of the heavy guns, and approached Lord Gough, but were put to flight by the personal escort under Lieut. Stanners, who received a severe wound. On the same occasion, Mr. Cocks, of the Civil

* This corps lost in the action and pursuit, one European officer killed and two wounded, and four rank and file wounded.

Service, who accompanied his Lordship, met a Sikh who had dismounted to attack the latter in single combat, and, after receiving a very severe wound in the leg, succeeded in slaying the bold assailant.

The enemy opened a feeble fire on White's Cavalry Brigade, which was soon silenced by the guns of Huish and Duncan. Observing that the Sikhs had abandoned one of their guns, a party of Huish's troop, on securing it, discovered it to be one of their own, which had been taken at Chillianwalla.

During the battle, a large Sikh gun had drawn a very heavy fire on itself from the British Artillery, and all its gunners were *hors de combat*, save two men. These, however, continued to serve it, as the line approached. At length, one of these heroic men was killed; but, so indomitable was the courage of the last survivor, that alone, and unaided, he succeeded in firing two rounds, and then "took to flight," or, as in European warfare it would be described,—abandoned his gun when further resistance was impossible.

A wounded Sikh, in the same proud spirit, exclaimed, as a British officer passed by—"God has given you the battle."

The cannonade was magnificent, and terrible in its effect.

The Sikh guns were served with their usual rapidity; and the enemy well, and resolutely, maintained his position as long as it was tenable under the British fire, and sullenly fell back.

The heavy guns continued to advance with extraordinary celerity, taking up successive forward positions, and driving the enemy from those to which he had retired, while the rapid advance, and splendid practice of the Horse Artillery and Light Field batteries,—strengthened by two troops of the former, under Brind, brought from the reserve, the whole being under the superintendence of Brigadier Brooke,—broke the ranks of the enemy at all points.

Large bodies of Sikh Cavalry hovered in front, while the Afghans, on their right, under Akram Khan, threatened the British left. The Scinde Horse, however, headed by the dauntless Malcolm, and supported by two squadrons of the 9th Lancers, dashed with impetuosity upon them, and sent them flying in retreat, leaving in the hands of the victors two standards, gallantly captured.

The rout of the Afghans was immediately followed by a wavering in the enemy's right wing, which was soon converted into a flight, followed by the remainder of his forces.

The whole Infantry line now rapidly advanced, and drove the enemy before it; the nullah was cleared, the guns in position carried, the camp captured, and the enemy routed in every direction,—the right wing with Campbell's division in pursuit, passing to the eastward of the town of Googerat, while the Bombay column advanced on the westward.

The British Cavalry was launched in pursuit. The whole country was strewn with the wreck of the Khalsa power,—guns, bullocks, wagons, tents, standards, and merchandize, &c. For miles around the country presented a dreary spectacle of the dead and the dying. Many cast away their arms and uniform to disguise their profession. Others hid themselves in the corn-fields and villages, but, the cavalry of Hearsey and Lockwood, dispersing in every direction, drove them out with great slaughter.

Corporal Payne, of the 14th Dragoons, captured a standard from a fugitive, and cut him down at the same time, while Major Scudamore, received a severe wound from a Sikh whose life he had spared.

The troopers did not draw rein until they had proceeded a distance of fourteen miles, by which time, evening had closed in. General Thackwell intended to bivouac for the night, and resume the pursuit next morning, but was recalled by Lord Gough. Had the pursuit continued, however, there can be little doubt that it must have been kept up by the Cavalry alone, for, even during the heat of the pursuit, Blood's magnificent troop of Bombay Horse Artillery, was the only one that rendered any assistance.

Unlike their followers, it is said that the majority of the Sikh chieftains, early in the day, deserted the field, and fled towards the Jhelum, taking with them the English officers made prisoner at Peshawur and Attock.

The Afghans never halted till they had reached the Jhelum, a distance of more than thirty miles. Akram Khan, their leader, who was wounded, did not stop until he had crossed that river, and approached close to Rawul Pindee.

After the battle, small detachments were posted at the principal fords of the Chenab, to disarm any fugitives returning home, but, to allow them their liberty, and the retention of their horses.

Meantime, on reaching Googerat, the 2nd Brigade of Whish's force took possession of the eight gates, and then of the fort, where about eighty of the enemy laid down their arms, and were made over as prisoners to the 30th Regiment, along with other detachments, found in different parts of the town, that, with few exceptions, made no resistance.

Four companies (two of the 32nd Foot, and two of the 51st Native Infantry), while proceeding to occupy the town, captured a gun, standard, and some horses, with the loss of one man killed, and an officer of the former corps wounded; and, about the same time, a sub-division of the 10th Foot, and the Grenadier Company of the 52nd Native Infantry, gallantly stormed and captured a temple and garden defended by the enemy, who suffered severely, between thirty and forty having been put *hors de combat*, and a great number taken prisoners.

The Sikhs left their picturesque camp standing near the Bura-daree, a kind of pleasure house, in an orange grove, close to the town. But, before the order was issued the following day, commanding all persons possessed of spoil, to deliver it up, the whole encampment, to the very tents themselves, had vanished piece-meal amongst the British camp-followers.

An Infantry offieer, entering one of the enemy's tents, was taken by surprise. A stalwart Sikh had ventured to remain, and now confronted him! Drawing his sword, the latter dashed past him, at the same time inflicting a severe wound, and escaped.

The Bombay troops saw little of the battle; the enemy gradually retired as they advanced. The 60th Rifles were extended in skirmishing order, but did not come into collision with the foe.

Immediately after the battle, life and property were, by a proclamation, assured to the terrified citizens of Googerat, most of whom had temporarily sought safety in concealment, and, next morning, the town presented its ordinary appearance.

The troops that remained at Googerat were, for some days, occupied with the explosion of the different magazines and tumbrils, with which the camp abounded, and, in the course of doing so, two European soldiers, and four Sepoys, thoughtlessly sitting down to smoke on an ammunition wagon, were blown into the air.

The total loss sustained by the British in this crowning victory, was ninety-six (including five European officers) killed; and 711 (including twenty-four European officers) wounded,—in all 807.

The British captured fifty-three * of the enemy's guns, some of which, however, were of very small calibre, and it is only surprising, what an admirable use was made of them against the overwhelming artillery of the victors,—namely, eighteen pieces of heavy ordnance, and sixty-six 9-pounders, exclusive of the Bombay Artillery.

From the point of view of the author, then an officer of Campbell's division, the general features of the action may be thus described:—

The battle of Googerat was a magnificent scenic display. The day was bright, and the sky cloudless. The immense level expanse of young corn, about four inches high, presented a sea of verdure, bounded, in the far distance, by the snowy range of Cashmere. To the left rose the towers of the walled city of Googerat, with orange groves in great part surrounding it, while the mid-distance was occupied by three nearly equi-distant mounds, on which stood ancient and isolated mud and brick villages, each with a small pond of water close to it. Here and there

* The total number finally captured, including fifty at Mooltan, was 158. The British actually had at Googerat 106 pieces.

a few light and graceful Arabian acacia and wild plum trees, alone broke the view, and from one to the other, flights of small birds, scared by the advancing red line, and the thunder of artillery, were twittering to and fro, in their alarm.

This great cultivated plain was bisected by a deep dry nullah or watercourse.

The first note of battle was a cloud of white smoke curling up into the blue sky, on the right of the enemy's line, and immediately afterwards came the booming of a gun, as a round shot ploughed the ground in front.

The order was then given to engage, whereupon the batteries of artillery, from the intervals of brigades, galloped about 300 yards to the front of the line, which lay down, and opened fire. These batteries were connected by skirmishers in extended order,—while, in the centre of the British force, and on the right of the nullah, advanced the stately elephants, the central one bearing on its back the banner of St. George, with its red cross on a white field, waving in the light breeze. These animals were drawing the heavy guns, which had only a few days before reached the army.

After each interval of cannonading, as the enemy slackened fire, and retired, the Infantry advanced, preceded by the Artillery, and skirmishers in the same order; and, again and again, the same tactics were repeated.

The striped red and white tents of the enemy's camp, below the walls of Googerat, were now in sight, when a cloud of horsemen rushed past the skirmishers of the 24th, from the direction of the elephants and heavy guns. The men prepared to fire, but some one cried out, "They are our own Irregulars,"—when another, seeing two sowars on the same house, shouted,—"Our men would not ride in that fashion *towards* the enemy!" and taking instant aim, he brought them down. Before the remainder could profit by the momentary hesitation of the skirmishers, about half-a-dozen more were struck by the fire now fully opened upon them.

Lieut. Hinde, a young officer always cheerful and calm in danger, observing one of the slain horsemen to be very handsomely dressed, said to the narrator, "Come, let us see who the fellow is," and both proceeded to the spot. The fallen man seemed to be an Afghan of note, and was remarkably handsome. On his finger was a gold ring, on the stone of which, in Persian characters, was engraven his name, followed by "Chief of Ghorchurhas" (Afghan Cavalry). This trophy was secured by the officer mentioned.

Later on in the day many large triangular red and green gold embroidered silken standards were picked up, and three of these afterwards come into the possession of the same officers, but were lost or stolen some weeks later.

But, to return.—After the repulse of the enemy's Cavalry, which, as it appeared, had made a dash to capture the heavy guns, there arose a dense cloud of reddish dust, which completely obscured the Sikh position. The monotonous sound of familiar tom-toms or drums, had suddenly ceased, and, in their stead came a rushing sound as of feet, from the cloud of darkness. The explanation was simple. The enemy had taken to flight, entirely abandoning all his guns, and camp equipage.

The British Cavalry was now launched in pursuit, while the Infantry, advancing through the gaily striped tents which had been abandoned, drew up in line on the left, and a little in advance of the town of Googerat.

It was now nearly sunset; arms were piled; and, while here and there, mines and combustibles were exploding, the bands of the various regiments struck up, at the hour of retreat, their martial music, dominated by the spirit-stirring "Rule Britannia."

In Indian battles, it may be observed, that *quarter* is rarely ever *given* or *taken,* and never can be forgotten the expression on the countenances of two severely wounded Sikhs, who were discovered secreted in a small house, after the battle had ceased. On lifting the purdah, or curtain, behind which they lay, they looked steadily at the intruder, as much as to say, "*We are in your power,—do your worst.*" It was evident that they were prepared to die without any further struggle, and listened with indifference to the officer's assurance that they were safe, and should be sent to hospital, and taken care of.

This indifference to death, is not always, however, paralleled by indifference to pain and danger.

Sometimes, through what might be regarded as mere whimsicality, the natives of India display considerable indifference to danger. Thus, at the battle of Googerat, an officer skirmishing in front, was surprised to find that his young Khidmutgar (Mahomedan table attendant), had followed under fire, to offer him a small bottle of sherry and water, with a biscuit. Yet, some month's later, the same man stole his horse!

CHAPTER XII.

On the morning of the 22nd, two flying columns were despatched in pursuit of the enemy. The smaller under Brig.-Gen. Campbell, which included the 24th Foot, proceeded to the Bimbu Pass, to secure any guns which might have taken that route, and returned in a few days without any result.

The larger, under Sir Walter R. Gilbert, proceeded by Dinghee to the Jhelum, and crossing that river, followed up the enemy with such vigour, that, on the 6th March, the Sikh Commander allowed his prisoners,—taken at Peshawar and Attock, to go over to Gilbert's camp; and, on the 8th, Shere Singh had an interview with that General and Major Mackeson, and was informed of the only terms admissible, namely, unconditional surrender.

On the 14th, Sirdar Chuttur Singh, Rajah Shere Singh, and the principal Sikh leaders, delivered their swords into the hands of the British General; and, at the same time, were surrendered forty-one pieces of artillery; while the remnant of the Sikh army, without provisions, with Abbot's force on their rear, the Cashmerians on their right, Sheik Eman ood Deen and Gilbert in front,—to the number of 16,000 men, laid down their arms in presence of the British troops.*

On the 21st March, Gilbert came in sight of Peshawar, and occupied that important stronghold.

Galloping to Attock with his staff, and a small escort of Cavalry, the General surprised the Afghans, who, on the farther side of the Indus, were in the act of destroying the bridge of boats; but, at once, in presence of a troop of the British Horse Artillery, abandoned their attempt, when seventeen of their best boats fell into the hands of the indefatigable General.

The Afghan Army, commanded by the Ameer Dost Mahomed Khan in person, had, in the meantime, on the 19th, precipitately retreated from Peshawar; and, thus "these brilliant results," says Lord Gough in his despatch of March 25th,—"have been obtained without a single shot being fired by our troops, since the victory of Googerat."

The annexation of the Punjab was proclaimed, on the 30th March 1849.

In April, the leaders Chuttur Singh, and his two sons, Shere Singh and Outar Singh, were dismissed to their native village, Attari, with a competence.

Moolraj, the traitor or patriot of Mooltan, was sentenced in July (1849), to imprisonment for life.

---

* This incident is represented on the reverse of the medal granted to the army of the Punjab.

Dhuleep Singh, the titular sovereign of the Punjab, yielded up his rights for an annual pension of 50,000*l.*, with liberty to dwell wherever he might choose, beyond the limits of his late kingdom.

The Royal treasures of Lahore were secured, and from the spoil, the celebrated diamond, the Koh-i-noor, was reserved for the Queen of England.

The remainder of the spoil, valued at many millions, was adjudged to the army by whose instrumentality it had been acquired, and, in the meantime, *six month's batta* was all that the captors of Mooltan, the victors of Googerat, and, the final conquerors of a warlike nation, were permitted to receive; and, with a few exceptions among the higher grades, this was all that the officers and men ever had; for, under an extraordinary arithmetical coincidence, it was ascertained, when millions came to be apportioned, that the latter had received, in batta, the exact equivalent of their share of prize money, and, accordingly, as the donative was deducted from the latter, the balance was found to have been already struck! A more equitable system, as regards the proportion of shares, in the distribution of prize-money has, since then, been established. But, as the fate of the *Kirwee*, and other prize property has shown, there is no absolute security for the soldier, against the necessities of the State,—if, indeed, *only* the State.

CHAPTER XIII.

Until the appearance of Thackwell's "Narrative of the Second Seikh War," the Parliamentary Blue Book of that campaign, could scarcely have afforded to the reader, unacquainted personally with the subject, without a very careful analysis of its contents, any very perspicuous idea of the sequence of events. Moreover, many incidents of that remarkable campaign, have been overlooked, either unavoidably, or owing to circumstances of a peculiar nature; and it is remarkable, that Lord Gough himself should not have considered it necessary to correct any of the numerous errors that crept into public notice, affecting, in some instances, his own reputation as a commander.

In the annals of war, there are certain campaigns that have given rise to more than ordinary diversity of criticism, even when the principal events might appear to have been the easiest of narration.

As regards the wars of Great Britain, one of the causes of this difficulty, prior to the period of the Crimean, appears to have arisen, in distant parts, such as India, from the absence of those unprofessional, and consequently, untrammelled correspondents of the Press, whose accounts of operations in the field, have rarely been influenced by official prescription which dictated who should, and who should not, irrespective of merit, be brought to the notice of their countrymen.

It has been said by an eminent German, that "it is a kind of piety to move along without consideration." But in war, on the other hand, it seems to be a disparagement of Providence to be hindered from motion through the apprehension of stumbling.

With all his proverbial personal gallantry, Lord Gough, has been accused by his detractors of timidity as well as rashness of judgment. But, his fault may rather have been, that he relied too much, in the Council, on the opinions of those whose plausible assurance, animated by doubtful motives, were mistaken by him for the evidence of superior ability.

While a striking vigour marked his conduct of the First Seikh Campaign, extreme vacillation,—no doubt, in a great measure, due to political and distant influences, to which the field operations were subordinated—characterised the Second.

At the very outset, orders and counter-orders succeeded each other so rapidly, that a state of feverish excitement, prejudicial to the public interests, was unnecessarily, as time has shown, kept up; and regiments showed the effects of varying and harassing rumours, in their hospital returns.

The intelligence department of the army was defective, strategical blunders were very naturally the result, and in order to cover these, the chronology of events, was obscured in the General's despatches,—an instance of which is to be found in those relating to the affair of Sadoolapore,* when Sir Joseph Thackwell, in command of a detached force, making a forced march to Wuzeerabad, missed his way, and being discovered by the enemy, was himself surprised by the sudden appearance of the Sikh army in his front, while Lord Gough, supporting as was believed this diversion, delayed a whole day, cannonading the evacuated Sikh position at the ford of the Chenab, near Ramnuggur—which were long suppressed.

It ought not, however, to be forgotten, that, although Lord Gough † had at first ignored the signs of revolt at Mooltan, and, had only thrown off his inactivity on the urgent remonstrance of Lord Dalhousie, it was the latter who restrained him, from the 5th of December (1848), until the 12th of January following.

According to the belief of Sir Henry Lawrence, not more than 10,000 Sikhs were opposed to Thackwell, at Sadoolapore, on the 3rd December, and, it is not improbable that, had Lord Gough, instead of listening to

---

* The able compiler of a certain Dictionary of Dates was excusably led into an error through the same cause.

† Lord Gough seems to have attributed nervousness to Sir F. Currie as Resident at Lahore, and absurd stories were afloat on the subject.

timid counsels, crossed the Chenab on that day, the result would have been a decisive victory.

But, there was no efficient co-operation between the two forces of the British; and Thackwell, equally uncertain of the movements of the Commander-in-Chief and of the enemy, was satisfied to hold his ground. Arnold says, "Thackwell's guns, however, after two hours fighting, completely subdued the Sikh fire." But this is incorrect, as the particulars related elsewhere show, that Thackwell, having passively sustained the enemy's fire for nearly four hours without returning a shot, at length opened fire, but, only when the enemy's object of keeping him in check had succeeded, and they were, in conformity to their original design, already retiring.

Lord Dalhousie, conscious of the possession of commanding talents, was, perhaps, too ready to overlook the fact, that, although his inferior in mental calibre, Lord Gough, with many noble qualities, was also the favourite of fortune; and, as a successful General, had won the devoted attachment, and even confidence of the army, which, appreciating his great personal gallantry in the field, was reconciled, in a measure, to such losses as might be occasioned by a strategy, which, however, always resulted in victory.

Thackwell, in his "Narrative of the Second Sikh War," while reflecting on the capacity of Lord Gough as a commander, to some extent neutralizes his strictures, by referring to the tutelage imposed upon him by a distant civilian, whose representative in camp, practically relieved the General of much of his responsibility. As an instance of this subordination of military to political considerations, it was well known, that while negociations with Shere Singh were pending, shortly after the battle of Chillianwalla, beef was not killed in the British camp, in deference to the enemy's veneration of the sacred animal.

At the same time, it seems only reasonable that, under the peculiar circumstances of the British rule in India, some political authority should always be present with the Commander in the field.

Sir C. J. Napier, the successor of Lord Gough, resisted any such check upon his military operations and command. But, this arose from his self-confidence, which was quite equal to that of the Governor-General. Each seemed to regard the other as his intellectual inferior,—and, at the same time, the talents of both were too much alike, to admit of harmony between them. The consequence was, that this incompatibility of temper weakened the authority of both, and might have been detrimental to the Imperial interests.

Lord Dalhousie, with the same autocratic disposition as Lord Ellenborough, missed the popularity of the latter, who invariably recognised the fact, that India is ruled by the sword, whereas, the former had the reputation of affecting to undervalue the true source of power, and was even unworthily suspected of seeking to intercept the glory of the Commander by the subtleties of diplomacy.

In the army of former times,—or, thirty years ago,—the great difficulty was, *not* to induce officers to acquire a knowledge of the higher duties of their profession, but rather to overcome the jealousy of superior and yet limited, knowledge, which was supposed by the higher grades to be the special privilege of each, in progressive degrees. Under that system, young officers who, after perhaps three years service, and who had never really been taught a knowledge of drill, were, sometimes, invested with independent command, while others, with a sufficient amount of instruction, for the period, but who happened to have, on first appointment, joined their corps, might be rigourously relegated to the supernumerary rank, for years, and never be afforded, all the while, a single opportunity of commanding their own companies.

Thus, under an arbitrary Colonel, or one whose authority was delegated to an Adjutant, majors were ciphers, and subalterns grew to be captains without confidence in themselves, while their special powers were usurped,—and the terrorism of the confidential and secret report induced them, too often, to submit to an abridgment of their authority.

It has always been the bane of the army of India, that a jealousy between the officers of the European and Native Infantry regiments has subsisted, which used, sometimes, to be fomented even by those who had risen to high command.

The imputation that the best officers of a Native infantry corps were almost invariably removed to the staff, was felt, by those who remained with their regiments, as a disparagement. At the same time, these favoured officers, and those of the Queen's corps seemed to coalesce, while the latter, in many instances, asserted an unintelligent exclusiveness.

But, in the course of time, the advantages have been reversed, by the amalgamation of the two services, and the local officer has not only secured a superior retirement, but, has acquired official rank in England, for which the former had been a compensation. Hence, many remarkable anomalies.

A new era dawned with the struggle on the banks of the Jhelum and the Chenab. The conquest of the Punjab led to the annexation of Oude, and both events exercised a powerful, although opposite, influence during the subsequent revolt of the Bengal army.

When the kingdom of the Sikhs was reduced to the position of a British province, Sir Henry Lawrence was appointed its first Governor, and, although he was blamed for a generous policy of *non-exaction*, by justice, conciliation, and tact, such as might have graced the narrative of "The Anabasis," he won the confidence of a proud race, enhanced the reputation of the English name, and lived to see the fruits of an enlightened administration, in the devotion and fidelity of those brilliant soldiers who fought shoulder to shoulder with the British, for the maintenance of an Empire which they had themselves disputed and lost.

APPENDICES.

APPENDIX A.

GENERAL NOTES, FROM PRIVATE JOURNALS, &c.

CHILLIANWALLA.

I. WHEN the 24th had cleared the jungle, and were advancing on the enemy's battery in front the dâk trees (*Butea frondosa*), between the large pools of water which stood there, were entirely denuded of their foliage by the successive discharges of grape-shot.

Here was found, it has been said, the body of a poor bhestie, or water-carrier, attached to the regiment, who, with singular generosity, and without any hope of reward, had followed the Europeans with his massick (skin) of water to afford a drink to such as might require it.

There were many poor camp-followers of the same class, equally disinterested.

II. The antelope, which used to walk in front of the band of the 24th, was here also, in the thickest of the fight, and seemed to bear a charmed life. Perhaps he was spared through the superstition of the enemy, or perhaps his life was of no consequence.

III. The placid expression on the countenances of the dead was remarkable; but, in those cases in which the enemy had had time, in the fierce struggle, to cut open the lips of dying or dead, to the ears, the expression was, of course, very different. In one instance, an officer had had all his fingers sliced off with a tulwar, ere he received the fatal blow. His arms in death were still upraised, as though in defence of his head, while the contortion of his features was dreadful.

Most of the bodies were stripped during the darkness of the night, probably by the country-people, who had, perhaps, taken advantage of the opportunity to plunder the dead.

As the brigade was being driven from the guns, Major Harris, a tall portly old officer, appeared to be much fatigued, and scarcely able to walk. In this condition, one of the enemy's sowars, who had ridden out from between the intervals of the guns, rushed upon him unperceived from the rear, and cut him down with one blow of his powerful tulwar.

Some of the dead appeared afterwards to have been dragged completely through the thorny bushes, as evidenced by their bodies, the flesh of which was torn in long ribbons by the peculiar crooked thorns of this jungle.

IV. To give some idea of the nature of the disaster, it is noticeable, that one of the senior officers of this ill-fated corps, on passing another, like himself, wounded, exclaimed, "This is a bad day for the 24th."

V. Lieut. Grant, of this regiment, who was orderly officer to Brig.-Gen. Campbell, as soon as the latter perceived that Pennicuick's brigade was advancing unflanked by artillery, despatched him to look for guns, and bring them up. But the mistake was even then irretrievable.

VI. When the 24th were rallying at the village of Chillianwalla, an officer of rank, splendidly mounted on an iron-grey Cabul horse, dashed wildly past, crying out to them, to save themselves, in the belief that the enemy's Cavalry were in pursuit. But, the men knew better. The horseman was evidently not a good judge of distance; but with this exception, he was considered a good officer, as indeed appears from the fact, that he received promotion, and the Companionship of the Bath.

VII. The martial spirit of the artillerymen was very conspicuous on this occasion, and the following incident should not be passed over:—

In the darkness and rain that succeeded to the action, while some groups were arranging themselves in circles, each man reclining on the side of his next neighbour,—a apital protection against cold,—and others were seeking unclaimed quilts which had been brought up, but which now had no owners, an officer parched with thirst accosted a gunner, who, with a bucket, was about to take some water from a pool, and offered him a rupee for a drink. But the latter drew himself up proudly, and replied, "No, Sir, a soldier never sells water on a battle-field: you may have what you like, free."

There was another instance of liberality, amongst many more which have been forgotten. A soldier of the 61st, named Watson, hearing in the darkness, an officer complaining that he could find nothing to smoke, suddenly started up from the ground, and offered half of a pipeful which was all that he possessed. The officer accepted it; and, while walking about in the dark, came upon one of the Brigadier-General's orderly officers, who, being a personal friend, gave him a surprise, in the shape of half a bottle of ale, and a piece of cold mutton and bread. It was now the officer's opportunity to repay a kindness, and, after calling out several times for Watson, at length the man himself appeared, whereupon the former, to his great satisfaction, shared with him the *bon bouche*.

VIII. A day or two after this battle, the dead, stripped naked and blood-stained, were brought into camp, slung up by ropes, three or four, on each camel; but the sight was so repugnant to the feelings of the men, that the remainder were buried where they fell, in shallow graves; and it was a tragic sight, afterwards, in the peculiar light of the gloamin,—jackals or dogs, dragging at the protruding limbs of the dead, while on others, completely exposed, these animals, and vultures, with flapping wings, were contending for the carrion meal, on the body itself.

IX. The European regiments at Chillianwalla, observed uniformity in dress. Thus, while the 24th Foot wore full attire, with the then inconvenient chaco,* the 29th were in undress jackets and forage caps. Some officers wore their blue frock coats, some dark trowsers, and shell jackets, and others, long red or blue cotton coats, quilted, with turbans or *pugrees* wound round their forage caps.

Considering the character of the ground, and the practice of the enemy, of always, where possible, directing their principal fire on the colours of regiments, thus exposing the centre and commanding officer to increased danger, the 29th Foot wisely and judiciously disregarding the mere pomp and circumstance of war, advanced in more business-like fashion, with their standards cased.

X. Having learnt a lesson from the disaster that befell the 24th, the troops, whenever practicable, were subsequently exercised by corps, in advancing and firing in loose order, a principle now fully established.

XI. It is a curious fact, as compared with the large promotion of officers, in subsequent campaigns, that the only officer of the Queen's army, under the grade of Captain, rewarded with a step of brevet rank, after Chillianwalla,

* Many of these were lost, even in the advance.

was Lieutenant and Adjutant Macdonnell, Brigade Major of Mountain's Brigade, in Sir W. R. Gilbert's division.

XII. Sir Henry Lawrence, and Lord Gifford, who had attended Lord Gough on the field of Chillianwalla, left the camp for Lahore on the 18th January.

XIII. A curious story is told, by Thackwell, of the 5th Bengal Light Cavalry. Lord Gough, for some unexplained reason, presented this corps with 100 rupees; but, with rare modesty, under the circumstances, the men declined to accept the donation, as not due to themselves, and with considerable magnaminity, purchased with it a piece of plate, which they presented to the 14th Dragoons.

XIV. We have a suggestive incident in the following:—
A subaltern officer, being one very dark night, on out-lying picquet, after visiting the European chain of sentries, conceived the idea of testing the vigilance of those who continued the line of his own men, and, having a quick ear, and keen sight, after passing far to the front, succeeded in re-entering the British lines without detection.

APPENDIX B.

The name Punjab, it is scarcely necessary to say, signifies the region of the five waters or rivers (*panj-âb*), bounded on the north-west by, but not including, the Indus. These five rivers are:—

1. The Hydaspes, or Jhelum (Sanskrit, *Vi-tasta*, "never standing").
2. The Ascesines, or Chenab (*Asikni*, "the black or dark").
3. The Hydraotes, or Ravi (*Irawati*, "the water"; *Ravi*, "the sounding").
4. The Hyphasis, Bibasa, or Beas (*Vipasa*, "uncontrollable").
5. The Sutlej (*Satadru*, "the hundred currents").

Between these rivers, the country is divided into Doabs, 1, the Sind Saugor,—Indus and Jhelum; 2, the Chuj, or Jetch; 3, the Rechna; 4, the Bari, or that between the Beas and the Ravi.

"The people of the Punjab," says the Rev. C. E. Moberly (in his Introduction to "Alexander the Great in the Punjab, from Arrian, Book V."), "have always been warlike by necessity;" and, their struggle against the Macedonian Conqueror, is but a type of subsequent conflicts in defence of their liberty. In A.D. 1000, Mahmoud of Ghuznee here encountered the stoutest resistance, while

Jenghis Khan, Timour, and others, were, successively, unable to proceed to the conquest of India proper, until this resistance had been subdued. In the seventeenth century, arose the fanatical "Sikhs" (disciples), or followers of the Hindu schismatist Nanuk.

An invader, emerging from the Afghan passes, and crossing the Indus, as Alexander the Great did, opposite Attock (*the forbidden*, beyond which a Hindu loses his caste), would reach a point where two great roads bifurcate. The western one, followed by Alexander, crossed the Jhelum, below, Jelapur, the Chenab, below Ramnuggur, the Ravi, below Lahore, and the Sutlej, at its junction with the Beas. The eastern road was, by Jhelum, Wuzeerabad, and Umritsir (fountain of the water of life).

Alexander was compelled to take the former road, by the position of Porus (*Purusha*, "the hero") king, as is supposed, of the Bari Doab.*

The battle with Porus has been described by Sir W. Napier, and more recently by General Cunningham. Both writers have drawn attention to the admirable skill displayed by the invader in his passage of the Jhelum, and it has been observed, that "Alexander managed *his* 'battle of Chillianwalla' in a way which it is profitable to compare" with the advance of Lord Gough from the Chenab, to "the identical ground" where, in April or May, B.C. 326, the Indian monarch was so utterly defeated.†

The characteristic of Alexander's strategy and tactics, was, a caution and preparation, which left little or nothing

* No sufficient reason seems to have been given for the exclusion of the Jetch and Rechna Doabs.

† The village of "Mong," mentioned in connection with the battle of Chillianwalla, is identical with the Νικαιαν of the Greek historians; and the Greek coins are still occasionally found there with the inscription "NIK."

to fortune. His lieutenants never failed when acting independently in the execution of his orders, for he had imbued them with the power of his own commanding intellect; and this fact, they seemed to recognise. One mind animated the whole mass, and, the result was, harmony. How different from divided command, and "dual government" in the field!

APPENDIX C.

The Second Advance of the 24th Foot, at Chillianwalla.

"On the second advance of the 24th Regiment," . . . at the battle of Chillianwalla, "Lieut. Archer commanded No. 6 company," and, "although wounded in the leg, he continued on the field till the close of the day," &c. (Signed) A. G. Blachford, 20th September 1853.

The following are also extracts from subsequent letters written by Maj.-Gen. Blachford, the originals of which are in the possession of the officer to whom they were addressed, and have been periodically referred to the Horse-Guards and War Office.

After the regiment had been rallied, and was advancing *in line*, "Lieut. Archer LED, and commanded No. 6 company," *—*i.e.*, *before* Captain Blachford had overtaken the advance, and *after*, the Adjutant-General Queen's Troops (Lugard) had ridden out of sight. The former

* This officer continued in command of the same company, until a captain, on the staff of the Governor-General, was temporarily attached to the corps, when, by order of Lieut.-Col. M. Smith, it was transferred to him, and its late commander was posted to another company, as subaltern. But, he commanded the latter, on all OUT-LYING picquets, until the close of the campaign, but not within the regimental camp.

continues—"I found myself senior officer on the field with only *seven* officers to command. . . . Lieut. Archer had, *previously* to this, rallied No. 7 company, with the help of Colour-Sergeant Eastall. . . . ." "I know that you (Lieut. A.) got hold of the Colour-Sergeant, —Eastall was his name, and rallied the company (No. 7). . . . This was the first company rallied . . . you got (*took*) charge of *No*. 6 company, and *led* in the second advance (in LINE)."

Capt. Blachford, succeeding to the temporary command of the corps, prepared the *Regimental Record*.

Amongst other documentary references to the above incidents,—and which, at the time, might have been multiplied, are the following:—

From James Michal. "I was with the Light Company of the 24th Regiment at Chillianwalla. I was in the second advance, in which Mr. Hinde commanded my company. The Brigadier-General (Campbell) rode up, and told the regiment *before* the *first* advance, that the battery before them must be taken without firing, and at the point of the bayonet. No. 7 company being the first rallied, and drawn up for the second advance, the Light Company was next rallied under Ensign Hinde, and formed on its left. I was present when it did so."

From Sergeant Thompson. "Colonel Brookes addressed the regiment in the (earliest) advance on the mound, from which the enemy had retired (saying), '*Men, we are going to charge the mound, and, by the grace of God, we shall gain a glorious victory!*' With that, he waved his sword. In the next (and disastrous) advance, Colonel Brookes did *not* again wave his sword, (after) Brig.-Gen. Campbell had ridden up, and told us, '*You must not fire,—steel*' (or '*the bayonet*') 'must do the work,'" &c.

From Sir E. Lugard. "War Office, 8th June 1865. . . . I am desired by Sir Edward Lugard . . . to acquaint you that he will have much pleasure in corroborating your statement, that when, at the battle of Chillianwalla, he rode up and assumed command of the 24th Foot, in order to lead it again against the enemy, you were, though wounded, one of the *seven* officers that followed him in that advance . . ."

The following narrative is the more necessary, as the above extracts contain (as will be noticed on comparing them), some obscurities :—

"Lieut. Archer, at his own request, was, in the absence of his regiment, appointed to serve with the 24th Foot, by the Commander-in-Chief in India, with the approval of the Governor-General, and accordingly joined the latter corps, on the eve of the combat of Ramnugger (22 Nov. 1848), at which he was present. He continued throughout the Punjab campaign, with the corps to which he was attached. At the passage of the Chenab, and action of Sadoolapore, he was with the skirmishers covering the advance; and afterwards, at the final victory of Googerat. In the meantime, however, was fought the battle of Chillianwalla (the occasion of these remarks), when he was still doing duty with No. 7 company, which, in consequence of Captain Blachford's acting as field-officer, was commanded by Lieut. Clark. On line of battle being formed (Jan. 13, 1849), Brigadier Colin Campbell (Lord Clyde) rode up to the regiment, and impressed upon the men that "there must be no firing," but that the bayonet must do the work. He then rode away, and the corps advanced into the dense jungle, under the command of Lieut.-Colonel Brookes. The real cause of the ensuing disaster, appears to have been the absence, in the brigade, of flanking batteries of artillery, &c. On the violent repulse of the 24th Regiment from the enemy's guns, the former retreated on the village of Chillianwalla.* No vestiges of the brigade being observable in the open, Lt. Archer (who had been held at bay by a Sikh horseman) entered this village, and discovering the men there called on them to follow him into the field, and recognising Sergt. Eastall, ordered the latter to stand opposite to him, about twenty paces off, and shout out incessantly, 'Fall in, number seven.' This proved effectual; and the remnant of that company was soon reformed, and told off in sections, &c., by Lieut. A. Lieut. Clark then came up (followed by Ensign Hinde, who at once began to form up the Light company in alignment with No. 7), and resumed command of the company. Thereupon Lieut. Archer directed his attention to No. 6 company, which was reforming on the right of No. 7, and assumed command of it. The other companies gradually followed the example, and the corps was at length ready for the *second* advance. At this conjuncture, the Adjt.-General Queen's Troops (Colonel Lugard) rode up, and, having inquired of Lieut. Archer the above circumstances, ordered him to follow—he giving the direction, and the word of command from Lieut. Archer being taken up by the Commanders of the other companies. Thus commenced the *second advance.* Colonel Lugard then rode ahead, and was scarcely out of sight, when Captain Blachford rejoined the regiment—made some brief inquiries of Lieut. Archer (whom he *confirmed* in command of No. 6 company), and thus ascertaining the orders of Colonel Lugard from him, continued the advance. The Assistant Adjt.-General afterwards met the regiment, and it was *then* that the orders referred to by

* On passing to the rear, wounded, Capt. —— hurriedly exclaimed, with much emotion, for he had considerable *esprit de corps*, "This is a bad day for the 24th."

Major-General Blachford, were given. Col. Lugard's orders having been taken over by Capt. Blachford FROM Lieut. Archer.

The *seven* officers, in the order of their rallying, referred to by Sir E. Lugard were,—Archer, Hinde, Clark, Bailley, Mackechnie, Drew, and Lutman. Capt. Blachford, who having AFTERWARDS joined in the second advance, made the *eighth*.

He had not, however, been with the corps when, in the earlier advance, it suffered so severely.

APPENDIX D.

DETAILED STATEMENT OF THE NUMERICAL STRENGTH OF CORPS ENGAGED IN THE SEVERAL ACTIONS DURING THE PUNJAB CAMPAIGN.

	All ranks.	Authority.
I.—RAMNUGGUR.		
1st Troop 2nd Brigade Horse Artillery.	125	Monthly Return.
3rd ditto ditto	148	Do.
1st Troop 3rd ditto 2nd ditto ditto	330	General Quarterly Return, dated 1st October 1848.
No 5 Lt. Field Battery and 3rd Co. 7th Bn. Foot Artillery.	157	Monthly Return.
No. 10 ditto and 1st Co. 1st ditto	172	Do.
Her Majesty's 3rd Light Dragoons.	693	General Quarterly Return, dated 1st October 1848.
Ditto 14th ditto	648	Do.
5th Light Cavalry - -	514	Do.
8th ditto - -	513	Do.
Her Majesty's 24th Foot -	1190	Do.
Ditto 61st Foot -	1046	Do.
2nd European Bengal Fusiliers -	818	Do.
22nd Native Infantry - -	952	Monthly Return.
25th ditto - -	905	Do.
31st ditto - -	949	Do.
36th ditto - -	1051	Do.
46th ditto - -	905	Do.
56th ditto - -	1008	Do.
II.—SADOOLAPORE.		
1st Troop 2nd Brigade Horse Artillery.	114	Chillianwallah figures plus the casualties at Sadoolapore.
2nd ditto ditto	154	Do.
3rd ditto ditto	143	Do.
No. 10 Light Field Battery -	184	Do.
No. 5 ditto -	92	Do.
Her Majesty's 3rd Light Dragoons	710	Do.
5th Light Cavalry - -	511	Do.
8th ditto - -	509	Do.
3rd Irregular Cavalry - -	610	Do.

	All ranks.	Authority.
II.—SADOOLAPORE—*cont.*		
Her Majesty's 24th Regiment (Exact Figures)	*1006	*Bayonets.
Ditto 61st Regiment (Exact Figures)	813	Do.
25th Native Infantry (Exact Figures)	610	Do.
31st ditto (Exact Figures)	756	Do.
36th ditto (Exact Figures)	768	Do.
46th ditto (Exact Figures)	599	Do.
56th ditto (Exact Figures)	838	Do.
2 Companies Pioneers - -		
III.—CHILLIANWALLAH.		
1st Troop 2nd Brigade Horse Artillery.	109	Monthly Return.
2nd ditto ditto	154	Do.
3rd ditto ditto	143	Do.
4th ditto ditto	147	Do.
1st Troop 2nd Brigade Horse Artillery. / 2nd ditto ditto	300	
No. 1 Co. 1st Bn. and No. 10 Battery Foot Artillery.	181	Do.
No. 3 Co. 1st Bn. and No. 17 Light Field Battery.	178	Do.
No. 3 Co. 7th Bn. and No. 5 Battery Foot Artillery - -	92	Do.
No. 1 Co. 4th Bn. Foot Artillery. (Reserve)	158	Do.
No. 2 Co. 4th Bn. ditto (Reserve)	118	Do.
No. 4 Co. 4th Bn. ditto (Reserve)	69	Do.
Her Majesty's 3rd Light Dragoons	709	Quarterly General Return, dated 1st January 1849.
Ditto 9th Lancers -	768	Do.
Ditto 14th Light Dragoons	673	Do.
1st Light Cavalry - -	517	Do.
5th ditto - -	510	Do.
6th ditto - -	516	Do.
8th ditto - -	508	Do.
3rd Irregular Cavalry - -	604	Do.
9th ditto - -	607	Do.
Her Majesty's 24th Foot -	1176	Do.
Ditto 29th Foot -	1134	Do.
Ditto 61st Foot -	1136	Do.
2nd European Bengal Fusiliers -	976	Do.
15th Native Infantry - -	1026	Monthly Return.

	All ranks.	Authority.
III.—CHILLIANWALLAH—*cont.*		
20th Native Infantry - -	1008	Quarterly General Return, 1st January 1849.
25th ditto - -	920	Monthly Return.
30th ditto - -	972	Do.
31st ditto - -	983	Do.
36th ditto - -	963	Do.
45th ditto - -	976	Do.
46th ditto - -	908	Do.
56th ditto - -	1040	Quarterly General Return, 1st January 1849.
69th ditto - -	1008	Monthly Return.
70th ditto - -	1081	Quarterly General Return, 1st January 1849.
6 Companies Pioneers - -	336	Do.
IV.—GOOJERAT.*		
4th Troop 1st Brigade Horse Artillery.	145	Monthly Return.
1st Troop 2nd ditto	118	Do.
2nd ditto ditto	118	Do.
3rd ditto ditto	145	Do.
4th ditto ditto	148	Do.
1st Troop 3rd ditto 2nd ditto ditto 4th ditto ditto	470	Quarterly General Return, 1st January 1849.
1st Co. 1st Bn. Foot Artillery with No. 10 Lt. Field Battery.	185	Monthly Return.
3rd ditto ditto No. 17 ditto	172	Do.
2nd Co. 2nd Bn. Foot Artillery -		
3rd Co. 3rd Bn. ditto -	97	Do.
4th ditto ditto -	92	Do.
1st Co. 4th Bn. Foot Artillery - 2nd ditto ditto - 4th ditto ditto (Dett.)	400 including absent dett. 4th Co.	Quarterly General Return, 1st January 1849.
3rd Co. 7th Bn. Foot Artillery (Dett.)	166 full strength	Do.
3rd Co. 7th Bn. Foot Artillery, with No. 5 Lt. Field Battery.	98	Monthly Return.
6th ditto ditto	102	Quarterly General Return, 1st January 1849.

* In this return of the force at Goojerat it will be observed that the following European Regiments are omitted, viz., the 24th Foot and 1st Bn. 60th, the King's Royal Rifle Regiment. These two corps may be estimated at about a total of 1500 rank and file and 44 officers.

IV.—GOOJERAT—*cont.*	All ranks.	Authority.
3rd Troop Bomb. Horse Artil. -	167	Monthly Return.
Her Majesty's 3rd Light Dragoons.	669	Quarterly General Return, 1st January 1849, deducting casualties at Chillianwallah.
Ditto 9th Lancers - -	756	Do.
Ditto 14th Light Dragoons	654	Do.
1st Light Cavalry - -	510	Do.
5th ditto - -	488	Do.
6th ditto - -	499	Do.
8th ditto - -	505	Do.
3rd Irregular Cavalry - -	604	Do.
9th ditto -	607	Do.
11th ditto (2 Ressallahs)	—	——
12th ditto - -	592	Quarterly General Return, 1st January 1849.
13th ditto - -	551	Do.
14th ditto (2 Ressallahs)	—	——
Guide Corps - - -	—	——
Scinde Horse - - -	—	——
Her Majesty's 10th Foot -	1106	Monthly Return.
Ditto 29th Foot - -	893	Quarterly General Return, 1st January 1849, deducting casualties at Chillianwallah.
Ditto 32nd Foot - -	1139	Quarterly General Return, 1st January 1849.
Ditto 61st Foot - -	958	Monthly Return.
2nd European Bengal Fusiliers -	909	Quarterly General Return, deducting loss at Chillianwallah.
8th Native Infantry - -	917	Monthly Return.
13th ditto - -	993	Quarterly General Return, 1st January 1849.
15th ditto - -	970	Ditto, deducting loss at Chillianwallah.
20th ditto - -	1008	Quarterly General Return, 1st January 1849.
25th ditto - -	661	Monthly Return.
30th ditto - -	567	Do.
31st ditto -	804	Do.
36th ditto -	833	Do.
45th ditto -	897	Quarterly General Return, deducting loss at Chillianwallah.
46th ditto - -	854	Do.

	All ranks.	Authority.
IV.—GOOJERAT—*cont.*		
51st ditto - -	955	Monthly Return.
52nd ditto - -	822	Do.
56th ditto - -	894	Do.
69th ditto - -	941	Quarterly General Return, 1st January 1849, deducting loss at Chillianwallah.
70th ditto - -	1056	Do.
72nd ditto - -	1019	Quarterly General Return, 1st January 1849.
2nd Co. and detachment 3rd Co. Sappers.	300	Do.
6 Companies Pioneers - -	333	Do.
[Total of all ranks imperfect for the reason explained in note.]		

P. S. LUMSDEN, *Major-General.*
Adjutant-General in India.

BESIEGING FORCE BEFORE MOOLTAN, 1848-9.

ARTILLERY.

Officers and Men.		Guns.*
H. A. - -	146	8 24-prs.
Other Artillery -	391	19 18-prs.
Sappers and Miners	583	5 10-in. mortars.
Pioneers (no returns obtainable in England).		13 8-in. „
		4 5½-in. „
		3 10-in. howitzers.
		8 ...-pr., Horse Artillery.

CAVALRY.

No Returns in England.

INFANTRY.

H.M. 10th Foot, 1088.
H.M. 32nd Foot. No Returns at H. G. or W. O.

8th N.I.
49th „
51st „
52nd „
72nd „
} No Returns in England.

* The expenditure of ammunition or guns during the siege of Mooltan was 42,347 rounds.

APPENDIX E.

Chillianwalla and Goojerat.

In the columns of the *Dehli Gazette* may be found some interesting particulars relative to the "Army of the Punjab," under the following dates:—

1849, Jan. 24th, p. 54.—Lord Gough at Chillianwalla.

„ Jan. 31st, p. 69.—Brig.-Gen. Campbell.

„ Feb. 7th, p. 83.—"The Sikhs have 20,000 regular troops and 51 guns . . . . they fought manfully."

„ Feb. 14th, p. 99.—"The 61st went on (Chillianwalla) file firing and advancing, and whenever the enemy seemed inclined to make a stand charging. The Sikhs tried to turn its right, which attempt was defeated by the left companies and 46th Native Infantry bringing up left shoulders. The front rank of the Grenadiers went on the knee, and thus, by their fire, compelled the enemy to abandon two guns. The 46th Native Infantry behaved as men and soldiers." &c.

„ Feb. 21st, p. .—"On the 13th . . . . the sick were sent to Ramnuggur under the impression that the Sikhs had retreated. On the same day also the Commander-in-Chief, went in person to examine the abandoned position of Russool. But the large body of the enemy at Kooree, remained on the same ground as before, our intelligence department remaining in blessed ignorance of their proceedings."

(14th.) "Orders were issued for the immediate march of the army at 9. It was then deferred till 12, when the order was that the march would be next morning."

1849, Feb. 24th, p. 124.—"Orders were despatched to Brig.-Gen. Dundas, through General Whish, to leave the Native portion of his force, and hurry on with his artillery and two European regiments, so as to ensure his arriving at Ramnugger on the 17th. Instead of hastening to obey the order of the officer in question, he replied to the effect, that he saw no necessity for altering the rate of his progress, which was in accordance with the instructions previously sent to him, and that as an European court-martial was then sitting, of which Major Blood was president, he wished to have the proceedings concluded before he moved forward." "Lord Gough (thereupon) sent off such a peremptory order that, we will venture to say, Brig.-Gen. Dundas did not wait to read it a second time. A second despatch desired him to send on the 60th Rifles by a forced march of 30 miles on the 18th; and intimated to the Brigadier-General that he might remain with the Native troops if he chose."

" March 10th, p. 157.—Relative to the audacity of the Sikhs.

APPENDIX F.

DESPATCHES RELATING TO THE CAMPAIGN IN THE PUNJAUB, 1848-9.

General Lord Gough, G. C. B., Commander-in-Chief, to the Governor-General of India.

Ramnugger, November 23, 1848.

Deeming it necessary to drive the rebel force at this side the river across, and to capture any guns they might have had on the left bank, I directed Brigadier-General Campbell, with an infantry brigade of the troops under his command, accompanied by the cavalry division, and three troops of horse artillery under Brigadier-General Cureton, to proceed, during the night of the 21st, from Saharun, four miles in front of my camp at Noewulla, to effect this object. I joined the Brigadier at 3 in the morning to witness the operation.

I hope to be able to inclose Brigadier-General Campbell's report, with a return of the killed and wounded, which I regret to say is much greater than I could have anticipated, in a great measure from the officers leading being unacquainted with the difficult nature of the ground in the vicinity of the river, and of which no native information ever gives you a just knowledge; and in some measure to the impetuosity of the artillery and cavalry, who, notwithstanding these difficulties, charged to the bank of the river, thereby exposing themselves to the fire of about twenty-eight guns. I deeply regret to say a gun was left behind, but spiked, having actually, in the impetuosity of the advance plunged down a bank close under the fire of the enemy's guns. It was reported to me it would occasion a fearful loss of life to bring it away, which alone could be effected by manual labour, and scarping the banks under even the fire of the matchlockmen on the opposite bank; I could not, therefore, consent to such a sacrifice. Though blameable as it may appear to have taken the guns into such close proximity to the enemy's guns in position, which could not, from the river intervening, be captured, it is impossible not to admire the daring gallantry exhibited by the troops, both of cavalry and artillery.

I witnessed with intense anxiety, but equally intense admiration, a charge made by Lieutenant-Colonel Havelock, at the head of the 14th Light Dragoons, who, I fear, misconceived the orders he received from the officer commanding the cavalry division, or from the inequalities of the ground, and the fearful dust occasioned by such a rapid movement, mistook the body he was instructed to charge, and moved upon and overwhelmed another much closer to the river, which exposed him to a cross fire from the enemy's guns. I never witnessed so brilliant a charge, but I regret to say the loss was considerable, were it only in that of Brigadier-General Cureton, than whom a better or a braver soldier never fell in his country's service. The brave leader of the 14th, Lieutenant-Colonel Havelock, is missing; he charged into a gole of the enemy, and has not since been seen, regretted by every sodier who witnessed his noble daring.

The enemy suffered severely; numbers were precipitated into the river and drowned, and a standard was captured.

The Goorchurras were more daring than I have before seen them, but the brilliant charges both of the 3rd and 14th Light Dragoons will have taught them a lesson they will not readily forget. This was a cavalry affair alone; the infantry never was, nor could have been, brought into play without an unnecessary exposure of life; but the cavalry and artillery engaged under Brigadier-General Campbell, whose judicious arrangements were most creditable to him, nobly supported the well-earned fame of the Indian army, and is but a prelude to, I have no doubt, the honourable fulfilment of what their country expects of them.

Brigadier White conducted the movements of the force, of which the 3rd formed a part, and as usual acted with gallantry and judgment; and Lieutenant-Colonel Grant commanded the artillery arm with much credit. I regret to say that gallant old soldier, Lieutenant-Colonel Alexander, has lost an arm, but I am thankful that all are doing well.

Lord Gough to the Governor-General.

Camp before Ramnugger, November 27, 1848.

In continuation of my letter to your Lordship of the 23rd instant, I now do myself the honour to forward the report of Brigadier-General C. Campbell, C.B., commanding the troops on the morning of the 22nd instant, of the operations of that day.

I also beg to inclose a copy of a general order which I have caused to be issued to the army of the Punjab on the occasion.

Brigadier-General Campbell, C.B., commanding the 4th Division, to the Adjutant-General of the Army.

Camp near Ramnugger, November 24, 1848.

I have the honour to report to you, for the information of the Commander-in-Chief, that, in obedience to his Lordship's instructions the troops in advance under my orders, moved, at 3 o'clock A.M., on the morning of the 22nd instant, from their encampment near Saharung, with a view to attack a considerable portion of the enemy's regular troops, who were, with several guns, stated to be on this bank of the Chenab, in the vicinity of Ramnugger. On reaching the high ground to the right of the town, it was ascertained that these troops, with their guns, had crossed to the encampment of the enemy on the opposite bank, where his whole force was in position; at the same time, however, several small parties of the enemy were observed to be retiring from the town of Ramnugger in the direction of the ford in front of the enemy's encampment, when Captain Warner and Lieutenant-Colonel Lane's troops of horse artillery were ordered by Brigadier Cureton, in command of that arm and of the cavalry of the army, to pursue these parties, and to open fire on them while crossing at the ford. These troops of horse artillery, in their eagerness to overtake the enemy, pushed forward through the deep and heavy sand which extends for a long distance on this side to the very margin of the river, and through which the guns could only be moved with great difficulty. Their fire inflicted considerable loss on the enemy while crossing.

In withdrawing from this position, which was effected under the whole of the enemy's artillery, amounting to 28 guns, posted on the high ground which immediately overhangs the river on the opposite bank, I regret to say that one gun and two ammunition-wagons belonging to Colonel Lane's troop, got so imbedded in the heavy sand behind a deep bank, that they could not be recovered.

The enemy, upon observing the difficulty in which this gun was placed, immediately crossed with great confidence the whole of his cavalry, in numbers between three and four thousand. They clung to the banks of the river, and kept constantly under cover of the fire of their artillery on the opposite bank.

This cavalry was charged on separate occasions by Her Majesty's 3rd and 14th Light Dragoons, and 5th and 8th Regiments of Light Cavalry. His Lordship the Commander-in-Chief was an eye-witness of the brilliant conduct of these several corps, and of the intrepid manner they were led by their officers. The enemy were overthrown upon every occasion, who fled for shelter to the river side to be under the cover and protection of their artillery; but, I lament to say, that these several defeats of the enemy's cavalry were not effected without loss.

Brigadier-General Cureton, commanding the cavalry of the army, was killed while leading a squadron of Her Majesty's 14th Light Dragoons to the support of the 5th Light Cavalry. In this officer, who had the honour of enjoying his Lordship's entire confidence and warmest regard, the service has lost one of its most distinguished officers, and one who was beloved by the whole army.

I regret also to have to report that Lieutenant-Colonel Havelock, commanding Her Majesty's 14th Light Dragoons, is reported to be missing. He was last seen charging the enemy at the head of his noble regiment, and has not since been heard of.

I am sorry to have further to report that Lieutenant-Colonel Alexander, commanding the 5th Regiment Light Cavalry, has been severely wounded, and lost his arm. Some other officers and men have also been wounded, whose names are mentioned in the inclosed return of casualties.

(Return of killed, wounded, and missing, of the advance force of the army of the Punjaub, under the command of Brigadier-General C. Campbell, C.B., in the action with the enemy on the 22nd of November 1848,—14 killed; 59 wounded; 12 missing.

Names of officers killed, wounded, and missing:—Ensign G. N. Hardinge, extra aide-de-camp, severely wounded; Brigadier-General C. R. Cureton, C.B., commanding cavalry division, killed; Brevet Lieutenant-Colonel W. Alexander, 5th Light Cavalry, severely wounded; Brevet Captain J. S. G. Ryley, same regiment, severely wounded; Captain A. Wheatley, same regiment, wounded; Captain R. H. Gall, Her Majesty's 14th Dragoons, severely wounded; Captain J. F. Fitzgerald, same regiment, very severely wounded; Captain A. Scudamore, same regiment, slightly wounded; Lieutenant W. McMahon, same regiment, severely wounded; Cornet Honourable R. W. Chetwynd, same regiment, slightly wounded; Lieutenant-Colonel W. Havelock, K.H., same regiment, missing; Lieutenant J. S. Holmes, 12th Irregular Cavalry, severely wounded.)

NOTIFICATION.

Foreign Department,
Camp Umballah, 8th December 1848.

The Right Honourable the Governor-General has much pleasure in publishing, for general information, the following despatch from his Excellency the Commander-in-Chief:—

Head-Quarters,
Flying Camp, Hillah, 5th Dec. 1848.

My Lord,—It has pleased Almighty God to vouchsafe to the British arms the most successful issue to the extensive combinations rendered necessary for the purpose of effecting the passage of the Chenab, the defeat and dispersion of the Sikh force under the insurgent Rajah Shere Sing, and the numerous Sikh sirdars, who had the temerity to set at defiance the British power. This force, from all my information, amounted to from 30,000 to 40,000 men, with 28 guns, and were strongly entrenched on the right bank of the Chenab, at the principal ford, about two miles from the town of Ramnugger.

My despatch of the 23rd November will have made your Lordship acquainted with the motives which induced me to penetrate thus far into the Punjaub, and the occurrences of the previous day, when the enemy were ejected from the left bank of the Chenab. My daily private communications will have placed your Lordship in possession of the difficulties I had to encounter in a country so little known, and in the passage of a river, the fords of which were most strictly watched by a numerous and vigilant enemy, and presenting more difficulties than most rivers, whilst I was surrounded by a hostile peasantry.

Finding that to force the passage at the ford in my front must have been attended with considerable loss, from the very strong entrenchments and well-selected batteries which protected the passage, I instructed the field-engineer, Major Tremenhere, in co-operation with the quartermaster-general's department, to ascertain (under the difficulties before noticed) the practicability of the several fords reported to exist on both my flanks, while I had batteries erected and made demonstrations so as to draw the attention of the enemy to the main ford in my front, and with the view, if my batteries could silence their guns, to act simultaneously with the force I proposed to detach under an officer of much experience in India, Major-General Sir Joseph Thackwell.

On the night of the 30th November, this officer, in

command of the following force, and more particularly detailed in the accompanying memorandum :—

	European.	Native.	Total.
3 troops horse artillery	3	0	3
2 light field batteries	2	0	2
1 brigade of cavalry	1	4	5
3 brigades of infantry	2	6	8

—two 18-pounders with elephant draft and detail artillery, pontoon train, with two companies sappers, moved up the river in light marching order, without tents and with three days' provisions, upon a ford which I had every reason to consider very practicable (and which I have since ascertained was so), but which the major-general deemed so difficult and dangerous, that he proceeded (as he was instructed should such turn out to be the case) to Wuzeerabad, a town 22 miles up the river, where Lieutenant Nicholson, a most energetic assistant to the resident at Lahore, had secured 16 boats, with the aid of which this force effected the passage on the evening of the 1st and morning of the 2nd instant.

Upon learning by an aide-de-camp sent for the purpose that the major-general's force had crossed and was in movement, I directed a heavy cannonade to commence upon the enemy's batteries and encampment at Ramnugger, which was returned by only a few guns, which guarded effectually the ford, but so buried, that although the practice of our artillery was admirable under Major Mowatt and Captain Sir Richmond Shakespear, we could not, from the width of the river, silence them. This cannonade, however, inflicted very severe loss to the enemy in their camp and batteries, and forced him to fall back with his camp about 2 miles, which enabled me, without the loss of a man, to push my batteries and breastworks, on the night of the 2nd, to the bank of the river, the principal ford of which I then commanded;

by this I was enabled to detach another brigade of infantry, under Brigadier Godby, at daylight on the 3rd, which effected the passage, with the aid of pontoon train, six miles up the river, and got into communication with Major-General Sir Joseph Thackwell.

The cannonade and demonstration to cross at Ramnugger was kept up on the 2nd and 3rd, so as to fix a large portion of the enemy there to defend that point. Having communicated to Sir Joseph my views and intentions, and although giving discretionary powers to attack any portion of the Sikh force sent to oppose him, I expressed a wish that, when he covered the crossing of Brigadier Godby's brigade, he should await their junction, except the enemy attempted to retreat: this induced him to halt within about 3 or 4 miles of the left of their position. About 2 o'clock on the 3rd, the principal part of the enemy's force, encouraged by the halt, moved to attack the detached column, when a smart cannonade on the part of the enemy took place, and an attempt to turn both Major-General Sir Joseph Thackwell's flanks, by numerous bodies of cavalry, was made. After about one hour's distant cannonade on the part of the Sikhs, the British artillery never returning a shot, the enemy took courage and advanced, when our artillery, commanded by that excellent officer Lieutenant-Colonel C. Grant, poured in upon them a most destructive fire, which soon silenced all their guns and frustrated all their operations, with very severe loss upon their side; but the exhausted state both of man and horsc induced the major-general to postpone the attack upon their flank and rear, as he was directed, until the following morning, the day having nearly closed when the cannonade ceased.

I regret to say that, during the night of the 3rd, the whole of the Sikh force precipitately fled, concealing or carrying with them their artillery, and exploding their magazines. I immediately pushed across the river the 9th Lancers and 14th Light Dragoons in pursuit, under that most energetic officer, Major-General Sir Walter Gilbert. The Sikhs, it appears, retreated in the greatest disorder, leaving in the villages numerous wounded men. They have subdivided into three divisions, which have become more a flight than a retreat; and I understand a great portion of those not belonging to the revolted Khalsa army have dispersed and returned to their homes, thus, I trust, effectually frustrating the views of the rebel Shere Sing and his rebel associates.

I have not received Major-General Sir Joseph Thackwell's report, nor the returns of his loss, but I am most thankful to say that our whole loss, subsequent to the 22nd November, does not much exceed 40 men; no officers have been killed, and but three wounded. Captain Austin, of the artillery, only appears severely so.

I have to congratulate your Lordship upon events so fraught with importance, and which will, I have no doubt, with God's blessing, tend to most momentous results. It is, as I anticipate, most gratifying to me to assure your Lordship that the noble army under my command has, in these operations, upheld the well-established fame of the arms of India, both European and Native, each vying who should best perform his duty. Every officer, from the general of division to the youngest subaltern, well supported their commander-in-chief, and cheerfully carried out his views, which at a future period, and when we shall have effected the views of the Government, I shall feel proud in bringing to your Lordship's notice.

I have, &c.

(Signed) GOUGH.

Return of the Strength of the Force sent under the command of Major-General Sir J. Thackwell, K.C.B.

Camp Ramnugger, 5th December 1848.

3 troops of horse artillery, 2 light field batteries, 1 European dragoon regiment, 2 light cavalry regiments 1 irregular cavalry regiment, 2 regiments of European infantry, 5 regiments and 2 companies of Native infantry, and 1 company of pioneers, proceeded with Major-General Sir J. Thackwell.

Reinforcement sent:—1 regiment of European infantry, 1 regiment and 2 companies of Native infantry.

N.B.—Two 18-pounders, two 9-pounders, pontoon train, and detachment of irregular cavalry, returned from Wuzeerabad. European regiments employed:—3rd Light Dragoons, 24th, 61st, and 2nd European Infantry.

(Signed) GOUGH.

By order of the Right Honourable the Governor-General of India. H. M. ELLIOT,

Secretary to the Government of India,

With the Governor-General.

Foreign Department,

Fort William, 2nd February 1849.

The President of the Council of India in Council is pleased to direct the publication of the following general order by the Right Honourable the Governor-General, with the Commander-in-Chief's despatch, dated the 16th of January, detailing the operations of the army under his Excellency's command at Chillianwallah.

By order of the President of the Council of India in Council. FRED. JAS. HALLIDAY,

Officiating Secretary to the Government of India.

General Order by the Right Honourable the Governor-General of India.

Foreign Department,
Camp Mukko, the 24th January 1849.

The Governor-General, having received from the Commander-in-Chief in India a despatch, dated the 16th instant, directs that it shall be published for the information of the army and of the people of India.

In this despatch, his Excellency reports the successful operations of the troops under his immediate command, on the afternoon of the 13th instant, when they attacked and defeated the Sikh army under the command of Rajah Shere Sing.

Notwithstanding great superiority in numbers, and the formidable position which he occupied, the enemy, after a severe and obstinate resistance, was driven back, and retreated from every part of his position in great disorder, with much slaughter, and with the loss of 12 pieces of artillery.

The Governor-General congratulates the Commander-in-Chief on the victory so obtained by the army under his command; and, on behalf of the Government of India, he desires cordially to acknowledge the gallant services which have been rendered on this occasion, by his Excellency the Commander-in-Chief, the generals, the officers, non-commissioned officers, and soldiers of the army in the field.

The Governor-General offers his thanks to Major-General Sir Joseph Thackwell, K.C.B. and K.H., for his services; and to Brigadier White, for his conduct of the brigade of cavalry on the left.

Major-General Sir W. R. Gilbert, K.C.B., and Brigadier-General Campbell, C.B., are entitled to the special thanks of the Governor-General, for the admirable manner in which they directed the divisions under their orders.

To Brigadier Mountain, C.B., and to Brigadier Hoggan, the Governor-General tenders his acknowledgments for the gallant example they offered in the lead of their men; and to them, to Brigadier Godby, C.B., and Brigadier Penny, C.B., for their able conduct of their respective brigades.

The warm thanks of the Governor-General are due to Brigadier-General Tennant, commanding the artillery division, to Brigadier Brooke, C.B., and Brigadier Huthwaite, C.B., for their direction of the operations of that distinguished arm, and for the effective service which it rendered.

To the heads of the various departments, and to the officers of the General and Personal Staff, whose services are acknowledged by the Commander-in-Chief, the Governor-General offers his thanks.

The Governor-General deeply regrets the loss of Brigadier Pennycuick, C.B., and of the gallant officers and men who have honourably fallen in the service of the country.

It has afforded the Governor-General the highest gratification to observe, that the conduct of the troops generally was worthy of all praise.

The Governor-General, indeed, is concerned to think that any order or misapprehension of an order could have produced the movements by the right brigade of cavalry which his Excellency the Commander-in-Chief reports.

To the artillery, European and Native, to the cavalry on the left, and to the European and Native infantry, the Governor-General offers his hearty thanks; especially to those corps, European and Native, which his Excellency reports to have acted under trying circumstances with a gallantry worthy of the greatest admiration.

The Governor-General will have sincere satisfaction in bringing the services of this army under the favourable notice of Her Majesty's Government and the Honourable East India Company.

A salute of 21 guns has been ordered to be fired from every principal station of the army in India.

The Governor-General repeats to the Commander-in-Chief and to the army the assurance of his cordial thanks; and expresses his confident belief, that the victory which, under Divine Providence, they have won, will exercise a most important influence on the successful progress of the war in which they are engaged.

By order of the Right Honourable the Governor-General of India.

H. M. Elliot,
Secretary to the Government of India,
With the Governor-General.

Copy.

From his Excellency the Commander-in-Chief, to the Right Honourable the Governor-General of India.

Dated Head-Quarters,
Camp Chillianwallah, January 16th, 1849.

My Lord,—Major Mackeson, your Lordship's political agent with my camp, officially communicated to me, on the 10th instant, the fall of Attock and the advance of Sirdar Chutter Sing in order to concentrate his force with the army in my front, under Shere Sing, already amounting to from 30,000 to 40,000 men with 62 guns, concluding his letter thus:—"I would urge, in the event of your Lordship's finding yourself strong enough with the army under your command to strike an effectual blow at the enemy in our front, that the blow should be struck with the least possible delay."

Concurring entirely with Major Mackeson, and feeling that I was perfectly competent effectually to overthrow

Shere Sing's army, I moved from Loah Tibba, at daylight on the 12th, to Dingee, about 12 miles. Having learnt from my spies, and from other sources of information, that Shere Sing still held with his right the village of Lukhneewalla and Futtehshaw-ke-Chuck, having the great body of his force at the village of Woolianwalla, with his left at Russool, on the Jhelum, strongly occupying the southern extremity of a low range of hills, intersected by ravines, which extend nearly to that village. I made my arrangements accordingly that evening, and communicated them to the commanders of the several divisions; but to ensure correct information as to the nature of the country, which I believed to be excessively difficult and ill-adapted to the advance of a regular army, I determined upon moving on this village with a view to reconnoitre.

On the morning of the 13th the force advanced. I made a considerable detour to my right, partly in order to distract the enemy's attention, but principally to get as clear as I could of the jungle, on which it would appear that the enemy mainly relied.

We approached this village about 12 o'clock, and I found, on a mound close to it, a strong piquet of the enemy's cavalry and infantry, which we at once dispersed, obtaining from the mound a very extended view of the country before us, and the enemy drawn out in battle array, he having, either during the night or that morning, moved out of his several positions, and occupied the ground in our front, which, though not a dense, was still a difficult jungle, his right in advance of Futtehshaw-ke-Chuck, and his left on the furrowed hills before described.

The day being so far advanced, I decided upon taking up a position in rear of the village, in order to reconnoitre my front, finding that I could not turn the enemy's flanks, which rested upon a dense jungle, extending nearly to Hailah, which I had previously occupied for some time, and the neighbourhood of which I knew, and upon the raviney hills near Russool, without detaching a force to a distance; this I considered both inexpedient and dangerous.

The engineer department had been ordered to examine the country before us, and the quartermaster-general was in the act of taking up ground for the encampment, when the enemy advanced some horse artillery, and opened a fire on the skirmishers in front of the village.

I immediately ordered them to be silenced by a few rounds from our heavy guns, which advanced to an open space in front of the village. Their fire was instantly returned by that of nearly the whole of the enemy's field artillery; thus exposing the position of his guns, which the jungle had hitherto concealed.

It was now evident that the enemy intended to fight, and would probably advance his guns so as to reach the encampment during the night.

I therefore drew up in order of battle, Sir Walter Gilbert's division on the right, flanked by Brigadier Pope's brigade of cavalry, which I strengthened by the 14th Light Dragoons, well aware that the enemy was strong in cavalry upon his left. To this were attached three troops of horse artillery under Lieutenant-Colonel Grant.

The heavy guns were in the centre.

Brigadier-General Campbell's division formed the left, flanked by Brigadier White's brigade of cavalry, and three troops of horse artillery under Lieutenant-Colonel Brind.

The field batteries were with the infantry divisions.

Thus formed, the troops were ordered to lie down, whilst the heavy guns under Major Horsford, ably seconded by Brevet-Majors Ludlow and Sir Richmond Shakespear, opened a well-directed and powerful fire upon the enemy's centre, where his guns appeared principally to be placed; and this fire was ably supported on the flanks by the field batteries of the infantry divisions.

After about an hour's fire, that of the enemy appeared to be, if not silenced, sufficiently disabled to justify an advance upon his position and guns.

I then ordered my left division to advance, which had to move over a great extent of ground, and in front of which the enemy seemed not to have many guns. Soon after, I directed Sir Walter Gilbert to advane, and sent orders to Brigadier Pope to protect the flank and support the movement. Brigadier Penny's brigade was held in reserve, while the irregular cavalry under Brigadier Hearsey, with the 20th Native Infantry, was ordered to protect the enormous amount of provision and baggage that so hampers the movement of an Indian army.

Some time after the advance, I found that Brigadier Pennycuick's brigade had failed in maintaining the position it had carried, and immediately ordered Brigadier Penny's reserve to its support; but Brigadier-General Campbell, with that steady coolness and military decision for which he is so remarkable, having pushed on his left brigade and formed line to his right, carried everything before him, and soon overthrew that portion of the enemy which had obtained a temporary advantage over his right brigade.

This last brigade, I am informed, mistook for the signal to move in double time, the action of their brave leaders, Brigadier Pennycuick and Lieutenant-Colonel Brooks (two officers not surpassed for sound judgment and military daring in this or any other army), who waived their swords over their heads as they cheered on their gallant comrades. This unhappy mistake led to the Europeans outstripping the Native corps, which could not keep pace, and arriving completely blown at a belt of thick jungle, where they got into some confusion, and Lieutenant-Colonel Brooks, leading the 24th, was killed between the enemy's guns. At this moment a large body of infantry, which supported their guns, opened upon them so destructive a fire, that the brigade was forced to retire, having lost their gallant and lamented leader, Brigadier Pennycuick, and the three other field-officers of the 24th, and nearly half the regiment before it gave way. The Native regiment, when it came up, also suffering severely. In justice to this brigade, I must be allowed to state, that they behaved heroically, and, but for their too hasty, and consequently disorderly advance, would have emulated the conduct of their left brigade, which, left unsupported for a time, had to charge to their front and right, wherever an enemy appeared. The brigade of horse artillery on their left, under Lieutenant-Colonel Brind, judiciously and gallantly aiding, maintained an effective fire.

Major-General Sir J. Thackwell, on the extreme left and rear, charged the enemy's cavalry wherever they showed themselves.

The right attack of infantry, under that able officer Major-General Sir Walter Gilbert, was most praiseworthy and successful. The left brigade, under Brigadier Mountain, advanced under a heavy fire upon the enemy's guns, in a manner that did credit to the brigadier and his gallant brigade, which came first into action and suffered severely: the right brigade, under Brigadier Godby, ably supported the advance.

This division nobly maintained the character of the Indian army, taking and spiking the whole of the enemy's guns, in their front, and dispersing the Sikhs wherever they were seen.

The major-general reports most favourably of the fire of his field-battery.

The right brigade of cavalry, under Brigadier Pope, was not, I regret to say, so successful. Either by some order, or misapprehension of an order, they got into much confusion, hampered the fine brigade of horse artillery, which, while getting into action, against a body of the enemy's cavalry that was coming down upon them, had their horses separated from their guns by the false movements of our cavalry, and notwithstanding the heroic conduct of the gunners, four of those guns were disabled to an extent which rendered their withdrawal, at the moment, impossible. The moment the artillery was extricated and the cavalry reformed, a few rounds put to flight the enemy that had occasioned this confusion.

With this exception, the conduct of the troops generally was most exemplary. Some corps, both European and native, acting under most trying circumstances (from the temporary failure in our left centre and right, and the cover which the jungle afforded to the enemy's movements), and with a gallantry worthy of the highest admiration.

Although the enemy, who defended not only his guns, but his position, with desperation, was driven in much confusion, and with heavy loss, from every part of it; and the greater part of his field-artillery was actually captured: the march of brigades to their flanks to repel parties that had rallied, and the want of numbers and consequent support to our right flank, aided by the cover of the jungle and the close of the day, enabled him, upon our further advance in pursuit, to return and carry off unobserved the greater portion of the guns we had thus gallantly carried at the point of the bayonet.

I remained with Brigadier-General Campbell's division, which had been reinforced by Brigadier Mountain's brigade, until near 8 o'clock, in order to effect the bringing in of the captured ordnance, and of the wounded, and I hoped to bring in the rest of the guns next morning. But I did not feel justified in remaining longer out. The night was very dark. I knew not how far I had advanced. There were no wells nearer than the line of this village. The troops had been arduously employed all day, and there was every appearance of a wet night: rain did fall before morning.

I should have felt greater satisfaction if I were enabled to state, that my expectations in regard to the guns had been realised; but although a brigade of cavalry, under Brigadier White, with a troop of horse artillery, were on the ground soon after daylight, we found that the enemy, assisted by the neighbouring villagers, had carried off their guns, excepting twelve, which we had brought in the night before. Most of the captured waggons I had caused to be blown up before leaving the ground.

The victory was complete, as to the total overthrow of the enemy; and his sense of utter discomfiture and defeat will, I trust, soon be made apparent, unless indeed the rumours prevalent this day of his having been joined by Chutter Sing, prove correct.

I am informed that the loss of the Sikhs has been very great, and chiefly amongst their old and tried soldiers. In no action do I remember seeing so many of an enemy's slain upon the same space: Sobraon perhaps only excepted.

I have now, my Lord, stated the general movements of this army previous to and during the action of Chillianwallah, and as that action was characterised by peculiar features, which rendered it impossible for the Commander-in-Chief to witness all the operations of the force, I shall beg leave to bring prominently to your Lordship's notice, the names of the several officers and corps particularly mentioned by the divisional commanders.

I have already stated the obligations I am under to Major-General Sir Joseph Thackwell, and Sir Walter Gilbert, and to Brigadier-General Campbell, for their most valuable services. I warmly concur with them in the thanks which they have expressed to the several brigadiers and officers commanding corps, and to the troops generally.

Sir Joseph Thackwell names, with much satisfaction, Brigadier White's conduct of his brigade; Major Yerbury, commanding 3rd Light Dragoons; the gallant charge of Captain Unett, in command of a squadron of that corps; Major Mackenzie, commanding tne 8th; and Captain Wheatley, commanding the 5th Light Cavalry; and the conduct of Captain Moore, of the 8th, with a squadron detached in support of the artillery. He further notices the assistance he derived from the zeal and activity of Captain Pratt, assistant adjutant-general, and Lieutenant Tucker, deputy-assistant quartermaster-general of his division, of Captain Cautley, major of brigade, of his aide-de-camp, Lieutenant Thackwell, and of Lieutenant Simpson, sub-assistant commissary-general.

Brigadier-General Campbell speaks in terms of admiration of the 5th brigade, led on by that distinguished officer, Brigadier Pennycuick; and particularly of the gallant exertions of Her Majesty's 24th Foot, under the command of Lieutenant-Colonel Brookes; and the good and steady advance of the 25th and 45th Native Infantry, under the command of Lieutenant-Colonel Corbett and Major Williams. He particularizes the undaunted example set to his brigade by Brigadier Hoggan; the continued steadiness and gallantry of Her Majesty's 61st Regiment, commanded by Lieutenant-Colonel Macleod, under the most trying circumstances; the distinguished conduct of Major Fleming and the officers of the 36th Native Infantry; and of the 46th Native Infantry, under Major Tudor; as also the able and zealous exertions of the Brigade-Major, Captain Keiller. The Brigadier-General also brings to notice his obligations to Major Tucker, assistant adjutant-general of the army; and to Captain Goldie and Lieutenant Irwin, of the Engineers, who were sent to his assistance, and the cordial and able support which he received from Major Ponsonby, his assistant adjutant-general; and he particularly mentions the conduct of Ensign Garden, his deputy assistant quartermaster-general; and Captain Haythorne, his aide-de-camp; further naming Lieutenant Grant of Her Majesty's 24th Regiment; Lieutenant Powys, of Her Majesty's 61st, who attended him as orderly officers; and of Lieutenant and Adjutant Shadwell, of Her Majesty's 98th, who was with him as a volunteer.

Sir Walter Gilbert speaks warmly of the charge led by Brigadier Mountain, against a large battery of the enemy, and followed up on the right by Brigadier Godby; and of the subsequent conduct of these officers; as also of the conduct of Major Chester, assistant adjutant-general; and Lieutenant Galloway, deputy assistant quartermaster-general of the division; of Lieutenant Colt, his aide-de-camp; of Captain Sherwill, and Lieutenant Macdonnell, majors of brigade; and of Captain Glasfurd; and Lieutenant W. E. Morton, of the Engineers.

The major-general further mentions the undaunted bravery on this occasion of Her Majesty's 29th Regiment, under Lieutenant-Colonel Congreve; the distinguished conduct of the 2nd European Regiment, under Major Steel; and the manner in which Majors Smith and Way, of the 29th, and Major Talbot, of the 2nd Europeans, seconded their able commanders. He also expresses his thanks to Lieutenant-Colonel Jack, commanding the 30th Native Infantry; Major Bamfield, commanding the 56th Native Infantry, who was mortally wounded; Major Corfield, commanding the 31st Native Infantry; and Major McCausland, commanding the 70th Native Infantry; for the manner in which they led their regiments into action: naming likewise Captain Nembhard, of the

56th, who succeeded to the command of that corps; Captain Dawes, commanding the field-battery of the division; and Captain Robbins, of the 15th, who acted as his aide-de-camp.

The reserve, consisting of the 15th Native Infantry, and eight companies of the 69th Native Infantry, was ably handled by Brigadier Penny, well seconded by Lieutenant-Colonels Sibbald and Mercer, commanding the corps. The brigadier particularly mentions the steady conduct of the Rifle Company of the 69th, under Captain Sissmore; and acknowledges the services of Captain Macpherson, his major of brigade; and Brevet Captain Morris, of the 20th Native Infantry, who attended him as orderly officer.

Brigadier-General Tennant, commanding the artillery division, rendered me every aid, and presided over the noble arm, of which he is the head, most creditably to himself and most beneficially to the service. The brigadier-general particularly mentions Brigadier J. Brooke, who commanded the whole of the horse artillery; Brigadier Huthwaite, commanding the foot artillery; Lieutenant-Colonels C. Grant and F. Brind; Major R. Horsford and Major Mowatt; all of whom were in important commands. He further brings to notice Captain J. Abercrombie, deputy assistant adjutant-general; Lieutenant Tombs, deputy assistant quartermaster-general, his aide-de-camp; Lieutenant Olpherts; Captain Hogge, commissary of ordnance; and Lieutenant de Tessier, who attended him as orderly officer.

I have, in the beginning of this despatch, noticed the services of Brevet-Major Sir Richmond Shakespear and Brevet-Major Ludlow, in command of the heavy batteries under the general superintendence of Major Horsford; and it only remains for me to add, that the conduct of Major Fordyce; Captains Warner and Duncan; Lieutenants

Robinson and Walker, commanding troops and field-batteries; as well as the officers and men of the artillery generally, have been named in terms of praise by the divisional commander.

Lieutenants C. V. Cox and E. Kaye, brigade-majors of this arm, have been also named by their respective brigadiers.

From the engineer department, under Major Tremenhere, I received active assistance, ably aided by Captain Durand, Lieutenants R. Baird, Smith, and Goodwyn.

To the general staff I am greatly indebted. Lieutenant-Colonel Gough, C.B., quartermaster-general; and Major Lugard, acting adjutant-general; and Captain C. Ottor, acting assistant adjutant-general of Her Majesty's forces; Lieutenant-Colonel P. Grant, C.B., adjutant-general of the army; Major C. Ekins (killed), a valued and much regretted officer, deputy adjutant-general; and Major Tucker, assistant adjutant-general of the army; Lieutenant-Colonel W. Garden, C.B., quartermaster-general of the army; Lieutenant W. F. Tytler, assistant quartermaster-general; and Lieutenant Paton, deputy assistant quartermaster-general of the army; Lieutenant-Colonel Birch, judge-advocate-general; and Lieutenant G. B. Johnson, deputy judge-advocate-general; Major G. Thomson, assistant commissary-general; Lieutenant-Colonel J. G. W. Curtis, assistant commissary-general; Captain C. Campbell, paymaster to the army; Captain J. Lang, postmaster; and H. Franklin, Esquire, inspector-general of Her Majesty's hospitals.

To my personal staff I am also much indebted. Captain F. P. Haines, military secretary; Major H. Bates, aide-de-camp; Lieutenant A. Bagot, aide-de-camp; Lieutenant S. J. Hire, aide-de-camp; Captain Gabbett, aide-de-camp; Lieutenant G. N. Hardinge, aide-de-camp; and Lieutenant W. G. Prendergast, Persian interpreter.

The unwearied exertions of Dr. Renny, superintending-surgeon, and of Dr. MacRae, field-surgeon, in the care of the wounded, have been beyond all praise.

The Earl of Gifford kindly accompanied me throughout the operations, and was most useful in conveying my orders to the several divisions and brigades. I had also the advantage throughout the day of the active services of Lieutenant-Colonel Sir Henry M. Lawrence, Major Mackeson, Mr. Cocks, C. S., Captain Nicholson, and Lieutenant Robinson, as well as of Major Anstruther, of the Madras Artillery, and Lieutenant H. O. Mayne, of the 6th Madras Light Cavalry.

Captain Ramsay, joint deputy commissary-general, with the several officers of that department, has been most indefatigable, and has hitherto kept the army well supplied.

I have, &c.

(Signed) GOUGH, General,
Commander-in-Chief.

Returned of killed, wounded, and missing of the army of the Punjaub, under the personal command of the Right Honourable Lord Gough, G.C.B., in the action with the Sikh forces, under Rajah Shere Sing, at Chillianwallah, on the 13th January 1849.

General Staff—1 European officer, 1 horse, killed; 2 European officers wounded.

Artillery Division.—Horse Artillery Brigade.

1st Troop, 2nd Brigade—5 rank and file, 1 lascar, killed; 1 rank and file, 4 lascars, 2 horses, wounded; 1 rank and file, 22 horses, missing.

2nd Troop, ditto—4 rank and file, 1 lascar, wounded; 2 horses missing.

3rd Troop, 2nd Brigade—1 sergeant, 6 rank and file, killed; 1 European officer, 2 rank and file, 3 lascars, 1 Syce, wounded; 1 rank and file, 6 Syces, 31 horses, missing.

4th Troop, ditto—1 European officer, 1 Syce, 6 horses, killed; 2 rank and file, 2 horses, wounded; 4 horses missing.

1st Troop, 3rd Brigade—1 rank and file, 1 horse, killed; 1 rank and file, 1 horse, wounded.

2nd Troop, ditto—1 rank and file wounded.

Foot Artillery Brigade.

1st Company, 1st Battalion, No. 10 Battery—1 horse wounded.

3rd Company, ditto, No. 17 Battery—3 horses killed; 2 European officers, 1 trumpeter, 2 rank and file, wounded; 1 horse missing.

1st Company, 4th ditto—1 rank and file killed; 7 rank and file wounded.

2nd Company, ditto—1 rank and file killed; 1 sergeant, 2 rank and file, wounded.

4th Company, ditto—1 rank and file wounded.

6th Company, 7th ditto, No. 5 Battery—1 horse killed; 5 rank and file, 1 horse, wounded; 1 horse missing.

Park Establishment—1 sergeant killed.

Total—1 European officer, 2 sergeants, 14 rank and file, 1 lascar, 1 Syce, 11 horses, killed; 3 European officers, 1 sergeant, 1 trumpeter, 28 rank and file, 8 lascars, 1 Syce, 7 horses, wounded; 2 rank and file, 6 Syces, 61 horses, missing.

Engineer Department, 6th Company of Pioneers—3 rank and file wounded.

Cavalry Division.—1st Brigade.

H. M.'s 3rd Light Dragoons—1 sergeant, 23 rank and file, killed; 2 European officers, 14 rank and file, 14 horses, wounded.

H. M.'s 14th Light Dragoons—1 European officer, 1 rank and file, 2 horses, killed; 1 European officer, 2 sergeants, 12 rank and file, 2 horses, wounded; 2 rank and file, 4 horses, missing.

5th Light Cavalry—2 sergeants, 1 trumpeter, 3 rank and file, 7 horses, killed; 2 European officers, 1 native ditto, 2 sergeants, 11 rank and file, 7 horses, wounded.

8th Light Cavalry—1 rank and file killed; 2 rank and file, 1 horse, wounded; 2 horses missing.

2nd Brigade.

Brigade Staff—1 European officer wounded.

H. M.'s 9th Lancers—4 rank and file killed; 8 rank and file, 5 horses, wounded; 4 horses missing.

1st Regiment Light Cavalry—3 rank and file, 1 Syce, 1 horse, killed; 1 native officer, 1 sergeant, 2 rank and file, 1 Syce, 7 horses, wounded; 3 horses missing.

6th Regiment Light Cavalry—1 European officer, 2 native ditto, 4 rank and file, 2 horses, killed; 2 European officers, 1 warrant officer, 1 sergeant, 6 rank and file, wounded; 6 horses missing.

Total—2 European officers, 2 native ditto, 3 sergeants, 1 trumpeter, 39 rank and file, 1 Syce, 38 horses, killed; 8 European officers, 2 native ditto, 1 warrant officer, 6 sergeants, 55 rank and file, 1 Syce, 36 horses, wounded; 2 rank and file, 19 horses, missing.

2nd Infantry Division.—3rd Brigade.

2nd European Regiment—6 rank and file killed; 2 European officers, 5 sergeants, 54 rank and file, wounded.

31st Regiment of Native Infantry—1 havildar, 2 rank and file, killed; 1 European officer, 2 havildars, 12 rank and file, wounded.

45th Regiment of Native Infantry—4 havildars, 13 rank and file, killed; 4 European officers, 1 native ditto, 1 havildar, 53 rank and file, wounded; 3 rank and file, missing.

70th Regiment of Native Infantry—2 native officers, 3 rank and file, killed; 20 rank and file wounded.

4th Brigade.

H. M.'s 29th Foot—2 sergeants, 29 rank and file, killed; 4 European officers, 5 sergeants, 4 drummers, 194 rank and file, wounded; 3 rank and file missing.

30th Regiment of Native Infantry—2 European officers, 1 native ditto, 10 havildars, 1 drummer, 53 rank and file, killed; 9 European officers, 9 native ditto, 12 havildars, 1 drummer, 187 rank and file, wounded.

56th Regiment of Native Infantry—2 European officers, 4 native ditto, 7 havildars, 32 rank and file, killed; 6 European officers, 6 native ditto, 18 havildars, 4 drummers, 205 rank and file, wounded; 2 havildars, 36 rank and file, missing.

Total—4 European officers, 7 native ditto, 24 sergeants or havildars, 1 drummer, 138 rank and file, killed; 26 European officers, 16 native ditto, 43 sergeants or havildars, 9 drummers, 725 rank and file, wounded; 2 havildars, 42 rank and file, missing.

3rd Infantry Division.

Divisional and Brigade Staff—2 European officers killed, 2 ditto wounded.

5th Brigade.

H. M.'s 24th Foot—11 European officers, 4 sergeants, 1 drummer, 188 rank and file, 2 horses, killed; 10 European officers, 8 serjeants, 2 drummers, 256 rank and file, wounded; 38 rank and file missing.

25th Regiment of Native Infantry—1 European officer, 6 native ditto, 13 havildars, 2 drummers, 78 rank and file, killed; 2 European officers, 3 native ditto, 3 havildars, 2 drummers, 82 rank and file, 1 horse, wounded; 2 havildars, 10 rank and file, missing.

6th Brigade.

15th Regiment of Native Infantry—4 havildars, 4 rank

and file, killed; 3 European officers, 1 native ditto, 7 havildars, 37 rank and file, wounded.

69th Regiment of Native Infantry—1 havildar, 3 rank and file, killed; 2 European officers, 8 havildars, 2 drummers, 51 rank and file, wounded.

7th Brigade.

H. M.'s 61st Foot—11 rank and file killed; 3 European officers, 7 sergeants, 93 rank and file, wounded.

36th Regiment of Native Infantry—1 native officer, 2 havildars, 25 rank and file, killed; 6 European officers, 2 native ditto, 3 havildars, 66 rank and file, wounded.

46th Regiment of Native Infantry—3 rank and file killed; 3 native officers, 4 havildars, 1 drummer, 43 rank and file, wounded.

Total—14 European officers, 7 native ditto, 24 sergeants or havildars, 3 drummers, 312 rank and file, 2 horses, killed; 28 European officers, 9 native ditto, 40 sergeants or havildars, 7 drummers, 628 rank and file, 1 horse, wounded; 2 havildars, 48 rank and file, missing.

Grand Total—22 European officers, 16 native ditto, 53 sergeants or havildars, 5 trumpeters or drummers, 508 rank and file, 1 lascar, 2 Syces, 52 horses, killed; 67 European officers, 27 native ditto, 1 warrant officer, 90 sergeants or havildars, 17 trumpeters or drummers, 1439 rank and file, 8 lascars, 2 Syces, 44 horses, wounded; 4 sergeants or havildars, 94 rank and file, 6 Syces, 80 horses, missing.

Nominal Roll of European Officers, Killed, Wounded, or Missing.

General Staff—Killed: Brevet-Major C. Ekins, deputy-adjutant-general of the army. Wounded: Brevet-Major H. T. Tucker, assistant adjutant-general of the army, contusion; Lieutenant J. S. Paton, deputy assistant quartermaster-general, severely.

Artillery Division.

4th Troop, 2nd Brigade Horse Artillery—Killed: Lieutenant J. A. Manson.

3rd Troop, 2nd Brigade Horse Artillery—Wounded: Brevet-Major E. Christie, very dangerously, since dead.

3rd Company, 1st Battalion Artillery—Wounded: Captain M. Dawes, slightly; 1st Lieutenant C. S. Dundas, severely.

Cavalry Division.

Brigade Staff—Wounded: Brigadier A. Pope, C.B., commanding 2nd Cavalry Brigade, severely.

H. M.'s 3rd Light Dragoons—Wounded: Captain W. Unett, severely; Lieutenant T. H. Stisted.

5th Regiment Light Cavalry—Wounded: Lieutenant R. Christie, dangerously; Lieutenant A. P. C. Elliot, severely.

H. M.'s 14th Light Dragoons—Killed: Lieutenant A. J. Cureton. Wounded: Major C. Steuart.

6th Regiment Light Cavalry—Killed: Lieutenant A. M. Shepherd. Wounded: Captain W. J. E. Boys, Lieutenant H. R. Grindlay.

2nd Infantry Division.

2nd European Regiment—Wounded: Lieutenant M. R. Nightingale, very severely; Lieutenant J. Bleaymire, slightly.

31st Regiment of Native Infantry— Wounded: Captain W. R. Dunmore, slightly.

H. M.'s 29th Foot—Wounded: Major M. Smith, slight contusion; Lieutenant the Honourable H. M. Moncton, severely; Lieutenant H. T. Metge, very severely; Ensign G. H. Nevill, slightly.

30th Regiment of Native Infantry—Killed: Captain W. H. Ross, Ensign A. C. de Morel. Wounded: Brevet-Major M. E. Loftie, severely; Captain W. C. Campbell, slightly; Captain R. S. Ewart, ditto; Captain C. F. Fenwick, very severely; Captain J. Morrieson, slightly; Lieutenant H. Swinhoe, severely; Ensign T. Pierce, slightly; Ensign J. C. Wood, very severely; Ensign W. T. Leicester, ditto.

56th Regiment of Native Infantry—Killed: Lieutenant W. Warde, Ensign F. W. Robinson. Wounded: Major D. Bamfield, very severely, since dead; Lieutenant W. C. Gott, slightly; Lieutenant L. B. Jones, severely; Lieutenant F. V. R. Jervis, ditto; Lieutenant J. H. Bacon, slightly; Lieutenant J. W. Delamain, severely, arm since amputated.

45th Regiment of Native Infantry—Wounded: Captain R. Haldane, severely; Lieutenant J. Palmer, do.; Ensign M. H. Combe, slightly; Ensign W. L. Trotter, badly.

3rd Infantry Division.

Divisional Staff—Wounded: Brigadier-General C. Campbell, C. B., slightly.

Brigade Staff—Killed: Brigadier J. Pennycuick, C. B. and K. H.; Captain C. R. Harris, major of brigade. Wounded: Brevet-Captain A. B. Morris, officiating brigade-major, slightly.

H. M.'s 24th Foot—Killed: Lieutenant-Colonel R. Brookes, Major H. W. Harris, Captain C. Lee, Captain J. S. Shore, Captain R. W. Travers, Lieutenant G. Phillips, Lieutenant O. B. Payne, Lieutenant J. A. Woodgate, Lieutenant W. Phillips, Ensign H. E. B. Collis, Ensign A. Pennycuick. Wounded: Major H. Paynter, dangerously; Captain W. G. Brown, slightly; Captain L. H. Bazalgette, severely; Lieutenant G. E. L. Williams, dangerously; Lieutenant R. A. Croker, severely; Lieutenant G. F.

Berry, slightly; Lieutenant J. B. Thelwall, severely; Lieutenant and Adjutant W. Hartshron, slightly; Lieutenant A. J. Macpherson, severely; Lieutenant J. H. Archer (H. M.'s 96th), slightly.

25th Regiment of Native Infantry—Killed: Lieutenant A. Money. Wounded: Lieutenant A. G. C. Sutherland, slightly; Lieutenant F. A. Jeune, ditto.

45th Regiment of Native Infantry—Wounded: Lieutenant and Adjutant G. G. Anderson, severely; Lieutenant H. R. Shawe, slightly; Lieutenant W. G. Ellice, ditto.

69th Regiment of Native Infantry—Wounded: Captain J. A. James, severely; Lieutenant J. Nesbitt, ditto.

H. M.'s 61st Foot—Wounded: Captain J. Massey, severely; Ensign J. Nagel, ditto; Ensign J. H. H. Parks, slightly.

36th Regiment of Native Infantry— Wounded: Captain F. A. Carleton, severely; Lieutenant, Interpreter, and Quartermaster A. N. Thompson, since dead; Lieutenant and Adjutant C. S. Weston, severely; Lieutenant J. D. Meynay, slightly; Ensign F. J. S. Bagshaw, severely; Ensign C. J. Godby, dangerously.

(Signed) PAT. GRANT, Lieut.-Col.
Adjutant-General of the Army.

Adjutant-General's Office,
Head-Quarters, Camp Chillianwallah.
17th January 1849.

List of Ordnance and Ordnance Stores captured from the Enemy in the Action of the 13th January.

Camp Chillianwallah, 15th Jan. 1849.

No.	Calibre.	Nature.
1	3·84	7-pounders
2	3·80	7-pounders
3	3·79	7-pounders
4	3·40	5½-pounders
5	3·67	6-pounders
6	3·80	7-pounders
7	3·76	7-pounders
8	3·75	7-pounders
9	2·90	3-pounders
10	3·94	7¼-pounders
11	3·74	6½-pounders
12	3·60	6-pounders

Six of these guns have carriages and limbers, and six are without limbers; all of the pattern nearly in use with our field-pieces.

Two ammunition-carriages (one partly destroyed by explosion), 1 platform-cart, 144 cartridges, liners fixed to shot; 16 cartridges unfixed, and 18 port-fires have also been brought into park.

(Signed) J. Abercrombie, Captain,
Dep. Assist. Adj.-Gen. Arty., Army of the Punjaub,
(Signed) J. Tennant, Brig.-Gen.,
Commanding Artillery Division.

(True Copy.)
(Signed) P. Grant, Lieut.-Col.,
Adjutant-General of the Army.

(True Copies.)
H. M. Elliot,
Secretary to the Govt. of India,
with the Governor-General.

From the Right Honourable the Commander-in-Chief, to the Right Honourable the Governor-General of India, &c. &c. &c.

Head-quarters, Camp Ramnugger,
December 10, 1848.

My Lord,—In continuation of my letter of the 5th instant, I have now the honour to inclose to your Lordship a copy of Major-General Sir Joseph Thackwell's despatch, dated the 6th idem, but only received last night, detailing the operations of the force under his command, after it had been detached from my head-quarters.

I can only repeat the warm approval I have already expressed of the conduct of the Major-General and of every officer and man under his command, and I beg your Lordship's favourable consideration of the services of those named by Sir Joseph Thackwell.

I beg to inclose a rough sketch of the operations of the 3rd instant.

I have, &c.
(Signed) GOUGH.

From Major-General Sir Joseph Thackwell, K.C.B. and K.H., to Lieutenant-Colonel Grant, C.B., Adjutant-General of the Army.

Head-quarters, Camp Ramnugger, Camp Heyleh.
December 6, 1848.

Sir,—I have the honour to report, for the information of the Right Honourable the Commander-in-Chief, that agreeably to his Excellency's orders, I left the camp at

Ramnugger, with the troops named in the margin,* at about half-past 3 o'clock on the morning of the 1st December 1848, instead of at 1 o'clock, as I had ordered, some of the troops having lost their way among the intricacies of the rear of the encampment, and proceeded to the vicinity of the ford on the Chenab at Runnee-Khan-

---

* Major Christie's Troop Horse Artillery.
Captain Huish's Troop Horse Artillery.
Captain Warner's Troop Horse Artillery.
Captain Kinleside, No. 5 Light Field Battery.
Captain Austin, No. 10 Light Field Battery.
Captain Robinson and two 18-pounders, under the command of Lieutenant-Colonel Grant, Horse Artillery.
2 companies of pioneers.
The pontoon train.
1st Brigade of Cavalry, commanded by Brigadier White.
3rd Light Dragoons, commanded by Major Yerbury.
5th Light Cavalry, commanded by Captain Wheatley.
8th Light Cavalry, commanded by Captain Moore.
3rd Irregular Cavalry, commanded by Major Tait.
12th Irregular Cavalry, commanded by Lieutenant Cunningham.
3rd Brigade of Infantry, Brigadier Eckford.
31st Native Infantry, Major Corfield.
56 Native Infantry, Major Bamfield.
3rd Division of Infantry, Brigadier-General Campbell, commanding.
6th Brigade of Infantry, Brigadier Pennycuick.
H.M.'s 24th Foot, Major Harris.
2 flank companies, 2nd Battalion company, 22nd Native Infantry, Major Sampson.
8th Brigade of Infantry, Brigadier Hoggan.
H.M.'s 61st Foot, Lieutenant-Colonel McLeod.
36th Native Infantry, Major Flemyng.
46th Native Infantry, Major Tudor.
Of the above detail, the following returned in charge of the two 18-pounders and pontoon train:
2 guns of No. 10 Light Field Battery.
12th Irregular Cavalry.
2 companies 22nd Native Infantry.

ke-Puttun, distant thirteen miles from Ramnugger, which, owing to the broken ground and narrow roads, where any existed for the first four miles, I did not reach before 11 o'clock. The enemy had infantry at this ford, which report afterwards magnified to 4,000 men, but the villagers said it was much deeper than the one at Allee Shere-ke-Chuck, a mile higher up the river. I am much indebted to Lieutenant Paton, deputy assistant quarter-master-generel, for his anxious exertions in examining this ford; and from his report I came to the conclusion that this ford of Allee Shere-ke-Chuck could not have artillery on the left bank of the river to cover the passage of the troops, from the insecure bottom of the first ford, neither could the pontoon train be of much use for the same reason, and the deep sands which lay between the fords. The pontoon train might have been laid over the main stream under cover of a battery, near the enemy's infantry; but beyond the river the sands seemed wet and insecure, and a branch of the river beyond them was said to be deep with a muddy bottom. Under all these disadvantages, I came to the decision that it was more advisable to try the passage of the river near Wuzeerabad, where Captain Nicholson, assistant to the Resident at Lahore, informed me that at the ferry were seventeen boats, and a ford not more than 3 feet 10 inches deep, with a good bottom, than to run the risk of a severe loss by passing the river near the enemy. This survey of the ford occupied three hours, and at 2 o'clock I put the column in movement to the ford and ferry at Wuzeerabad, which was in possession of Lieutenant Nicholson's pattans, where the leading infantry arrived about 5 o'clock in the afternoon, having made a march of about twenty-five miles. The 6th brigade of infantry and some of the guns were passed over the Chenab immediately, and I am indebted to Brigadier-General Campbell, Lieutenant-Colonel

Grant, horse artillery, and Captain Smith of the Engineers, for their great exertions in forwarding this object. Brigadier Eckford I hoped would have crossed the river by the three fords that evening; but as it became too dark and hazy for such an operation, he halted for the night on the dry sands near the last branch of the river. Major Tait, 3rd Irregular Cavalry, was enabled to pass over three of his risallahs; in doing which, I am sorry to say, three sowars and one horse were drowned. On the morrow the infantry, cavalry, and all the troops were soon over the river by ferry and ford, and all the baggage and commissariat animals passed the same by 12 o'clock, without any further loss.

At 2 P.M., after the troops had dined, I marched in order of battle, three brigade columns of companies, at half distance left in front, at deploying interval. The 1st brigade of cavalry, in the same order on the right, with strong flanking parties and rear guard, and the 3rd Irregular Cavalry on the left, with orders to patrole to the river and clear the right bank, aided by infantry, if necessary: in this order I arrived at Doorawal at dusk, about twelve miles from the ferry, and halted for the night. On Sunday, December 3, at daylight, the troops proceeded in the same order towards the Sikh position, and I intended to have reconnoitred and commenced an attack upon it by 11 o'clock: hearing, however, when within about four miles of it or less, that reinforcements were expected to pass over the Chenab at the ford near Ghurree-ke-Puttun, it became necessary to secure that post, and which had been found without an enemy an hour before, but to which it now seemed that a body of about 600 of the enemy were seen approaching, and I detached a wing of the 56th Native Infantry, and two risallahs of the 3rd Irregular Cavalry under Major Tait, who secured the post and frustrated the attempt of the enemy. This caused so much delay, that enough of daylight would not be left for the advance and attack on the left and rear of the enemy's position. About 2 P.M. some of the enemy's guns opened on a patrol of the 5th Light Cavalry, and he was seen advancing in large bodies of cavalry and infantry, and the picquets which occupied three villages with large plantations of sugar-cane being too much in advance to be supported, fell back without any loss, and the enemy occupied these villages with cavalry on the right, guns and bodies of infantry, and the main body of their cavalry with horse artillery were on their left. When the enemy's guns opened, I ordered Brigadier-General Campbell to deploy the infantry into line in front of the village of Sudoolapoor, Brigadier Eckford and part of Brigadier Hoggan's brigade being extended in order not to be outflanked. It was not until the enemy came well within range of our guns that I caused them to open their fire, which they then did with great effect. The enemy tried to turn both our flanks, which having foreseen, I had caused Captain Warner to move his troop of artillery to the left of the infantry, and had sent the 5th Light Cavalry to the left to support these guns, and to act in conjunction with the two risallahs of the 3rd Irregular Cavalry under Captain Biddulph, who were posted on open ground, and these soon drove the enemy back. The attempt to turn our right was met by extending the 8th Light Cavalry and Her Majesty's 3rd Light Dragoons, supported by Major Christie's troop of artillery. As the cavalry of the right advanced, the enemy's suwars gave way, and they fell back on their infantry, having lost some men by the skirmishers of the 3rd Light Dragoons. After a cannonade of about two hours the fire of the enemy slackened, and I sent Lieutenant Paton to desire the cavalry on the right to charge and take the enemy's guns, if possible; intending to support them by moving the brigades in échelon from the right at intervals according to circumstances; but as no opportunity offered for the cavalry to charge, and so little of the daylight remained, I deemed it safer to remain in my position than attempt to drive back an enemy so strongly posted on their right and centre, with the prospect of having to attack their entrenched position afterwards. From this position the Sikhs began to retire at about 12 o'clock at night, as was afterwards ascertained, and as was conjectured by the barking of the dogs in their rear. I have every reason to believe that Shere Singh attacked with 20 guns, and nearly the whole of the Sikh army were employed against my position, which was by no means what I could have wished it; but the fire of our artillery was so effective, that he did not dare to bring his masses to the front, and my brave, steady, and ardent infantry, whom I had caused to lay down to avoid the heavy fire, had no chance of firing a shot, except a few companies on the left of the line. The enemy's loss has been severe; ours comparatively small. I regret not being able to capture the enemy's guns; but with the small force of cavalry, two regiments on the right only, it would have been a matter of difficulty for tired cavalry to overtake horse artillery, fresh and well mounted. In these operations the conduct of all has merited my warmest praise, and the patient endurance of the artillery, cavalry, European infantry and sepoys, under privations of no ordinary nature, has been most praiseworthy.

To Brigadier-General Campbell I am much indebted for his able assistance during these movements, and to Lieutenant-Colonel Grant, commanding the artillery, Major Christie, Captains Huish, Warner, Austin and Kinleside, and the officers and men under their command, I cannot bestow too much praise for their skill and gallantry in overcoming the fire of a numerous artillery, some of which were of heavy calibre. I am also greatly indebted to Captain Smith of the engineers, for his exertions in passing over guns at the Wuzeerabad ferry, and for his assistance in conveying my orders on various occasions. And my thanks are due to Lieutenants Yule and Crommelin of the same corps, and Lieutenant Bacon of the sappers; to Lieutenant Paton, deputy assistant quartermaster-general, my best thanks are due for his exertions and assistance in the advance of the troops and during the action; and to Captain Nicholson, assistant to the Resident at Lahore, I beg to offer my best thanks for his endeavours to procure intelligence of the enemy's movements, for his endeavours to procure supplies for the troops, and his able assistance on all occasions. Captain Pratt, my deputy assistant adjutant-general, Lieutenant Tucker, deputy assistant quartermaster-general, and Lieutenant Thackwell, aide-de-camp, have been most zealous in performing their respective duties, and have rendered me every assistance; and I feel assured that if the cavalry and infantry had been brought into close action, I should have had the great satisfaction of thanking brigadiers commanding, officers of corps, and the officers and men, for their gallantry and noble bearing in action, as I now do for their steadiness and good conduct. To Major Mainwaring, Captains Gerrard, Simpson, Faddy, and James, I am much indebted for their exertions in their respective departments.

I beg further to state that on the morning of the 4th I put the troops in motion to pursue the enemy, who had retreated during the preceding night, and encamped about eleven miles from the Chenab, on the road to Jullalpore, the 9th Lancers having been pushed to the front, but without seeing anything of the enemy, who had retreated by the Jhelum, Jullalpore, and Pind Dadun Khan roads. On the following day I arrived at this place, and sent two regiments of cavalry, on the road to Dingee; one of them, the 14th Light Dragoons and two regiments of cavalry, and a troop of horse artillery on the road to Jullalpore; the latter party observed two bodies of the enemy of about 800 and 400 men each, imagined to be a strong rear-guard, about eight miles from this, and behind a thick jungle which reaches to the river; and the former went to Dingee, which place the enemy had left, and the villagers said had gone over the Jhelum. Both parties returned to this camp without, I am sorry to say, having overtaken any of the enemy's troops or guns.

I beg leave to inclose a return of the killed and wounded.

I have, &c.

(Signed) Jos. Thackwell, Major-General,
Commanding the advanced post of the Army.

List of Officers killed, wounded, and missing, of a detachment of the army of the Punjaub, on the 3rd December 1848.

1st Troop, 2nd Brigade Horse Artillery—Lieutenant E. J. Watson, wounded.

10th Light Field Battery, 1st Company, 1st Battalion—Captain E. G. Austin, severely wounded.

22nd Regiment Native Infantry—Jemadar Sudar Khan, severely wounded; amputation of leg.

25th Regiment Native Infantry—Thunnoo Ram Jemadar, killed.

36th Regiment Native Infantry—Lieutenant Garstin, severely wounded.

3rd Irregular Cavalry—Lieutenant A. Gibbons, wounded.

Return of killed, wounded, and missing, of a detachment of the army of the Punjaub, in the action on the 3rd December 1848.

Camp Heyleh, December 6, 1848.

1st Troop, 2nd Brigade Horse Artillery—1 sergeant, 1 rank and file, 3 horses, killed; 1 European officer, 1 sergeant, 1 rank and file, 2 horses, wounded.

3rd Troop, 2nd Brigade Horse Artillery—2 horses wounded.

1st Troop, 3rd Brigade Horse Artillery—4 rank and file, 8 horses, killed; 7 rank and file, 4 horses, wounded.

Total—1 serjeant, 5 rank and file, 11 horses, killed; 1 European officer, 1 sergeant, 8 rank and file, 8 horses, wounded.

No. 5 Light Field Battery and 3rd Company 7th Battalion—1 horse killed; 2 Syce drivers, 1 Syce, 2 horses, wounded.

No. 10 Light Field Battery and 1st Company 1st Battalion—2 horses, killed; 1 European officer, 2 rank and file, wounded.

Total—3 horses killed; 1 European officer, 2 rank and file, 2 Syce drivers, 1 Syce, 2 horses, wounded.

Cavalry—1st Brigade.

H. M.'s 3rd Light Dragoons—3 horses, killed; 1 rank and file, 1 horse, wounded.

5th Light Cavalry—2 horses, killed; 1 havildar, 1 horse, wounded.

8th Light Cavalry—1 rank and file, 3 horses, killed; 1 horse, wounded.

Total—1 rank and file, 8 horses, killed; 1 havildar, 1 rank and file, 3 horses, wounded.

3rd Irregular Cavalry—1 havildar, 2 rank and file, 11 horses, killed; 1 European officer, 2 rank and file, 1 horse, wounded; 1 rank and file, 1 horse, missing.

12th Irregular Cavalry—1 rank and file, killed.

Infantry—3rd Brigade.

31st Regiment Native Infantry—1 havildar, 6 rank and file, wounded.

Total—1 havildar, 3 rank and file, 11 horses, killed; 1 European officer, 1 havildar, 3 rank and file, 1 horse, wounded.

6th Brigade.

Remarks—1 Bheestie wounded and drowned crossing the river on the night of the 1st December 1848; 3 sowars and 1 horse, not included in this.

H. M.'s 24th Regiment—1 sergeant, 1 rank and file, killed; 1 sergeant, 3 rank and file, wounded.

22nd Regiment Native Infantry—1 havildar, killed; 1 native officer, 2 rank and file, wounded.

25th Regiment Native Infantry—1 native officer, 4 rank and file, killed; 1 havildar, 7 rank and file, wounded.

Total—1 native officer, 1 sergeant, and 1 havildar, 5 rank and file, killed; 1 native officer, 1 sergeant, and 1 havildar, 12 rank and file, wounded.

8th Brigade.

H. M.'s 61st Regiment—2 rank and file, killed; 1 sergeant, 8 rank and file, wounded.

36th Regiment Native Infantry—1 native officer, 1 rank and file, killed; 1 European officer, 2 rank and file, wounded.

46th Regiment Native Infantry—1 rank and file, wounded.

Total—1 native officer, 3 rank and file, killed; 1 European officer, 1 sergeant, 11 rank and file, wounded.

Total—21 men, 33 horses, killed; 51 men, 14 horses, wounded; 1 man, 1 horse, missing.

Grand Total—73 men, 48 horses.

The Secretary with the Governor-General to the Adjutant-General of the Army.

Ferozepore, January 31, 1849.

I am directed to acknowledge the receipt of his Excellency the Commander-in-Chief's despatches, dated the 5th, 10th, and 16th ultimo, reporting the particulars of an action with the enemy at Sadoolapore, and the passage of the Chenab by Major-General Sir Joseph Thackwell, K.C.B.

The Governor-General regrets to find that he inadvertently omitted to issue instructions founded on a minute which he had recorded on the subject of the despatches under acknowledgment. His Lordship begs to congratulate the Commander-in-Chief on the success of the measures which he adopted for effecting the passage of the Chenab, and to convey to him the assurance of his satisfaction with, and his best thanks for, the judicious arrangements by which he was enabled, with comparatively little loss, to carry into execution his plans for the passage of that difficult river, and for compelling the retreat of the Sikh army from the formidable position which they occupied on its further bank, after they had been engaged, and beaten back by the forces under Major-General Sir Joseph Thackwell. The result of his Excellency's movements, in driving the Sikh army from their entrenchments, and forcing them to retire on the other extremity of the Dooab, was of much importance.

The Governor-General offers his best thanks to Major-General Sir Joseph Thackwell for his successful direction of the force under his command, and for the dispositions by which he compelled the enemy to retire, and ultimately to quit the ground he had occupied. The Governor-General tenders his best thanks to Brigadier-General Campbell for the able assistance which he rendered to Major-General Sir Joseph Thackwell, and to Lieutenant-Colonel Grant for the powerful and effective use which he made of the artillery under his command.

The Governor-General has had much gratification in observing the terms in which the Commander-in-Chief has spoken of the army under his command in the field; and he concurs with his Excellency in bestowing upon them the praise which is their due.

General Orders by the Right Honourable the Governor-General of India.

Camp Ferozepore, February 24, 1849.

The following notifications from the Foreign Department, are republished for the information of the army:

Notification.

Foreign Department, Camp Ferozepore,
February 23, 1849.

The Governor-General has the gratification of intimating to the President in Council, and notifying for public information, that he has this day received a despatch from Major Mackeson, C.B., agent to the Governor-General with the Commander-in-Chief, conveying the intelligence that the forces under his Excellency the Commander-in-Chief, on the 21st instant, attacked and routed the Sikh army in the neighbourhood of Goojerat.

The enemy was beaten at every point and retreated in disorder, leaving in the hands of the British troops, by whom he was pursued, a great portion of his artillery, his ammunition, and the whole of his standing camp.

The official despatches of his Excellency the Commander-in-Chief will be published as soon as they are received.

The Governor-General directs that a salute of 21 guns shall be fired, at every principal station of the army, on the receipt of this notification.

By order of the Right Honourable the Governor-General of India.

(Signed) H. M. Elliot,
Secretary to the Government of India,
with the Governor-General.

NOTIFICATION.

Foreign Department, Camp Ferozepore,
February 24, 1849.

The Right Honourable the Governor-General directs the publication of the following letter from his Excellency the Commander-in-Chief, reporting the complete defeat of the Sikh army on the 21st instant. The detailed despatches will be published hereafter.

From his Excellency the Commander-in-Chief in India to the Right Honourable the Governor-General.

Camp, in front of Goojerat, February 21, 1849.

My Lord,—I have the honour to report to your Lordship that I have this day obtained a victory of no common order, either in its character, or, I trust, in its effects.

I was joined yesterday by Brigadier Markham's brigade, Brigadier-General Dundas having joined late the preceding night. I moved on in the afternoon of yesterday, as soon as these troops were refreshed, from Trikur to the village of Shadiwal, and at seven this morning I moved to the attack, which commenced at half-past eight o'clock, and by one o'clock I was in possession of the whole of the Sikh position, with all his camp equipage, baggage, magazines, and I hope a large proportion of his guns; the exact number I cannot at present state, from the great extent of his position and length of pursuit, as I followed up the enemy from four to five miles on the Bimbur road, and pushed on Sir Joseph Thackwell with the cavalry. The rout has been most complete; the whole road for twelve miles is strewed with guns, ammunition waggons, arms, and baggage.

My loss was camparatively small (I hope within 300 killed and wounded) when it is considered I had to attack 60,000 Sikhs, in a very strong position, armed with upwards of 60 guns. The loss of the enemy must have been very severe.

The conduct of the whole army, in every arm, was conspicuous for steadiness in movement, and gallantry in action. The details I shall furnish hereafter.

I have, &c.

(Signed) GOUGH, General,
Commander-in-Chief in India.

By order of the Right Honourable the Governor-General of India.

(Signed) H. M. ELLIOT,
Secretary to the Government of India,
with the Governor-General.

J. STUART, Colonel,
Secretary to the Government of India, Military Department, with the Governor-General.

NOTIFICATION.

Fort William, Foreign Department,
March 9, 1849.

The President in Council is pleased to direct the publication of the following notification issued by the Right Honourable the Governor-General at his Lordship's head-quarters, with a despatch from his Excellency the Commander-in-Chief, reporting the details of the complete victory which was gained over the Sikh force at Goojerat, on the 21st ultimo by the army under his Excellency's command.

By order of the President of the Council of India in council.

FRED. JAS. HALLIDAY,
Officiating Secretary to the Government of India.

GENERAL ORDER BY THE RIGHT HONOURABLE THE GOVERNOR-GENERAL OF INDIA.

Foreign Department, Camp Ferozepore,
March 1, 1849.

The Governor-General, having received from his Excellency the Commander-in-Chief a despatch, reporting the details of the brilliant victory which was gained by the British army at Goojerat, on the 21st ultimo, directs that it be published for the information of the army and of the people of India.

The Sikh army, under the command of Sirdar Chutter Sing and of Rajah Shere Sing, combined with the Affghan troops in the service of the Ameer of Cabool, were posted in great strength near to the town of Goojerat.

Their numbers were estimated at 60,000 men, and 59 guns were brought by them into action.

On the morning of the 21st they were attacked by the forces under the personal command of his Excellency the Commander-in-Chief. A powerful and sustained cannonade by the British artillery compelled them, after some time, to retire from the positions they had well and resolutely maintained.

The subsequent advance of the British army drove them back at once from every point, and retreat having been speedily converted into rout, they fled in the utmost disorder, and abandoning their guns, and throwing away their arms, were pursued by the artillery and cavalry till the evening, for many miles beyond the town.

Fifty-three pieces of the enemy's artillery, his camp, his baggage, his magazines, and vast stores of ammunition left in the hands of the British troops, bear testimony to the completeness and to the importance of the victory that has been won.

The Governor-General, in the name and on behalf of the Government of India, most cordially congratulates his Excellency the Commander-in-Chief and the whole army on the glorious success which, under the blessing of Divine Providence, their skill and gallantry have achieved: and he offers to his Excellency, to the generals, the officers, non-commissioned officers and soldiers of the force, his grateful acknowledgments of the services they have thus rendered to the Government and to their country.

The Governor-General begs especially to thank Major-General Sir Joseph Thackwell, K.C.B. and K.H.; Major-General Sir W. Gilbert, K.C.B.; Major-General Whish, C.B.; Brigadier-General Campbell, C.B., and Brigadier-General the Honourable H. Dundas, C.B., for the ability and judgment with which they directed the operations of the divisions respectively under their command.

To the chief engineer, Brigadier Cheape, C.B.; to the officers commanding brigades, Brigadier Brooke, C.B.; Brigadier Huthwaite, C.B.; Brigadier Leeson; to Brigadier White, C.B., Brigadier Hearsey and Brigadier Lockwood, C.B.; to Brigadier Hervey and Brigadier Markham; to Brigadier Mountain, C.B.; Brigadier Penny, C.B.; Brigadier Capon and Brigadier Hoggan; Brigadier Carnegy and Brigadier McLeod, the best thanks of the Governor-General are due.

The services of Brigadier-General Tennant and of the artillery of the force have been recorded in the despatch of the Commander-in-Chief in terms of which they may justly be proud.

The Governor-General cordially joins with his Excellency

in acknowledging their merit, and in bestowing upon them the praise they have earned so well.

To Major Lugard, to Lieutenant-Colonel Gough, C.B., and to the officers of the general staff of Her Majesty's army; to Lieutenant-Colonel Grant, C.B.; to Lieutenant-Colonel Garden, C.B.; and to the officers of the general staff of the army; to Captain Ramsay and the officers of the commissariat department; to Mr. Franklin, inspector-general of Her Majesty's hospitals; to Dr. Renny and the officers of the medical department, and to the officers of his Excellency's personal staff, the Governor-General offers his best thanks, and assures them of his full appreciation of their services.

And to all the troops of every arm, European and native, the Governor-General desires to convey his entire approbation of their steady and gallant conduct throughout the day; particularly to a portion of the 9th Lancers and the Scinde Horse for their charge against the Affghan cavalry; to the 3rd brigade of infantry under Brigadier Penny, C.B., for their attack on the village of Kalra; and to a portion of Brigadier Hervey's brigade for their charge led by Lieutenant-Colonel Franks, C.B., all of which have been specially reported by his Excellency the Commander-in-Chief.

The Governor-General estimates highly the important results which the battle gained on the 21st ultimo is calculated to produce. He entertains a hope that the conviction, which the events of that day must force upon all, of the vast superiority which the British army derived from the possession of science and military resource, will induce the enemy shortly to abandon a contest which is a hopeless one.

The war in which we are engaged must be prosecuted with vigour and determination, to the entire defeat and dispersion of all who are in arms against us, whether Sikhs or Affghans.

The Governor-General has ever felt, and feels, unbounded confidence in the army which serves in India. He relies fully on the conviction that their services will be given cheerfully and gallantly, as heretofore, whatever may be the obstacles opposed to them; and he does not doubt that, with the blessing of Heaven, such full success will continue to follow their efforts, as shall speedily give to the Government of India the victory over its enemies, and restore the country to the enjoyment of peace.

The Governor-General will not fail earnestly to commend the past services of this army to the favourable consideration of Her Majesty's Government and of the Honourable East India Company.

A salute of 21 guns has been ordered at every principal station of the army in India.

By order of the Right Honourable the Governor-General of India.

(Signed) H. M. ELLIOT,
Secretary to the Government of India,
with the Governor-General.

From the Right Honourable the Commander-in-Chief in India, to the Right Honourable the Governor-General of India.

Head-quarters, Camp Goojerat,
February 26, 1849.

My Lord,—By my letter of the 21st instant, written on the field of battle immediately after the action, your Lordship will have been made acquainted with the glorious result of my operations on that day against the Sikh army, calculated from all credible reports at 60,000 men of all arms and 59 pieces of artillery, under the command of

Sirdar Chutter Sing and Rajah Shere Sing, with a body of 1500 Affghan horse led by Akram Khan, son of the Ameer Dost Mahomed Khan; a result, my Lord, glorious indeed for the ever victorious army of India! The ranks of the enemy broken, their position carried, their guns, ammunition, camp equipage, and baggage captured, their flying masses driven before the victorious pursuers from mid-day to dusk, receiving a most severe punishment in their flight; and, my Lord, with gratitude to a merciful Providence, I have the satisfaction of adding, that notwithstanding the obstinate resistance of the enemy, this triumphant success, this brilliant victory has been achieved with comparatively little loss on our side.

The number of guns taken in action and captured in the line of pursuit, I now find to be fifty-three (53).

The official report made by the adjutant-general of the army on the 20th instant, will have informed your Lordship that I had directed Brigadier-General the Honourable H. Dundas to join me by forced marches, and that I had closed up to so short a distance of the Sikh army, that they could not possibly attempt the passage of the Chenab, in order to put into execution their avowed determination of moving upon Lahore, make a retrograde movement by the Kooree Pass (the only practicable one for guns), or indeed quit their position, without my being able to attack them and defeat their movement.

On the 18th instant Brigadier Markham had proceeded from Ramnugger up the left bank of the river to Kanokee, to which I had directed forty-seven boats to be sent up. On the morning of the 20th this officer crossed the Chenab, by my instructions, and joined me at eleven o'clock A.M. At the same time Lieutenant-Colonel Byrne was directed to move down the left bank, from the position he held in front of Wuzeerabad with two corps of infantry and four guns, leaving two regiments of irregular cavalry to watch the fords, and to prevent any marauding parties or bodies of the routed enemy from effecting a passage.

On the same day a reconnoissance was made of the enemy's position, and it was ascertained that their camp nearly encircled the town of Goojerat, their regular troops being placed immediately fronting us between the town and a deep watercourse, the dry bed of the River Dwara. This nullah, which is very tortuous, passing round nearly two sides of the town of Goojerat—diverging to a considerable distance on the north and west faces, and then taking a southerly direction, running through the centre of the ground, I occupied at Shadiwal. Thus the enemy's position on the right was greatly strengthened, the nullah giving cover to his infantry in front of his guns, whilst another deep, though narrow wet nullah running from the east of the town and falling into the Chenab, in the direction of Wuzeerabad, covered his left.

The ground between these nullahs, for a space of nearly three miles, being well calculated for the operations of all arms, and presenting no obstacle to the movement of my heavy guns, I determined to make my principal attack in that direction and dispose my force accordingly.

On the extreme left I placed the Bombay column, commanded by the Honourable H. Dundas, supported by Brigadier White's brigade of cavalry and the Scinde horse, under Sir Joseph Thackwell, to protect the left and to prevent large bodies of Sikh and Affghan cavalry from turning that flank: with this cavalry I placed Captains Duncan and Huish's troops of horse artillery, whilst the infantry was covered by the Bombay troop of horse artillery under Major Blood.

On the right of the Bombay column, and with its right resting on the nullah, I placed Brigadier-General Campbell's division of infantry, covered by No. 5 and No. 10

light field batteries, under Major Ludlow and Lieutenant Robertson, having Brigadier Hoggan's brigade of infantry in reserve.

Upon the right of the nullah, I placed the infantry division of Major-General Sir Walter Gilbert, the heavy guns, eighteen in number, under Majors Day and Horsford, with Captain Shakespear and Brevet-Major Sir Richmond Shakespear, commanding batteries, being disposed in two divisions upon the flanks of his left brigade.

This line was prolonged by Major-General Whish's division of infantry, with one brigade of infantry under Brigadier Markham in support of second line, and the whole covered by three troops of horse artillery; Major Fordyce's, Captain Mackenzie's, and Anderson's, No. 17 light field battery, under Captain Dawes, with Lieutenant-Colonel Lane's and Captain Kinleside's troops of horse artillery, in a second line in reserve under Lieutenant-Colonel Brind.

My right flank was protected by Brigadiers Hearsay's and Lockwood's brigades of cavalry, with Captain Warner's troop of horse artillery.

The 5th and 6th Light Cavalry, with the Bombay light field battery, and the 45th and 69th Regiments, under the command of Lieutenant-Colonel Mercer, most effectually protected my rear and baggage.

With my right wing I proposed penetrating the centre of the enemy's line, so as to turn the position of their force in rear of the nullah, and thus enable my left wing to cross it with little loss and in co-operation with the right to double upon the centre the wing of the enemy's force opposed to them.

At half-past seven o'clock the army advanced in the order described with the precision of a parade movement. The enemy opened their fire at a very long distance, which exposed to my artillery both the position and range

13

of their guns. I halted the infantry just out of fire, and advanced the whole of my artillery, covered by skirmishers.

The cannonade now opened upon the enemy was the most magnificent I ever witnessed, and as terrible in its effect.

The Sikh guns were served with their accustomed rapidity, and the enemy well and resolutely maintained his position; but the terrific force of our fire obliged them, after an obstinate resistance, to fall back. I then deployed the infantry, and directed a general advance, covering the movement by my artillery as before.

The village of Burra-kabra, the left one of those of that name, in which the enemy had concealed a large body of infantry, and which was apparently the key of their position, lay immediately in the line of Major-General Sir Walter Gilbert's advance, and was carried in the most brilliant style by a spirited attack of the 3rd Brigade under Brigadier Penny, consisting of the 2nd Europeans, 31st and 70th Regiments of Native Infantry, which drove the enemy from their cover with great slaughter.

A very spirited and successful movement was also made about the same time against a heavy body of the enemy's troops, in and about second or Chota-kabra, by part of Brigadier Hervey's Brigade, most gallantly led by Lieutenant-Colonel Franks of Her Majesty's 10th Foot.

The heavy artillery continued to advance with extraordinary celerity, taking up successive forward positions, driving the enemy from those they had retired to, whilst the rapid advance and beautiful fire of the horse artillery and light field batteries, which I strengthened by bringing to the front the two reserved troops of horse artillery under Lieutenant-Colonel Brind, Brigadier Brooke having the general superintendence of the whole of the horse artillery, broke the ranks of the enemy at all points. The whole infantry line now rapidly advanced and drove the enemy before it; the nullah was cleared, several villages stormed, the guns that were in position carried, the camp captured, and the enemy routed in every direction! The right wing and Brigadier-General Campbell's division passing in pursuit to the eastward—the Bombay column to the westward of the town.

The retreat of the Sikh army thus hotly pressed, soon became a perfect flight, all arms dispersing over the country, rapidly pursued by our troops for a distance of twelve miles, their track strewed with their wounded, their arms, and military equipments, which they threw away to conceal that they were soldiers.

Throughout the operations thus detailed, the cavalry brigades on the flanks were threatened, and occasionally attacked, by vast masses of the enemy's cavalry, which were, in every instance, put to flight by the steady movements and spirited manœuvres of our cavalry, most zealously and judiciously supported by the troops of horse artillery attached to them, from whom the enemy received the severest punishment.

On the left, a most successful and gallant charge was made upon the Affghan cavalry and a large body of Goorchurras, by the Scinde Horse and a party of the 9th Lancers, when some standards were captured.

The determined front shown by the 14th Light Dragoons and the other cavalry regiments on the right, both regular and irregular, completely overawed the enemy, and contributed much to the success of the day; the conduct of all in following up the fugitive enemy was beyond all praise.

A competent force, under the command of Major-General Sir Walter Gilbert, resumed the pursuit towards the Jhelum on the following morning, with a view of cutting off the enemy from the only practicable gun road to the Jhelum. Another division of infantry, under Brigadier-

General Campbell, advanced on the road to Bimber, scouring the country in that direction to prevent their carrying off the guns by that route, and a body of cavalry, under Lieutenant-Colonel Bradford, successfully pushed on several miles into the hills and twenty-four from Goojerat, accompanied by that most energetic political officer, Captain Nicholson, for the same purpose, whilst I remained in possession of the field for the purpose of supporting these operations, covering the fords of the Chenab, and destroying the vast magazine of ammunition left scattered about in all directions. I am happy to add that these combinations have been entirely successful, the detached parties coming at every step on the wreck of the dispersed and flying foe.

Having thus endeavoured to convey to your Lordship the particulars of the operations of the battle of "Goojerat," I beg now to offer my heartfelt congratulations to your Lordship, and to the Government of India, upon this signal victory achieved under the blessing of Divine Providence by the united efforts and indomitable gallantry of the noble army under my command, a victory, my Lord, as glorious to the army that gained it, as it must be satisfactory to yourself and the Government of India, from the very important and decisive results to be expected from it.

It is quite impossible for me sufficiently to express my admiration of the gallant and steady conduct of the officers and men, as well Native as European, upon this occasion.

The brilliant service they have performed in so signally defeating so vastly a superior force, amongst whom were the élite of the old Khalsa army, making a last, united, and desperate struggle, will speak for itself, and will, I am confident, be justly estimated by your Lordship.

I cannot too strongly express to your Lordship my deep

sense of obligation to the general officers and brigadier-generals in command of divisions, who so ably carried out my views and directed operations of their troops on this day.

I beg to annex for your Lordship's information the reports I have received from them, and to bring most prominently to your Lordship's notice the brigadiers commanding brigades; the commanding officers of regiments and of troops of horse artillery and light field batteries, and the several officers of the divisional and brigade staff enumerated in these reports, in terms of such just commendation.

I feel much indebted to Major-General Sir Joseph Thackwell, for the able and judicious manner he manœuvred the cavalry with horse artillery attached, on the left, keeping in check the immensely superior force of the enemy, whose main object was to turn my flanks. I am also greatly indebted to this tried and gallant officer for his valuable assistance and untiring exertions throughout the present and previous operations as second in command with his force.

To Major-General Sir Walter Gilbert, whose services upon this, as on all former occasions, were invaluable, and ever marked by energy, zeal, and devotion; as well as to Major-General Whish, Brigadier-Generals Campbell and Dundas, for their able assistance, I am deeply indebted.

To Brigadier-General Tennant, commanding that splendid arm the artillery, to whose irresistible power I am mainly indebted for the glorious victory of Goojerat, I am indeed most grateful. Conspicuous as the artillery has ever proved itself, never was its superiority over that of the enemy, its irresistible and annihilating power, more truthfully shown than in this battle. The heavy batteries manœuvred with the celerity of light guns; and the rapid advance, the scientific and judicious selection of points of attack, the effective and well-directed fire of the troops of horse artillery and light field batteries, merit my warmest praise; and I beg most earnestly to recommend their brave and gallant commanders, with the several officers named in Brigadier-General Tennant's report, to your Lordship's most favourable notice.

From Brigadier Cheape, the chief engineer, and the talented officers in that department as named in the Brigadier's report, I have received the most valuable assistance in reconnoitring the enemy's position and on the field of battle. The Sappers and Pioneers, under that most able officer, Captain Siddons, did excellent service, and were ever in front to overcome any obstacle to the advance of the artillery.

To the officers of the general staff of Her Majesty's service, Major Lugard, acting adjutant-general and Lieutenant-Colonel Gough, quartermaster-general, of Her Majesty's troops in India, my best thanks are due; their exertions upon the present occasion and throughout the recent operations were most valuable, and I beg to bring them under your Lordship's most favourable notice. I am equally indebted to Captain Otter, acting assistant adjutant-genera of Her Majesty's forces for his valuable services.

To the officers of the general staff of the army, Lieutenant-Colonel Grant, adjutant-general, and Lieutenant-Colonel Garden, quartermaster-general, whose most onerous and very important duties have invariably been conducted to my entire satisfaction, I am under the greatest obligation. Their valuable assistance in the field, and their indefatigable exertions throughout operations of no ordinary character, deserve my warmest thanks and your Lordship's approbation.

To Lieutenant-Colonel Birch, judge-advocate-general, I am much indebted for his assistance upon every occasion.

To Major Tucker, deputy adjutant-general, a most gallant, energetic, and valuable officer; to Lieutenant-Colonel Drummond, deputy quartermaster-general, whose services have been most praiseworthy; to Major Chester, assistant adjutant-general, and Lieutenant Tytler, assistant quartermaster-general; Lieutenant Johnston, deputy judge-advocate-general; Major G. Thompson, and Lieutenant-Colonel Curtis, assistant commissary-general; Captain C. Campbell, paymaster to the army, I offer my best thanks for their services whilst attending me in the field, and the efficient manner they have performed their several duties.

Mr. Franklin, inspector-general of Her Majesty's hospitals, has been unceasing in his exertions in rendering every aid to the sick and wounded of the Royal service, and giving the benefit of his long professional experience in such duties; as has Doctor Renny, superintending-surgeon of this army, who has been indefatigable in his professional exertions and well-organized medical arrangements.

I feel I cannot too prominently bring to notice the valuable exertions of Doctor MacRae, field-surgeon, and of the medical officers of the army generally; they have been most unwearied and praiseworthy.

To Captain Ramsay, deputy commissary-general, and to the officers of his department, I am much indebted, and feel grateful for their unceasing and successful exertions amidst all difficulties to supply the troops, and thus preserve the efficiency of the army.

The officers of my personal staff have well merited my best thanks and your Lordship's favourable notice. Captain Haines, military secretary, who has rendered me most valuable aid; Brevet-Major Bates, A.D.C.; Lieutenant A. Bagot, A.D.C.; Lieutenant S. J. Hire, A.D.C.; Captain Gabbett, A.D.C.; Lieutenant G. Hardinge, A.D.C.; and Lieutenant W. G. Prendergast, my Persian interpreter.

I beg also to acknowledge the valuable assistance I have received from the political officers, Major Mackeson, Mr. Cocks, Captain Nicholson, and Lieutenant Robison, both in the field and throughout the operations. I regret to add that Mr. Cocks was seriously wounded during the action in a rencontre with a Sikh horseman.

I would also bring to your Lordship's notice the name of Lieutenant Stannus, of the 5th Light Cavalry; this officer has commanded the cavalry party attached to my escort throughout the operations to my entire satisfaction. He was severely wounded on the 21st, when gallantly charging a party of the enemy's horsemen.

Major Anstruther, of the Madras Artillery, Lieutenant Mayne, of the Madras Cavalry, and Captain Showers, of the 14th Native Infantry, attended me in the field.

I have most unwillingly been delayed from sooner forwarding this despatch, from the circumstance of having only this day received Brigadier-General the Honourable H. Dundas' report, and some of the casualty returns have not even yet reached me. As soon as the whole come in, a full amended general return shall be transmitted without loss of time for your Lordship's information.

I have the pleasure to inclose a plan of the battle of Goojerat. Also a return of the captured ordnance.

I have, &c.

(Signed) GOUGH, General,
Commander-in-Chief in India.

P.S.—The casualty lists having arrived, I have the honour to inclose the return of killed and wounded, which I am sorry to see is so much heavier than I at first anticipated. Several of these were occasioned by accidental explosions of the enemy's tumbrils and magazines after the action.

G.

To Lieutenant-Colonel P. Grant, C.B., Adjutant-General of the Army.

Sir,—I have the honour to report, for the information of his Excellency the Commander-in-Chief, that the Bengal Artillery of the army of the Punjaub were allotted, as follows, during the action of yesterday: —

Lieutenant-Colonel C. Grant.

1st troop, 3rd brigade, Captain W. R. Warner. Attached to Brigadier Lockwood's cavalry brigade, on the right.

Major Garbett.

4th troop, 1st brigade, Captain M. Mackenzie. 4th troop, 3rd brigade, Captain J. Anderson. With the 1st division of Infantry, commanded by Major-General W. S. Whish, C.B.

2nd troop, 2nd brigade, Major D. Fordyce. No. 17 light field battery, Captain M. Dawes. With the 2nd Infantry division, commanded by Major-General Sir W. R. Gilbert, K.C.B.

Major Mowatt.

No. 5 light field battery, Major E. Ludlow. No. 10 light field battery, Lieutenant Robertson. With the 3rd division of Infantry, under Brigadier-General Campbell, C.B.

4th troop, 2nd brigade, Captain F. Duncan. 1st troop, 2nd brigade, Captain A. Huish. With Brigadier M. White's cavalry brigade on the left.

Lieutenant-Colonel Brind.

2nd troop, 3rd brigade, Lieutenant-Colonel Lane, C.B. 3rd troop, 2nd brigade, Captain E. Kinleside, composing the reserve under Brigadier G. Brooke, C.B.

Brigadier E. Huthwaite, C.B.

Major Horsford.

Four 18-pounders, two 8-inch howitzers, drawn by elephants, Major Sir R. Shakespear.

Two 18-pounders, two 8-inch howitzers, drawn by elephants, Captain J. Shakespear.

Major E. Day.

Two 18-pounders, two 8-inch howitzers, Captain E. Masters.

Two 18-pounders, two 8-inch howitzers, Captain E. Austin, who, being unable from his wound to accompany his own battery, No. 10 did duty with the heavy guns.

These batteries engaged in action by those attached to the 1st and 2nd divisions, advancing within about 600 yards, and the heavy guns within 800 or 1000 yards of the enemy's artillery, on which they opened their fire about 9 o'clock A.M.; shortly after the action commenced, an opportunity was observed of enfilading one of the enemy's batteries, when the reserve artillery under Lieutenant-Colonel F. Brind was advanced, and placed by Brigadier G. Brooke, C.B., so as to do so. The batteries of the 3rd division engaged as they came up, and those with the cavalry brigades supported their movements as opportunity offered. Nearly the whole engagement being a cannonade, no movement of importance took place among the batteries, which maintained their fire until half-past 11 A.M., when many of the enemy's guns were observed to be dismounted and their line broke, and an advance was ordered in pursuit.

I have the honour to state for the Commander-in-Chief's information, my perfect satisfaction with the professional exertions of the officers and my high approbation of the steady conduct of both officers and men during the day.

To Brigadiers Brooke, C.B., and Huthwaite, C.B., in general direction of the horse and foot artillery respectively under my orders, Lieutenant-Colonel C. Grant and E. Brind, Majors R. Horsford, E. F. Day, and J. L. Mowatt, all of whom held commands, as well as to all the officers commanding troops and batteries above enumerated,

I have to acknowledge my best thanks for their exertions by which these results were obtained. To the divisional staff, Captain J. Abercrombie, deputy assistant adjutant-general, and Lieutenant H. Tombs, deputy assistant quartermaster-general, and to Lieutenant H. A. Olpherts, my aide-de-camp, I am much indebted for their exertions, and also to Captain C. Hogge, the commissary, and Lieutenant P. Christie, deputy commissary of ordnance, for their excellent arrangement of their department as well as for their assistance in the field.

Brigadiers Brooke and Huthwaite mention their majors of brigade, Lieutenant C. V. Cox and Lieutenant E. Kaye respectively, as having afforded them able assistance. I have great pleasure finally particularly to bring to his Excellency's notice, the zeal and attention of Mr. Deputy Commissary Spencer during the day, and beg to recommend that old and deserving officer to his kind consideration.

(Signed) J. Tennant, Brigadier-General,
Commanding Artillery Division,
Army of the Punjaub.

Camp Goojerat, the 22nd February 1849.

To Lieutenant-Colonel P. Grant, C.B., Adjutant-General of the Army.

Head Quarters, Camp Goojerat,
Februray 26, 1849.

Sir,—In reference to general orders of the 21st instant, I beg to submit for the information of the Right Honourable the Commander-in-Chief, a report on the conduct of the engineer department, during the late operations and the engagement of the 21st.

Major Napier, attended by Lieutenant Greathead, and Major Tremenheere, attended by Lieutenant Glover, were employed on the 21st, the former with the right, the latter with the left column of attack, and were very useful from their previous examination of the ground, and in particular of the position of the nullah on our right flank.

Captain Western, Lieutenants Goodwyn, Crommeline, and Taylor accompanied me, and to all those officers, my acknowledgments are due for conveying communications, and obtaining information on every point required during the day.

I have also the gratification to report to his Excellency, the zealous and able manner in which Captain Cunningham and Lieutenant C. Paton performed the duty assigned to them, of bringing up the fleet of boats ordered by his Excellency from Ramnugger, and placing them so as to enable the portion of the army on the other side of the Chenab to co-operate and to come up; the former officer arrived before the close of the action, and joined Brigadier-General Campbell's division.

The other officers of engineers were detached with the different divisions of the army, and no mention of these officers is needed from me, as whatever service they may have had an opportunity of rendering will be more appropriately reported to his Excellency, or acknowledged by the general officers commanding each division.

Captain Siddons, commanding the Sappers and Pioneers, was attached to the heavy guns, with a portion of his corps, the remainder being detached by companies to the different divisions. Such duty as was required from them, I need hardly say was effectively performed; and I trust it may not be considered by his Lordship out of place, my mentioning here the gallant behaviour and unwearied exertion displayed by these men throughout the present service. I allude, in particular, to the siege operations at Mooltan, and the conduct of that portion of the corps who were employed there.

Prior to the engagement on the 21st instant, the officers of engineers were employed in collecting information and in surveying and reconnoitering; and it is due to Captain Longden, of H. M.'s 10th regiment, who is attached to the engineer department, as surveyor and field engineer, to state the very able assistance he has rendered in all these duties during the whole operations, since I have joined the army.

I beg to add, that I am much indebted to Lieutenant J. H. Maxwell, for the very zealous performance of his duties on all occasions, as major of brigade of engineers; and to Lieutenant J. E. Cracroft, brigade quartermaster, my acknowledgments are also due. And I hope I may be permitted to recommend to his Excellency's favour Lieutenant Hutchinson, of engineers, a very promising young officer, who has been lately acting as my aide-de-camp, and who was very severely wounded on the 21st instant.

I have, &c.

(Signed) J. Cheape, Brigadier,
Chief Engineer, Army of Punjaub.

From Major-General Sir J. Thackwell, K.C.B. and K.H., commanding Cavalry Division, to Lieutenant-Colonel Grant, C.B., Adjutant-General of the Army.

Head-Quarters, dated Camp Goojerat,
Feb. 25, 1849.

Sir,—I have the honour to report, for the information of his Excellency the Right Honourable the Commander-in-Chief, the operations of the division of cavalry under my command, in the battle fought on the 21st instant, near the town of Goojerat.

The left column of cavalry, under the command of Brigadier White, C.B., consisting of the troops named in the margin,* was assembled in column of troops at half distance, right in front at deploying interval, on the left of the Bombay column of infantry, at 7 o'clock in the morning.

The right column, composed of troops named in the margin,† under the command of Brigadiers Hearsey, and Lockwood, C.B., were formed in column left in front at the same hour.

The 3rd division of infantry and the Bombay brigade, all on the left of the nullah, leading towards Goojerat, being under my immediate superintendence, I remained on the left flank of the army; and I make no doubt Brigadier-Generals Dundas and Campbell have made you fully acquainted with the operations of the troop under their command.

On approaching the village of Nurrawalla, just without the range of the enemy's batteries, the infantry deployed into line, and Brigadier White formed his cavalry in front of that village with its left back, and parallel to a gentle rising of the ground, on which was posted the enemy's right, consisting of a large body of Affghans and Goor-

* Left Column. 1st Brigade of Cavalry.

Brigadier White, C.B., commanding. H.M.'s 3rd Dragoons, Major Yerbury; H.M.'s 9th Lancers, Lieutenant-Colonel Fullerton; 8th Light Cavalry, Major Mackenzie; Scinde Horse, Captain Malcolm; Captain Duncan's Troop Horse Artillery; Captain Huish's Troop Horse Artillery.

† Right Column. 2nd Brigade of Cavalry.

Brigadier Lockwood, C.B., commanding. H.M.'s 14th Light Dragoons, Lieutenant-Colonel King; 1st Light Cavalry, Lieutenant-Colonel Bradford; 2 Risallahs 11th Irregular Cavalry, Captain Masters; 2 Risallahs 14th Irregular Cavalry, Lieutenant Robarts; Captain Warner's Troop Horse Artillery.

4th Brigade Cavalry.

Brigadier Hearsey, commanding. 3rd Irregular Cavalry, Major Tait, C.B.; 9th Irregular Cavalry, Major Christie. The 5th and 6th Light Cavalry were left in the rear to protect the baggage.

churra horse. From this position a fire of round shot was opened, and the enemy's cavalry extended to the right, so as to threaten to turn our left flank. To oppose the enemy's guns, I ordered Captain Duncan to move his troop of horse artillery to the front, which he did in good style, and opened his fire within 500 or 600 yards. This movement was followed by the advance of Captain Huish's troop; and both did considerable execution upon the enemy, but did not prevent the attempt of the Affghans to outflank our left. The Scinde Horse were on the left of my line; and I ordered them to advance with a squadron of the 9th Lancers, under Captain Campbell, a part of the former to be in reserve, and supported by a squadron of the 9th Lancers, under Major Grant, C.B., in échelon on the right. These troops made a most brilliant charge upon the enemy, at the same time I advanced the guns and cavalry towards the enemy's line. The fire of the guns soon put the Goorchurras in retreat, and the glorious charge of the troops on the left caused their whole force to seek safety in retreat by the Burradurree. A gun was captured during these proceedings; but as we were then considerably in advance of the left of the infantry—although Captain Duncan was enabled to enfilade a battery opposed to them—and ignorant of the force the enemy might have between the Burradurree, and the town, a space covered with trees, it became necessary to proceed with caution; yet I soon was enabled to open a fire upon the enemy, both on the right and left of the former place, which caused them considerable loss, and hastened their retreat.

I may here observe, that all the enemy's tents were left standing near the Bnrradurree, and on the Sikh right of the town, with probably much baggage in them, all of which were probably plundered by the camp-followers.

The enemy being now in full retreat, I moved Brigadier White's brigade well to the left front, and soon forced the enemy from the Jhelum road, and eventually from that of Beembur, also cutting off large bodies of the enemy, much baggage and many guns, which were secured by this brigade, as well as the troops of the 2nd and 4th brigades, which had been ordered to join in the pursuit. At twenty minutes past 4 P.M., none of the enemy being in sight, and being, as was said by the villagers, nine or ten miles from Goojerat, I discontinued the pursuit and returned to camp at this place. In this pursuit Captains Duncan and Huish's troops of artillery, latterly joined by Major Leeson and Major Blood's troop of the same arm, brought their guns to bear upon the enemy with good effect on several occasions, and their advance was as rapid as the intersected nature of the ground (by nullahs) would admit, and the 9th Lancers and 8th Light Cavalry made gallant attempts to close with the enemy's cavalry, which, however, were frustrated by the rapid retreat of the latter, yet a great number of the enemy were slain by this brigade in the pursuit. I witnessed the activity of Captain Unett, and part of his squadron of the 3rd Light Dragoons, and Brigadier White mentions that the whole of that regiment was actively engaged in this work of retribution.

Being an eye-witness to all the movements of the 1st Brigade, I have great satisfaction in stating that Brigadier White conducted them very much to my satisfaction. I am also well satisfied with the manner in which Lieutenant-Colonel Fullerton, Majors Yerbury and Mackenzie, commanded their respective regiments, and in which Major Grant supported the charge of cavalry on the left. The charge of the Scinde Horse reflects the highest credit on Captain Malcolm, and I have great pleasure in having witnessed the gallant bearing of all the officers and men of this brigade during the operations of the day; and I feel sure that their only regret was that the enemy's cavalry so often declined the attack.

To Captains Duncan and Huish and Majors Leeson and Blood, I am much indebted for the manner in which they brought their guns into action whenever an opportunity occurred, and the steadiness and good conduct of both officers and men were very conspicuous.

I have now the pleasing duty to state, that I have received every assistance and support from my deputy assistant adjutant-general, Captain Pratt, on the present occasion, as well as during the campaign. To my deputy assistant quartermaster-general, Lieutenant Tucker, I am greatly indebted for his zeal, activity, intelligence, and successful endeavours to procure intelligence of the movements of the enemy during the operations; he as well as my aide-de-camp, Lieutenant Thackwell, Lieutenant Young, of the Engineers, Lieutenant Carter, of the Pioneers, and Cornet Beatson, of the 6th Light Cavalry, accompanied me during the battle, and afforded me essential service in carrying my orders on various occasions during the operations of the day.

Brigadier White states how greatly he was satisfied with the conduct of his brigade-major, Captain Cautley, and the whole of the officers and men of his brigade.

As the operations of the 2nd and 4th brigades of cavalry did not come under my observations, except towards the latter end of the pursuit, I have the honour to forward Brigadier Lockwood's report, and it would appear therefrom that he conducted his brigade judiciously; and I am gratified to learn that both officers and men behaved greatly to his satisfaction, and that the 14th Light Dragoons and 1st Light Cavalry conducted themselves gallantly, and evinced every anxiety to close with the enemy. I am happy to observe that the brigadier has mentioned with great approbation the conduct of Lieutenant-Colonels Bradford and King, in command of their regiments; and I cannot avoid here stating, for the information of his Lordship, that I observed with much satisfaction the zeal and judgment evinced by both officers, when in command of considerable bodies of cavalry detached from the camp at Chillianwallah on important duties.

I regret that I have not yet received any report from Brigadier Hearsey, or return of casualties from his brigade, or the Scinde Horse: these will be forwarded when they arrive.

I have, &c.
(Signed) J. THACKWELL,
Major-General Commanding Cavalry Division.

To the Deputy Assistant Adjutant-General.
Cavalry Division, Army of the Punjaub.

Camp Goojerat, February 22, 1849.

Sir,—I have the honour to report for the information of Major-General Sir Joseph Thackwell, commanding the cavalry division, that, on the morning of the 21st, I formed my brigade, as directed by his Excellency the Commander-in-Chief, on the right rear of the 1st Division of Infantry, and parallel to Brigadier Markham's reserve; advancing in this order until the enemy opened their fire.

I then deployed the brigade in the following manner:—In the first line, five troops Her Majesty's 14th Light Dragoons, two squadrons 1st Light Cavalry with the 1st Troop, 3rd Brigade Horse Artillery on the left, escorted by a troop of the 14th and a Risallah 11th Irregular Cavalry. In support, the remainder of the Irregular Cavalry, and in reserve, one squadron 14th and one squadron 1st Light Cavalry.

In the commencement of the action I directed Captain Warner to open his fire upon a large body of the enemy near a village in our front; but as they returned a heavy fire within accurate range I changed position left back, and the horse artillery ceased firing.

The enemy's horsemen now appeared in great force upon our right, threatening to turn our flank, so I changed front to the right, directing the reserve to retain its front, and communicate with the infantry.

Captain Warner's guns opened with great effect upon the horsemen, and turned them, but they only retired a short distance, and then a regiment of their regular cavalry moved round by a circuitous route, and got completely into our rear. I immediately detached towards them three guns with a squadron of the 14th, who, in conjunction with Major Christie's corps of irregular cavalry, drove them off.

About this time a large gol of horse came on towards me, and I prepared to charge, but as they turned at once from the fire of the guns, and as there was a nullah in our front, I refrained from advancing after them. The reserve also now advanced in support of Colonel Hervey's brigade of infantry.

I then received orders from the Commander-in-Chief to bring on the brigade, which I did, and followed in pursuit of the enemy, until I found myself parallel to the cavalry under the Major-General, when I placed myself in communication with him.

In the pursuit, the 14th Dragoons and 1st Light Cavalry cut down or shot a considerable number of the Sikh infantry, both regular and irregular, and Corporal William Pain, of the 14th Dragoons captured a red silk standard, killing, in single combat, the horseman who bore it.

I beg to state to the major-general, that I had the greatest satisfaction in witnessing the steadiness of the troops composing the brigade, in performing several manœuvres under a heavy fire of artillery.

My best thanks are due to Captain Warner, horse artillery, for the able and efficient manner in which he employed his guns; also to Lieutenant-Colonel Bradford, commanding the 1st Light Cavalry; Lieutenant-Colonel King, 14th Light Dragoons; Captain Masters, 11th Irregular Cavalry; and Lieutenant Robarts, 14th Irregular Cavalry; and Lieutenant-Colonel Doherty, who commanded the reserve.

I am also under the greatest obligations to my brigade-major, Captain Yule, 9th Lancers, for the essential assistance he rendered me, not only during the action, but during the period I have commanded the 2nd brigade.

(Signed) C. H. Lockwood,
Commanding 2nd Cavalry Brigade.

To Captain Pratt, Assistant Adjutant-General, Cavalry Division.

Camp near Koree, February 23, 1849.

Sir,—I have the honour to report to Sir Joseph Thackwell, K.C.B., and K.H., commanding the cavalry division of the army of the Punjaub, for the information of his Excellency the Right Honourable the Commander-in-Chief, that agreeable to instructions received from Captain Pratt, assistant adjutant-general, cavalry division, I joined at about half-past 8 on the morning of the 21st instant, the brigade of cavalry on the right, under Brigadier Lockwood, with the 3rd and 9th Irregular Cavalry; and as senior cavalry officer in the field on that flank, I assumed command of the whole of that arm as detailed in the margin,* and a troop of horse artillery

* Brigadier Lockwood's Brigade:—
H.M.'s 14th Dragoons.
1st Light Cavalry.
Captain Warner's Troop Horse Artillery.
Captain Fordyce's, at the end of the action.

under Captain Warner. Soon after, the action commenced by a cannonade, and heavy bodies of horse, amongst them apparently a regular regiment, showed in our front. The cavalry under my command advanced towards them, and the troop of horse artillery was sent to the front with its supports (a squadron of Her Majesty's 14th Dragoons and a squadron of irregular horse), and opened a well-directed fire of round shot and shrapnell, which made the enemy fall back to a respectable distance. On this, very numerous bodies of horse went off to our right, apparently with the intention of turning that flank. I manœuvred to the right with the irregular brigade and kept them in check. About this time I received orders from his Excellency the Commander-in-Chief not to separate the left of the cavalry too far from the column of infantry advancing in that direction. I was therefore necessitated to close to the left, which I did with Brigadier Lockwood's brigade. At the same time as they again pressed on my right, I ordered three guns to support it, the fire from which made the enemy again draw off. I now observed it was their determination to turn the right, and as I had been joined by Colonel Doherty with two squadrons, I placed him to fill the gap on my left, and ordered Brigadier Lockwood's brigade and three guns to join the irregulars on that flank. This checked the enemy, but a very large body now advanced on the space on our left, I immediately opposed it with the irregular brigade and Brigadier Lockwood's with a half-battery, and the enemy was again foiled, but they perceiving I had only the

---

Irregular Brigade:—
3rd Irregular Cavalry.
9th Irregular Cavalry.
11th Irregular Cavalry.
13th Irregular Cavalry, 1st squadron.

artillery supports and a rissalah of horse under the command of Lieutenant Robarts on my extreme right, made a last effort to turn it.

This was promptly met by the 3rd and 9th Irregulars being sent in that direction, the 9th advancing to meet them with the half battery; thus foiled, they returned to our left, Major Christie following their movement. This was their last attempt, a troop of horse artillery with supports of one squadron of 9th Irregulars, commanded by Lieutenant and Adjutant Tytler, pushed to the front and got under the fire of their artillery, when several men and horses suffered from round shot. It was now apparent from the distance of the sound of our guns, that the enemy were in retreat and Major Mackeson informed me it was his Excellency the Commander-in-Chief's wish, that all the cavalry should pursue and prevent the enemy carrying off their guns; I immediately directed Brigadier Lockwood's brigade to take a sweep to the right and pushed on myself with the 3rd Irregulars and Lieutenant Robarts' rissalah with Captain Warner's troop of horse artillery, the 9th Irregulars and 11th under Captain Masters, following as soon as they could get clear of a deep and quaggy nullah, and we perceived the enemy in full retreat, after a canter of four miles. The artillery opened upon the masses of men, whilst the cavalry advanced on the flank and overtook them near the village of Runnewall, where a great many of the Bunnoo troops were sabred and shot. In this manner the pursuit continued until a deep nullah prevented the horse artillery getting on without delay. Here I left them with two squadrons and pushed on again, overtaking another body and punishing them. I detached Captain Biddulph with half a rissalah to ascertain the cause of a heavy cloud of dust to our left. He reported it was Sir J. Thackwell's division, and I soon after heard his battery of horse artillery open.

Both divisions of cavalry were now closing on the enemy, and Captain Biddulph was so fortunate as to capture five guns, and Major Christie another, that had been left in a nullah by the retreating foe. (Major Christie informs me that this gun would have been left behind if he had not made great exertions in having it brought into camp. He disclaims the capture of it.—J. B. H.) The pursuit continued to the village of Sainthul, when I met and reported to Sir J. Thackwell, and from whence we returned to camp. The distance the cavalry under my command went over in pursuit was fifteen miles. We did not get to the camp of the Irregulars, near the Baradurree of Goojerat, until 10 o'clock at night, and had thus been fifteen hours on horseback.

I have every reason to be pleased with the conduct of all the officers under my command. Some difference arose as to carrying my orders into effect by Brigadier Lockwood, in consequence of his receiving directions from supreme authority, of which I was not at the time aware, but I found him most zealous and desirous of having an opportunity to charge the enemy at the head of Her Majesty's 14th Dragoons. The conduct of that regiment throughout the day was most exemplary and steady, and I have not the least doubt, had an opportunity occurred, it would have been most eagerly seized, to the utter destruction of any body opposed to it. Brigadier Lockwood's report will bear testimony to the energy of the officers commanding regiments in his brigade, as I do most assuredly of those officers commanding and in the regiments of irregular cavalry. My thanks are due to Major Tait, C.B., commanding 3rd Irregulars, Major Christie, commanding 9th Irregulars, Captain Masters, commanding 11th Irregulars, and Lieutenant Robarts, commanding a rissalah of the 14th Irregulars. The conduct of the horse artillery was beyond all praise, and I feel much indebted to Captain Warner, his officers and men, for the able manner in which that noble arm was employed.

I feel myself much indebted also to Lieutenant Neville Chamberlain, Brigade-Major 4th Brigade Irregular Cavalry, for his assistance in the field during the forenoon, which I cannot too much appreciate, and for the example he set in several hand-to-hand affairs with a furious and exasperated enemy during the pursuit. Lieutenant Crawford Chamberlain, second in command 9th Irregular Horse, although still suffering from his wound, was present with the regiment the whole day, thus showing his usual energy.

Lieutenant and Adjutant Tytler, 9th Irregulars, also brought to my notice the steadiness of a squadron of that regiment when under severe artillery fire, by which one sowar was killed and several men and horses wounded.

I shall forward a list of casualties as soon as I can get them from the different officers in command of regiments and parties, but from the constant marching we have had since the battle of Goojerat, and the inclement weather we are now enduring, I have not as yet been able to get them.

I have, &c,

(Signed) J. B. Hearsey,

Brigadier 4th Brigade,

Commanding Cavalry on the Right Flank of the Army.

P.S.—I have just got the return of the casualties of the 3rd and 9th Irregular Cavalry, which I have the honour to inclose.

To the Adjutant-General of the Army.

Head-quarters, Camp Goojerat,

February 22, 1849.

Sir,—I have the honour to report, for the information of the Right Honourable the Commander-in-Chief, that the 1st infantry division, with horse artillery attached (as detailed per margin* from right to left), marched at about half-past 7 A.M. yesterday, the 1st brigade commanded by Brigadier Harvey, in quarter distance column of regiments, right in front, at deploying distance, with a troop of native horse artillery on either flank, drawn up in corresponding order.

The 2nd brigade in reserve, commanded by Brigadier Markham, and three to four hundred yards in rear, proceeded in contiguous quarter distance columns.

After advancing about two miles or more, the enemy opened their fire, and after the army had made some further progress, both brigades, agreeably to his Lordship's orders (and taken up from the left), deployed, the horse artillery conforming thereto. Immediately afterwards the troops of horse artillery and skirmishers (of the 1st brigade) were ordered to the front, the latter at 300 yards distance. I then requested Brigadier Markham to take ground on the left, that the interval made by the advance of Captain Anderson's four guns might be covered by the 72nd Native Infantry. Both troops began a spirited cannonade and continued it for about three hours, at the rate of forty rounds per gun per hour, until the enemy's guns in our front (like those, I believe, in front of every part of the line through a similar treatment) were silenced.

---

* 4th Troop 1st Brigade Horse Artillery.—Captain McKenzie.

1st Infantry Brigade.—52nd Native Infantry; H.M.'s 10th Foot; 8th Native Infantry.

4th Troop, 3rd Brigade Horse Artillery.—Captain J. Anderson (except guns at Wuzeerabad).

3rd Company of Pioneers.—Lieutenant McMullin. In reserve.

2nd Infantry Brigade.—51st Native Infantry; H.M.'s 32nd Foot; 72nd Native Infantry.

During the cannonade, on first receiving an order for the further advance of both troops, I learnt from Major Garbett who was in command of them, that the guns in our left front had had so many horses killed and disabled, that they must await the arrival of others from the rear, which I observed were making quick progress to their troop; and which shortly afterwards, I regret to say, lost its gallant captain, who was mortally wounded by a cannon-ball. The duties continued, however, to be efficiently prosecuted under the superintendence of Lieutenants Francis and Mecham, to the former of whom the command immediately devolved.

After this, both troops being well advanced to the front, and the enemy making one or two threatening demonstrations, I thought it right to make a requisition in the cavalry for a small detachment for their protection, which was promptly complied with by Brigadier Lockwood.

On the advance of the line being directed, the right brigade found the enemy's infantry in great force in its front, with a strong body of cavalry on their left, which rendered it necessary for Brigadier Hervey to make a short flank movement to the right and throw back the 52nd Native Infantry, in order to counteract any attack the enemy might have in contemplation.

As this unavoidably caused a great gap in the line, I thought it advisable to direct Brigadier Markham at once to occupy it by his brigade, which was accordingly done, and the arrangement immediately reported to his Excellency. The enemy were otherwise preparing to take advantage of this opening, but on seeing the 2nd Brigade advancing to it, halted and gave a few rounds of grape and matchlock fire, which was returned with full effect by file firing from the right divisions and Lieutenant Francis's guns, which latter were being replenished with ammunition, and for the moment in rear of the infantry.

Lieutenant Need, aide-de-camp, on noticing the enemy's cavalry and infantry immediately in front of the 2nd Brigade, had made known the same to Lieutenants Francis and Mecham, who, on his suggestion, instantly galloped to the front through an interval made for the purpose by Her Majesty's 32nd Regiment, and with a few rounds of grape, co-operated with the infantry (who were advancing to charge) in sending back the enemy in great confusion.

In the flank movement by the 1st Brigade, already adverted to, and which, under a heavy fire from the enemy, of round, grape, and matchlock, with the reformation to line (on discovering that the enemy did not make the anticipated attack) was effected in the most steady and orderly manner. Captain Mackenzie, by his able and judicious co-operation, made his troop particularly useful, and on the enemy's declining to receive the charge of Her Majesty's 10th and the 8th and 52nd Native Infantry, poured in such a continued fire of shrapnell and round upon their retiring masses, as, with what had occurred from the 2nd brigade, effectually to prevent any further threat or molestation to the division under my command, and as far as I could observe, every part of the line had been equally succesful in defeating the purposes of the enemy, who, long before noon, must have discovered that the entire loss of their guns, ammunition, camp equipage, and cattle, was inevitable.

On reaching Goojerat, the 2nd brigade, agreeably to his Lordship's orders, commenced collecting the enemy's abandoned guns, nineteen of which were sent in by them forthwith, and occupied the town with the following details, under Major Case, Her Majesty's 32nd Regiment (which was afterwards reinforced by the 36th Regiment Native Infantry).

Two Companies H. M.'s 32nd Regiment under Captain Pigott.

Two Companies 51st Regiment Native Infantry, under Lieutenant Wallace.

Possession of the eight gates was first taken, and then of the fort, where about eighty of the enemy laid down their arms, and were made over as prisoners to the 36th Regiment Native Infantry, with other small parties found in different parts of the town, that with few exceptions, made no resistance. The above four companies captured a gun, standard, and some horses, with the loss of one man killed of Her Majesty's 32nd, and an officer of the same corps wounded, Lieutenant Jeffry. The 1st brigade, on halting here, detached a subdivision of Her Majesty's 10th Regiment and the Grenadier Company of 52nd Native Infantry, to expel a party of 200 of the enemy in occupation of the temple and garden, in rear of which the 8th Regiment Native Infantry is now encamped, which was effected with trifling loss on our side, but the enemy had 30 or 40 killed and wounded, and a great number taken prisoners.

It is particularly satisfactory to me to bring to the favourable notice of the Right Honourable the Commander-in-Chief the conduct of the division under my command during the services of yesterday, performed under his Lordship's immediate orders and direction, and consisting of, in fact, the Horse Artillery and Infantry of the (Bengal) Mooltan Field Force, with the exception of the 49th Regiment Native Infantry on detached duty. Brigadiers Hervey and Markham conducted their brigades, under the various circumstances of the day (some of which I have briefly specified), in a manner that merits the strongest commendation, and they were, as heretofore, admirably supported by the officers in command of regiments, viz.:

Lieutenant-Colonel Franks, C.B., H. M.'s 10th Regiment; Lieutenant-Colonel Brooke, H. M.'s 32nd Regiment.

Major Farquharson, 8th Regiment Native Infantry, and, on his being severely wounded, Brevet-Major Williams.

Brevet-Major Griffin, 51st Regiment Native Infantry; Captain Jamieson, 52nd ditto; Captain Lloyd, 72nd ditto.

I cordially unite with both Brigadiers, in the expression of thanks to the above officers, for the intelligence and zeal with which they carried out their orders, and to all the officers and men under their command, for the steadiness and prompt obedience so uniformly evinced throughout the division.

Brigadier Hervey acknowledges the services of his Brigade-Major Captain Wiggins, in high terms of commendation; and the active assistance he received throughout the day from Lieutenant B. Reid (34th Regiment Native Infantry), interpreter to Her Majesty's 10th Regiment; as does Brigadier Markham those of his Brigade-Major Captain Balfour, Her Majesty's 32nd Regiment (who has happily recovered from the wound he received in the action of the 12th September last), and of Ensign Fraser, 23rd Regiment, appointed acting interpreter of 49th Regiment Native Infantry, who is awaiting the arrival of his regiment from Mooltan, and who gladly made his services useful to the Brigadier.

To Major Garbett, commanding the Horse Artillery attached to my division, my best acknowledgments are due, for his unremitting attention to both troops under his command, and particularly in matters the officers commanding them were not so able of themselves to give directions about. He mentions in the highest terms (as does Brigadier Hervey) Captain Mackenzie and his troop, and notices that, after the lamented death of Captain J. Anderson, the four guns of his troop were well commanded by Lieutenant Francis; and I heartily concur in the testimony he bears to the admirable conduct of the officers and men of both troops, who worked their guns with a rapidity and precision that would have been impracticable except from their uniform coolness and steadiness under a heavy fire from the enemy at both positions, first at 1000 yards and secondly at 500 yards. Major Garbett also notices in most favourable terms, the able assistance rendered him by Lieutenant De Tessier, Acting Adjutant, 1st Brigade Horse Artillery.

Lieutenant McMullin and his company of pioneers deserve much credit, having continued with the 4th Troop, 1st Brigade Horse Artillery, and rendered useful service whenever called upon.

Having but recently had my attention drawn to the circumstances I am about to mention, I think, in justice to the gallant officer affected by them, I may be permitted so to do though they refer to anterior conflicts with the enemy. On the 12th September last, after Lieutenant-Colonel Pattoun was mortally wounded, the command of the six companies, Her Majesty's 32nd Regiment, devolved on Major Inglis, and through the exertions of the gallant troops employed, the enemy's strong position was carried: and a similar result occurred on the 7th of November last, when, from Lieutenant Colonel-Brooke having the command of one of the two columns of attack, that of Her Majesty's 23nd Regiment again devolved on Major Inglis, whose conduct in that important trust was highly satisfactory to the brigadier commanding, and I have accordingly great satisfaction in soliciting the favourable notice of his Excellency to the same.

Major Napier (attended by Lieutenant Greathead), of Engineers, who was attached for the day to the two divisions on the right, aided me much by occasionally reconnoitring positions we were approaching; and in giving me the advantage of his reconnoissance of the preceding day. Captain Glasfurd and Lieutenant J. B. Smith, of Engineers, having been directed to join me, were extremely useful during the day; and I feel much indebted to both; as also to Captain Cheape (51st Native Infantry), late treasurer to the Mooltan Field Force, who attended me throughout, and for whom it was not difficult to find frequent and active employment.

Major Becher, assistant quartermaster-general, and Captain Whish, deputy assistant adjutant-general of the division, as also my aides-de-camp, Captain J. C. Kennedy, Her Majesty's 18th Foot, and Lieutenant A. Need, Her Majesty's 14th Light Dragoons, afforded me every assistance, and are entitled to my best thanks for their attention and zeal. The horse of the deputy assistant adjutant-general, from which he had just dismounted, having on the commencement of our cannonade been severely wounded by a cannon-shot, it was some time before another could join from the rear, and intermediately a camel served him as a tolerable substitute.

I beg respectfully, in conclusion, to offer to the Right Honourable the Commander-in-Chief my hearty congratulations on the complete success of his Lordship's arrangements for the day, and on an issue, which, under Divine Providence, has been permitted to be most triumphant.

I have, &c.

(Signed) W. S. Whish, Major-General,
Commanding 1st Infantry Division, Army of the Punjab.

To Lieutenant-Colonel P. Grant, C.B., Adjutant-General of the Army.

Camp Nowrungabad, Feb. 24, 1849.

Sir,—I have to apologize for the delay which has taken place in complying with general orders of the 21st instant, directing reports of the proceedings of the troops employed against the enemy to be forwarded for the information of his Excellency the Right Honourable the Commander-in-Chief; but having been, as you are aware, constantly on the move since the morning after the action near Goojerat, in pursuit of the fugitive Sikh army, I have not had an opportunity of doing so.

I have now to report, for the information of his Lordship, the 2nd infantry division, consisting of the troops mentioned in the margin,* advanced from Shadawalla on the morning of the 21st instant, in line of quarter distance columns, at deploying distance, leaving a battery of heavy guns under Major Horsford, of artillery, between the two brigades, No. 17 light field battery under command of Captain Dawes, and, Brevet-Major Fordyce's troop of horse artillery, between the right regiments of the left and right brigades respectively.

Having received orders to push forward my light troops, to force the enemy to show their position, I immediately advanced the troop of horse artillery and Dawes' light field battery, which instantly drew a very heavy and well-directed fire from two large batteries which the enemy had established on either side of the village of Kalerah, by which they were nearly screened from the fire of our guns, which, with the light companies, were then still further pushed forward, followed by the division which had deployed into line; the heavy guns in our centre, at this time, opening a very destructive cannonade. Up to this time the village above named seemed to be unoccupied, and I directed a party of infantry to take possession of it. Upon the approach of this party a tremendous fire of musketry was opened from the walls,

---

* 3rd Brigade:—31st Native Infantry; 2nd European Regiment; 70th Native Infantry.

4th Brigade:—30th Native Infantry; H.M.'s 29th Foot; 56th Native Infantry.

which were loopholed in every direction; the 2nd European regiment was then ordered up in support, under the command of Major Steel, and soon carried it after a most obstinate resistance, in which that gallant regiment suffered rather severely, as well as upon its emerging from the village; soon after which the enemy left many of their guns, and fled in the greatest confusion.

It affords me the highest satisfaction to record the valuable services of Brigadier A. S. H. Mountain, C.B., and of Brigadier N. Penny, C.B., who led the 2nd European Regiment to the attack of the village, in the most gallant and exemplary manner. I should wish particularly to mention the very great assistance I received from Major Horsford, commanding the heavy battery, and Major Fordyce, commanding 2nd troop, 2nd brigade horse artillery, and Captain Dawes, commanding No. 17 light field battery. It is impossible to praise too highly their conduct, and that of all those under their command.

I beg likewise to bring to his Excellency's notice the valuable asistance I received from my divisional and personal staff, Brevet Captain J. A. D. Fergusson, deputy assistant adjutant-general, Lieutenant A. S. Galloway, deputy assistant quartermaster-general, Lieutenant Colt, aide-de-camp, Captain Sherwill and Lieutenant MacDonnell, majors of brigade, and Captain Goldie and Lieutenant Irwin, of the engineers.

Captain W. P. Robbins, 15th Native Infantry, who acted as my aide-de-camp during the action, afforded me great and active assistance, as did also Lieutenant H. B. Hopper, 31st Native Infantry (orderly officer).

My warmest thanks are due to Lieutenant-Colonel Congreve, C.B., Her Majesty's 29th Foot, Lieutenant-Colonel Jack, 30th Native Infantry, and Lieutenant-Colonel Holmes, 56th Native Infantry, and to Majors J. Steel, 2nd European Regiment, W. R. Corfield, 31st Native Infantry,

15

and J. R. McCausland, 70th Native Infantry (severely wounded in the attack on the village of Kalerah), for the exemplary manner in which they led their regiments. I trust I may be permitted to bring to his Excellency's notice the name of Brevet Captain G. Gordon, 50th Native Infantry, officiating sub-assistant commissary-general, who, at my request, destroyed the enemy's camp equipage and loose ammunition.

The conduct of all the troops under my command, European and Native, under a terrific and well-directed cannonade, was such as to call forth my highest commendation.

In conclusion, I regret, that in consequence of our being so constantly on the move since the action, I am unable to forward herein the return of casualties; but I shall do myself the honour to transmit them with the least possible delay.

I have, &c.

(Signed) W. R. Gilbert, Major-General,
Commanding 2nd Infantry Division,
Army of the Punjaub.

P.S.—In the absence of the regular returns I may here add that the amount of loss is very trifling, considering the heavy fire kept up by the enemy's artillery on the centre of the division, where the heavy guns were, the 2nd European Regiment having only lost 8 men killed, and 135 wounded; the 31st Native Infantry, 11 men killed, and 131 wounded; and 70th Native Infantry, 20 killed and 40 wounded.

In the 4th Brigade H. M's. 29th Regiment lost only 2 men and 6 wounded, the 30th Native Infantry 3 men wounded, and the 56th Native Infantry only 1 man wounded.

To Lieutenant-Colonel P. Grant, C.B., Adjutant-General of the Army.

Camp Dowlutnuggur, February 23, 1849.

Sir,—I have the honour to report to you, for the information of the Right Honourable the Commander-in-Chief, that in obedience to the orders I received from his Lordship, at daylight of the 21st instant I formed the brigades of the 3rd Division, commanded by Brigadiers Carnegie and McLeod, with the light field batteries attached to them, close to the left bank of the nullah, which passed in front of the village of Shadawal, a little after 7 A.M. The brigade under Brigadier Hoggan was formed at the same time in rear to act as a reserve to the whole force intended to be employed on that side of the nullah.

In the advance to the attack of the enemy's position, his Lordship desired me to keep close to the left side of the nullah, and to preserve my communication with the heavy guns, which were placed on the opposite bank.

His Lordship further directed me to approach, but not to pass that part of the nullah, behind which the right of the enemy's army was formed, without further instructions from him.

With a view to the effectual fulfilment of his Lordship's wishes to maintain close communication with the heavy guns on my right, and to prevent their molestation by the enemy from the nullah, I directed the light company of H. M's. 24th to occupy and move along the nullah in advance of the heavy guns, and to render the communication more secure, I supported this company with two guns from No. 10 light field battery, which moved close along the bank of the nullah.

The two brigades were formed, in the first instance, in contiguous columns of regiments (the brigades at full distance), covered by a strong line of skirmishers, and these immediately supported by Nos. 5 and 10 light field batteries, attached to them respectively. These skirmishers, communicated on the left with those covering the front of the Bombay division, which were likewise supported by the troop of horse artillery belonging to that force. The whole line moved forward at ¼ before 8 A.M., in this order, with the regularity of troops at a review. The country we passed over in our advance was perfectly level, highly cultivated and without an obstruction, being merely dotted here and there with an occasional tree.

At ½ past 9, the skirmishers having arrived within long range of the enemy's guns, the columns were deployed into line, when we again moved forward; at this time the right wing of the enemy's army was plainly to be seen, formed directly in our front beyond a turn in the nullah which seemed to run parallel to the front of their position, in the centre of which and nearly opposite to Nos. 5 and 10 light field batteries, they had two very heavy guns, and several 6 and 9-pounders field guns, which then opened fire; that from the former, in the first instance, caused some loss in the batteries; and here it was, I regret to say, that Lieutenant Day, of the Artillery, a very brave and most promising young officer, was killed by a cannon-ball.

The line moved onwards to the front, keeping in communication with, and as much as possible, in the allignment of the heavy guns, while the field batteries kept up so destructive a fire upon the enemy in their front, in position behind the nullah, that they finally obliged the whole force to abandon it, and take shelter under cover of the bank of the nullah, and from which they were afterwards driven in confusion and flight, by an enfilading fire from these same field batteries.

About three-quarters of an hour before the enemy had been finally driven in flight from the nullah and from the field, a great effort was made by many, apparently of the principal chiefs, to bring forward a large body of their cavalry, which was followed in a tumultuous manner by the infantry, which had taken shelter in the nullah to attack the centre of the Bombay division. This attack was taken in flank by No. 5 field battery, and caused great loss to the enemy, both in his short advance and subsequent retreat.

The infantry of the 3rd Division had not occasion to fire a shot. The enemy were driven from their different positions, and from the field, by the fire of those two field batteries, aided by that of the Bombay troop of horse artillery.

I cannot find language to express my sense of the calm, steady and admirable manner, in which these two batteries were commanded and worked by Major Mowatt, the commanding officer, and by Major Ludlow and Lieutenant Robertson, the former commanding No. 5, the latter No. 10 battery; nor am I able adequately to express my admiration of the bravery and gallantry of the other officers of these batteries, and of their non-commissioned officers and men, all of whom I beg to recommend, in an especial manner to the favourable notice of the Right Honourable the Commander-in-Chief.

After the troops had crossed the nullah, I received his Lordship's orders to follow the troops of the right wing, in their movement towards the east side of Goojerat, while the Bombay division passed the town on the other side. After clearing the town, the division again resumed its communication with the Bombay troops, and proceeded with them in advance, together with the troops of the 2nd Division on our right, until ordered to halt and encamp.

I beg leave to bring to the favourable notice of the Commander-in-Chief the conduct of Brigadiers Carnagie and McLeod, to whom I feel much indebted for the brave example they set to their men, and for the officer-like manner in which they managed their respective brigades during the day. Brigadier Hoggan, commanding the reserve, was under the immediate orders of Brigadier-General Dundas on the left.

The two former brigadiers speak in strong terms of the merits and services during the day of their respective brigade-majors, Captain Clarke, of the 25th Native Infantry, and Captain Keiller, of the 6th Native Infantry; and I can confirm their opinion of the zeal, activity, and value of these officers' services, from my own personal observation.

I beg also to recommend to the favourable notice of the Commander-in-Chief, the conduct of the several officers commanding regiments, who all set an example of the greatest gallantry to their respective corps, viz., Lieutenant-Colonel Smith, Her Majesty's 24th Regiment, Lieutenant-Colonel Corbett, 25th Native Infantry, Lieutenant-Colonel Jones, Her Majesty's 61st, Major Tudor, 46th Native Infantry, and Captain Lang, 36th Native Infantry, they are all truly deserving of his Lordship's favourable notice and approbation. Lieutenant-Colonel Jones, of Her Majesty's 61st, speaks in terms of praise of the assistance he received from the two majors of that regiment, Major Campbell and Major Stephens; and Lieutenant-Colonel Smith, of Her Majesty's 24th Regiment, in a similar manner, notices the conduct of Major Blachford of that corps.

I received, during the day, the most cordial and valuable assistance from Major Ponsonby, assistant adjutant-general of the division, with whom I have found a real pleasure in being associated on service, and to whom I owe great obligation for the able and careful manner in which he conducts the duties of his department.

I beg to recommend to the particular notice of his Lordship the Commander-in-Chief the conduct of Ensign

Garden, deputy assistant quartermaster-general, to whom I am also under many obligations for the zeal and ability with which he performs his various duties.

Captain Durand and Lieutenant Morton, of the Engineers, were attached to the 3rd Division, during the action, and accompanied me during the day; they rendered me valuable assistance, and I owe to them, accordingly, my warmest acknowledgments.

I cannot conclude this report without also bringing to the notice of the Commander-in-Chief the willing and valuable assistance afforded me by my aide-de-camp Captain Haythorne, and also by my brother officer Lieutenant Shadwell, of Her Majesty's 98th Regiment, who was present in the action as a volunteer.

I beg herewith to inclose a return of the killed and wounded, together with a present state of the troops actually engaged, and returns of the quantity of ammunition expended.

I have, &c.

(Signed) C. Campbell, Brigadier-General,
Commanding 3rd Division, Army of the Punjaub.

From Brigadier-General H. Dundas, C.B., commanding Bombay column, Army of the Punjaub, to the Adjutant-General of the Bengal Army.

Head-Quarters, Camp Saikerwalla, February 22, 1849.

Sir,—I have the honour to inform you that, agreeably to the orders I received, the Bombay Infantry division was formed on the left of the line. I advanced for some distance in contiguous columns at quarter distance, the 60th Rifles, under Lieutenant-Colonel Bradshaw, and the 3rd troop Horse Artillery, under Major Blood, being thrown in advance. The division deployed into line, and gradually advanced as the attack on the right developed itself. A party of the enemy's horse made a demonstration of attacking the line, but speedily moved off to their own right, on receiving one or two rounds from Major Blood's troop. A battery of the enemy, which was in front of the Bengal division, was also quickly silenced by this troop, which made excellent practice. The division kept gradually advancing without firing a shot, the enemy moving off so fast we could not reach him, the artillery taking every advantage of opening its fire that was afforded. The infantry kept constantly advancing, passing through the enemy's camp, which was left standing, and round the town of Goojerat on the left, bringing up the left shoulders. The ground at the first was studded with bushes and hedges of prickly pear, which caused some delay in getting through, and on reaching the open country again, not a sign of the enemy was to be seen. Two guns were abandoned by him on this side of the town. Not a casualty occurred in the infantry division or in the troop, with the exception of two horses. The troop afterwards accompanied Major-General Sir Joseph Thackwell's division of cavalry in pursuit of the enemy, and it has been reported to me, by Brigadier Leeson, commanding Bombay Artillery, that it rendered good service. The Scinde Horse, under Lieutenant Malcolm, having been attached for the day to Major-General Sir Joseph Thackwell's division, I had not an opportunity of witnessing a most successful and gallant charge which was made by that distinguished regiment against a party of the enemy's horse, which was completely overthrown with the loss of their standards, and the attempt to turn our left, which the enemy showed a disposition to try, altogether frustrated. This success was not gained without some loss, which amounted to 3 killed and 16 or 17 wounded. The field battery under Captain Turnbull was attached to the force protecting the baggage, where the troops never came in contact with the enemy, who moved off with the utmost rapidity; there is little room for remark on their conduct, beyond making a steady and regular advance, and for a long distance, and preserving a good order of formation. I had every reason to be satisfied with the conduct of all —and my thanks are due to Brigadier Capon, commanding the 1st Infantry Brigade, to Lieutenant-Colonel Bradshaw, commanding 60th Rifles, Major Hallett, commanding 3rd Regiment Native Infantry, Major Mignon, commanding 1st Bombay Fusiliers, Major Maut, commanding 19th Regiment Native Infantry, Brigadier Leeson, commanding the artillery, rendering every assistance, and Major Blood, in command of the troop, is entitled to every credit for the efficient service the troop was enabled to perform.

The steady and good order in which the brigade of the Bengal army moved under Brigadier Hoggan, which was in support of the Bombay division, was very praiseworthy.

I am indebted to the officers of the divisional staff for the active assistance they afforded me, Major Greene, assistant adjutant-general, Captain Hart, deputy assistant adjutant-general, Captain Ramsay, the assistant quartermaster-general, Captain Skinner, the deputy judge-advocate-general, Major St. John, paymaster, Lieutenant Mules, of the 1st Fusiliers, postmaster, Lieutenant Ward, 60th Rifles, my aide-de-camp, and, Lieutenant Crawley, 15th Hussars, aide-de-camp to Major-General Aitchison, commanding Mysore division, who officiated as my aide-de-camp,* Lieutenant Stevenson, brigade-major of artillery, rendered every assistance in his department. The sappers and miners, under Lieutenant Kendall, were kept pre-

* Brigadier Capon also reports favourably of the assistance he derived from Captain Stiles, major of brigade, and Lieutenant Gordon, 60th Rifles, who officiated as aide-de-camp.

pared for any duty that might have been required in sloping down nullahs for the guns, &c., but the ground was so favourable for the movement of the troops that their exertions were not required in this duty. My thanks are also due to Captain Threshie, assistant commissary-general, on this occasion, as also for the efficient manner in which the duties of his department have been conducted.

Lieutenant Henry, 19th Regiment Native Infantry, aide-de-camp to the Right Honourable the Governor of Bombay, and who was placed in political charge of the prisoner of war, the Dewan Moolraj, joined me in the afternoon, having ridden post from Lahore on purpose to be present, after delivering over charge of his prisoner on the 20th instant.

Herewith I inclose a list of casualties, which is principally in horses, together with a return of ammunition expended.

I have, &c.

(Signed) H. Dundas, Brigadier-General,
Commanding Bombay column, Army of the Punjaub.

From Major J. S. Leeson, Brigadier commanding Artillery Brigade, Bombay Division, to the Assistant Adjutant-General, Bombay Division.

Camp Goojerat, February 22, 1849.

Sir,—In compliance with your order, I have the honour to report that the 3rd, or Major Blood's troop of horse artillery, was ordered to accompany the cavalry division under General Sir Joseph Thackwell, K.C.B., at about half-past one yesterday, to follow the enemy, who were then retreating. With this troop I proceeded, accompanied by Lieutenant Hamilton and my staff.

After proceeding at a trot and gallop for about nine miles, we joined the cavalry division, and soon joined the enemy's rear, and at a distance of about 400 yards opened fire with manifest good effect; they were then attempting to carry off three guns, and a considerable body of cavalry were hovering round to afford them protection; this they were unable to effect, as our well-directed fire soon obliged the enemy to abandon their guns, camels, carts, bullocks, &c., and a great proportion of their baggage, which fell into our hands.

The enemy still continuing to retreat in a most disorderly manner, we advanced at a gallop for about three miles, and again opened fire with such effect that they were compelled to abandon another gun.

We again advanced same distance further, and were halted by order of the general commanding, who proceeded, and at a quarter to 5 P.M. we began to fall back towards camp, which we reached at half-past 8 o'clock P.M.

I have, &c.

(Signed) J. S. Leeson, Maj., H. A.,
Brigadier Comdg. Arty. Bde., Bombay Division.

(True Copy,)

(Signed) Edward Green, Major,
Assistant Adjutant-General, F. F.

General Return of Casualties in the Army of the Punjaub in the Action of Goojerat, on the 21st February, 1849, between the British Forces under the personal command of General the Right Honourable Hugh, Baron Gough, G.C.B., Commander-in-Chief of all the Forces in India, and the Rebel Army under Sirdar Chutter Sing and Rajah Shere Sing.

General Staff—1 Provost-Marshal wounded.

Artillery Division.—Horse Artillery.

4th Troop, 1st Brigade—3 rank and file, 1 syce, 17 horses, killed; 1 native officer, 5 rank and file, 2 lascars, 5 syces, 11 horses, wounded.

2nd Troop, 2nd Brigade—7 rank and file, 1 lascar, 25 horses, killed; 1 sergeant, 1 trumpeter, 17 rank and file, 4 lascars, 13 horses, wounded.

3rd Troop, 2nd Brigade—1 syce, 7 horses, killed; 4 rank and file, wounded; 1 syce missing.

4th Troop, 2nd Brigade—1 rank and file wounded; 1 horse missing.

1st Troop, 3rd Brigade—1 trumpeter, 2 rank and file, wounded; 1 horse missing.

2nd Troop, 3rd Brigade—1 rank and file, 7 horses, killed; 2 sergeants, 3 rank and file, 1 syce, 1 horse, wounded; 2 horses missing.

4th Troop, 3rd Brigade—1 European officer, 1 sergeant, 6 rank and file, 1 lascar, 16 horses, killed; 1 sergeant, 4 rank and file, 1 lascar, 1 syce, 6 horses, wounded; 1 horse missing.

Foot Artillery.

1st Company, 1st Battalion (No. 10 Battery)—1 European officer, 1 rank and file, 2 horses, killed; 2 rank and file, 2 syce-drivers, 3 horses, wounded; 1 horse missing.

3rd Company, 1st Battalion (No. 17 Battery)—10 horses killed; 4 rank and file, 3 horses, wounded.

3rd Company, 3rd Battalion—2 rank and file, 5 bullocks, killed; 2 syce-drivers wounded.

4th Company, 3rd Battalion—5 bullocks killed; 2 rank and file, 1 lascar, 3 syce-drivers, wounded.

1st Company, 4th Battalion—1 European officer, 3 rank and file, 1 lascar, wounded.

4th Company, 4th Battalion—1 rank and file wounded.

3rd Company, 7th Battalion (No. 5 Battery)—1 syce-driver, 1 syce, 3 horses, killed; 2 rank and file, 1 lascar, 1 syce-driver, wounded.

Total—2 European officers, 1 sergeant, 20 rank and file, 2 lascars, 1 syce-driver, 3 syces, 97 horses or bullocks, killed; 1 European officer, 1 native ditto, 4 sergeants, 2 trumpeters, 50 rank and file, 10 lascars, 8 syce-drivers, 7 syces, 37 horses or bullocks, wounded; 1 syce, 6 horses, missing.

Engineer Department and Sappers and Pioneers—1 European officer, 1 native ditto, 2 sergeants or havildars, 5 rank and file, wounded.

Cavalry Division.—1st Brigade.

H. M.'s 3rd Light Dragoons—1 horse killed; 1 rank and file, 2 horses, wounded; 2 horses missing.

H. M.'s 9th Lancers—4 horses missing.

5th Regiment Light Cavalry—1 European officer, 4 rank and file, 1 horse, wounded.

8th Regiment Light Cavalry—1 syce, 1 horse, killed; 1 native officer wounded; 1 rank and file, 3 horses, missing.

2nd Brigade.

H. M.'s 14th Light Dragoons—1 European officer, 3 horses, killed; 2 European officers, 4 rank and file, 2 horses, wounded.

1st Regiment Light Cavalry—2 rank and file, 4 horses, wounded; 2 horses missing.

3rd Brigade.

11th Irregular Cavalry—2 horses killed; 3 rank and file wounded.

14th Irregular Cavalry (1 squadron)—2 rank and file, 4 horses, wounded; 2 horses missing.

4th Brigade.

3rd Irregular Cavalry—1 rank and file, 2 horses, killed; 1 native officer, 1 havildar, 5 rank and file, 2 horses, wounded.

9th Irregular Cavalry—1 rank and file, 10 horses, killed; 1 havildar, 12 rank and file, 3 horses, wounded.

Total—1 European officer, 2 rank and file, 1 syce, 19 horses, killed; 3 European officers, 2 native ditto, 2 havildars, 33 rank and file, 18 horses, wounded; 1 rank and file, 13 horses, missing.

1st Infantry Division.

Divisional Staff—1 horse wounded.

1st Brigade.

H. M.'s 10th Foot—7 rank and file, 1 horse, killed; 1 European officer, 53 rank and file, wounded.

8th Regiment Native Infantry—1 European officer, 1 native ditto, 3 rank and file, killed; 2 European officers, 3 native ditto, 4 havildars, 56 rank and file, wounded.

52nd Regiment Native Infantry—5 rank and file killed; 3 European officers, 1 havildar, 30 rank and file, wounded.

2nd Brigade.

H. M.'s 32nd Foot—1 rank and file killed; 1 European officer, 4 rank and file, wounded.

51st Regiment Native Infantry—5 rank and file killed; 1 European officer, 1 native ditto, 1 havildar, 46 rank and file, wounded.

72nd Regiment Native Infantry—1 rank and file killed; 8 rank and file wounded.

Total—1 European officer, 1 native ditto, 22 rank and file, 1 horse, killed; 8 European officers, 4 native ditto, 6 havildars, 197 rank and file, 1 horse, wounded.

2nd Infantry Division, 3rd Brigade.

2nd European Regiment—1 European officer, 2 sergeants, 6 rank and file, 1 horse, killed; 5 European officers, 12 sergeants, 123 rank and file, 1 horse, wounded; 3 rank and file missing.

31st Regiment Native Infantry—2 havildars, 9 rank and

file, killed; 1 European officer, 4 native ditto, 7 havildars, 119 rank and file, 1 lascar, wounded.

70th Regiment N. I.—10 rank and file killed; 5 European officers, 1 native ditto, 4 havildars, 34 rank and file, wounded.

4th Brigade.

H. M.'s 29th Foot—2 rank and file killed; 6 rank and file wounded.

30th Regiment Native Infantry—3 rank and file wounded.

56th Regiment Native Infantry—1 rank and file wounded.

Total—1 European officer, 4 sergeants or havildars, 27 rank and file, 1 horse, killed; 11 European officers, 5 native ditto, 23 sergeants or havildars, 286 rank and file, 1 lascar, 1 horse, wounded; 3 rank and file missing.

3rd Infantry Division, 5th Brigade.

25th Regiment Native Infantry—1 rank and file killed; 2 rank and file wounded.

7th Brigade.

H. M.'s 61st Foot—9 rank and file wounded.

36th Regiment Native Infantry—1 trumpeter, 3 rank and file, killed; 2 havildars, 7 rank and file, wounded.

Total—1 trumpeter, 4 rank and file, killed; 2 sergeants or havildars, 18 rank and file, wounded.

Bombay Division.

3rd Troop Horse Artillery—1 horse killed.

Scinde Irregular Horse—1 havildar, 1 rank and file, 24 horses, killed; 1 native officer, 1 havildar, 10 rank and file, 11 horses, wounded.

Total—1 sergeant or havildar, 1 rank and file, 25 horses, killed: 1 native officer, 1 sergeant or havildar, 10 rank and file, 11 horses, wounded.

Grand Total—5 European officers, 1 native ditto, 6 sergeants or havildars, 1 trumpeter, 76 rank and file,

2 lascars, 1 syce-driver, 4 syces, 143 horses or bullocks, killed; 24 European officers, 14 native ditto, 1 provost marshal, 40 sergeants or havildars, 2 trumpeters, 599 rank and file, 11 lascars, 8 syce-drivers, 7 syces or grass-cutters, 68 horses or bullocks, wounded; 4 rank and file, 1 syce, 19 horses or bullocks, missing.

Nominal List of European Officers.

General Staff—Wounded, Provost-Marshal S. Budd, severely.

Artillery Division.

4th Troop, 3rd Brigade Horse Artillery—Killed, Captain J. Anderson.

1st Company, 1st Battalion Artillery—Killed, Second Lieutenant E. W. Day.

1st Company, 4th Battalion Artillery—Wounded, Captain and Brevet-Major Sir R. C. Shakespear.

Corps of Engineers—Wounded, Second Lieutenant B. M. Hutchinson, very severely, leg amputated.

Cavalry Division.

H. M.'s 14th Light Dragoons—Killed, Lieutenant A. Lloyd; Wounded, Captain J. H. Goddard, severely; Captain A. Scudamore, dangerously.

5th Regiment Light Cavalry—Wounded, Lieutenant H. J. Stannus, severely.

1st Infantry Division.

H. M.'s 10th Foot—Wounded, Captain R. M. Best, slightly.

H. M.'s 32nd Foot—Wounded, Lieutenant G. Jeffrey, slightly.

8th Regiment Native Infantry—Killed, Lieutenant R. Cox; Wounded, Major G. Farquharson, dangerously; Ensign G. H. Griffiths, severely.

51st Regiment Native Infantry—Wounded, Lieutenant T. C. Darnell, severely.

52nd Regiment Native Infantry—Wounded, Captain J. W. H. Jamieson, severe contusion; Lieutenant W. H. Lowther, ditto: Lieutenant G. R. Smith, ditto.

2nd Infantry Division.

2nd European Regiment—Killed, Lieutenant G. H. Sprott; Wounded, Captain A. Boyd, slightly; Lieutenant A. Elderton, ditto; Ensign A. D. Toogood, ditto; Ensign D. A. Sandford, ditto; Ensign J. C. S. Matheson, ditto.

31st Regiment Native Infantry—Wounded, Ensign F. J. Gully, slightly.

70th Regiment Native Infantry—Wounded, Major J. K. McCausland, severely; Brevet Captain C. L. Edwards, slightly; Lieutenant A. Fytche, ditto; Ensign R. C. Whiting, severely; Ensign C. Murray, slightly.

(Signed) PAT. GRANT, Lieut.-Colonel,
Adjutant-General of the Army.

List of Ordnance captured from the Enemy, in the Action at Goojerat, on the 21*st February* 1849.

Camp Goojerat, February 22, 1849.

No.	Nature of Ordnance.		No.	Nature of Ordnance.	
1	Brass Gun . .	16-pounder	30	Brass Gun . .	6-pounder
	,,	6-pounder		,,	6-pounder
	,,	9-pounder		,,	8-pounder
	,,	8-pounder	35	,,	8-pounder
5	,,	9-pounder		,,	8-pounder
	,,	8-pounder		,,	8-pounder
	,,	8-pounder		,,	8-pounder
	,,	3-pounder		,,	8-pounder
	,,	8-pounder	40	,,	8-pounder

10	Brass Gun .	12-pounder	41	Brass Gun. . 7½-pounder
	,,	9-pounder	42	,, 7½-pounder
	,,	18-pounder	1	Brass Howitzer
	,,	8-pounder		,,
	,,	9-pounder		,,
15	,,	8-pounder		,,
	,,	2-pounder	5	,,
	,,	7-pounder		,,
	,,	8-pounder		,,
	,,	8-pounder	8	,,
20	,,	2-pounder	1	Brass Mortar
	,,	8-pounder		,,
	,,	16-pounder	3	,,
	,,	8-pounder	—	,,
	,,	9-pounder	53	Total pieces of ordnance captured.
25	,,	8-pounder	—	
	,,	6-pounder	17	Ammunition tumbrils unserviceable.
	,,	6-pounder		
	,,	8-pounder		
	,,	7-pounder		A considerable number of tumbrils were also blown up and otherwise destroyed.
30	,,	6-pounder		
	,,	7-pounder		

(Signed) J. Abercrombie, Captain,
Deputy Assistant Adj.-Gen., Artillery.

(Signed) J. Tenant, Brigadier-Gen.,
Commanding Artillery Division.

Notification.

Foreign Department, Camp Ferozepore,
March 10, 1849.

In the General Order, dated 1st March, publishing the details of the action at Goojerat, the name of Lieutenant-Colonel Birch (Judge-Advocate-General) having been inadvertently omitted, the Right Hon. the Governor-General is pleased to direct that, in that part of the General Order in which the Officers of the General Staff of the Army are thanked, the name of Lieutenant-Colonel Birch be inserted immediately after the name of Lieutenant-Colonel Garden, C.B.

(Signed) H. M. Elliot,
Secretary to the Government of India,
with the Governor-General.

(Signed) J. Stuart, Colonel,
Secretary to the Government of India, Military
Department, with the Governor-General.

General Order by the Right Hon. the Governor-General of India.

Foreign Department, Camp Ferozepore,
March 17, 1849.

The Governor-General has the utmost satisfaction in directing that the despatches which he has this day received from his Excellency the Commander-in-Chief, and from Major-General Sir Walter Gilbert, K.C.B., be published for the information of the army and of the people of India.

The British subjects, who were prisoners in the hands of the enemy, have all returned in safety.

On the 14th instant, Sirdar Chutter Sing, Rajah Shere Sing, and the principal Sikh Sirdars and Chiefs, delivered their swords into the hand of Major-General Sir Walter Gilbert.

Forty-one pieces of artillery were at the same time surrendered; and the remains of the Sikh army, to the number of 16,000 men, laid down their arms in the presence of the British troops.

The Governor-General offers to his Excellency the Commander-in-Chief, to Major-General Gilbert, and to the whole army, his heartfelt congratulations on this glorious result of the battle of Goojerat, and of the operations subsequent to it, so admirably conducted by the Major-General, in fulfilment of his Excellency's instructions.

But the war is not yet concluded; nor can there be any cessation of hostilities until Dost Mahomed Khan and the Affghan army are either driven from the province of Peshawur, or destroyed within it.

The British army has already resumed its march upon Attok; and the Governor-General confidently hopes, that the entire success which, with God's blessing, will attend it, may enable him soon to announce the restoration of peace.

The Governor-General directs that, in honour of the important events which have now been notified, a salute of 21 guns be fired from every principal station of the army in India.

By order of the Right Honourable the Governor-General of India.

(Signed) H. M. Elliot,
Secretary to the Government of India,
with the Governor-General.

From the Rt. Hon. the Commander-in-Chief to the Rt. Hon. the Governor-General of India, &c., &c.

Dated Head-Quarters, Camp Kuttala,
March 16, 1849.

My Lord,—I have the greatest gratification in reporting to your Lordship the further happy results of the decisive victory obtained at Goojerat on the 21st ultimo.

Major-General Sir Walter Gilbert, with that energy and judgment which induced me to select him to conduct the ulterior operations subsequent to that action, has well fulfilled the trust reposed in him, by rapidly pressing the routed enemy, which has led to their unqualified submission, the surrender of their remaining guns, and about 16,000 stand of arms, all of which are now in our possession; and I rejoice to add, that this fortunate consummation has been obtained without a single shot being fired.

The whole of the Sikh force, with their Sirdars, have now come in, with the exception of Bhae Maharaj and Colonel Richpaul Sing, who have absconded, but without followers.

We have now in our possession 56 guns taken at Goojerat and abandoned by the enemy in his retreat on the 21st February; 40 surrendered to Major-General Sir Walter Gilbert since that event; 12 captured at Chillianwallah, and 50 at Mooltan, making a total of 158 pieces of ordnance which have fallen into our hands during the present campaign.

Again heartily congratulating your Lordship at this most satisfactory termination of the Sikh war,

I have, &c.

(Signed) GOUGH, General.

No. 282.

From Major-General Sir W. R. Gilbert, K.C.B., Commanding Field Force, on Special Service, to H. M. Elliot, Esq., Secretary to the Government of India, with the Governor-General.

Dated Camp Rawul Pindee, March 14, 1849.

Sir,—Since I addressed you on the 11th instant, from Hoormuck, I have advanced to Rawul Pindee, which place I reached to-day. I have now the high gratification of reporting for the information of the Right Honourable the Governor-General of India, that the disarmament of the Sikh army, commenced at Manikyalla, has been this day completed by the surrender of their swords, by the Sikh Sirdars, in presence of the commanding officers of divisions and brigades and their staff.

The total number of guns surrendered is 41, of which a return shall be forwarded hereafter; and the number of stands of arms laid down before the force under my command is about 16,000.

I have, &c.
(Signed) W. R. GILBERT, Major-Gen.
Commanding Field Force, on Special Service.
(True Copies.)
(Signed) H. M. ELLIOT,
Secretary to the Government of India,
with the Governor-General.
(Signed) J. STUART, Colonel,
Secretary to the Government of India, Military
Department, with the Governor-General.

GENERAL ORDER BY THE RIGHT HON. THE GOVERNOR-GENERAL OF INDIA.

Foreign Department, Camp Ferozepore,
April 2, 1849.

The Governor-General has the gratification of publishing for general information, despatches which have been received from His Excellency the Commander-in-Chief and from Major-General Sir Walter Gilbert, K.C.B., announcing the termination of hostilities in the Punjaub.

The Governor-General declared that before the war could cease, every enemy, whether Sikh or Affghan, should be driven from before us; and the British army has well and gallantly made good his words.

The Sikh Sirdars and the remnant of their army were pursued, have surrendered, and have been disarmed.

The Ameer of Cabul with his troops has fled before the British force, and has been chased ignominiously from the territories he invaded.

The war has thus been brought to an end, and the Punjaub has been declared a portion of the British Empire in India.

Once again the Governor-General offers to His Excellency the Commander-in-Chief, to the general officers, the officers, non-commissioned officers, and soldiers of the army, the assurance of his deep and unfeigned gratitude for the great services they have rendered to the country by the zeal and gallantry they displayed, and for the sustained and cheerful exertions they have made.

In anticipation of the wishes of the Honourable Court of Directors, the Governor-General will grant to every officer and soldier who has been employed within the Punjaub in this campaign, to the date of the occupation of Peshawur, a medal, bearing the word "Punjaub," in commemoration of the honourable service they have done.

The Governor-General is also pleased to direct that every corps which has been so employed shall bear the same word on their standards, colours, and appointments.

The Governor-General desires to take the opportunity of acknowledging his obligations to officers who have been serving in various positions connected with the army in the field.

The Governor-General is sensible of the zeal and activity of Major-General Sir D. Hill, K.C.B., commanding the reserve: and he would have looked with confidence to his services if the division under his command had been called into operation.

Brigadier-General Wheeler, C.B., has executed the

several duties which have been committed to him with skill and success; and the Governor-General has been happy to convey to him his thanks.

The Governor-General is indebted to Brigadier Stalker, commanding at Mooltan, for the successful exertions which have been made under his directions, for placing the fort again in a condition of defence, and for maintaining the tranquillity of the country.

The Governor-General begs to acknowledge the service which has been rendered by Lieut.-Colonel McSherry, 1st N. I., commanding at Govindgurh. The energy, vigilance, and tact which he exhibited during his occupation of that important fortress, have been of much value to the Government of India.

From Sir F. Currie, Baronet, Resident at Lahore, previously to his return to his seat in Council, the Governor-General received at all times effective and most ready co-operation; and he has continued to receive from Lieut.-Colonel Sir H. Lawrence, K.C.B., the support which his known ability and experience enabled him to afford.

The meritorious conduct of the several assistants to the Resident has elicited the strong approbation of the Government. In addition to those whom he has before named, the Governor-General offers his especial thanks to Major George Lawrence, for the able management which so long enabled him to maintain his position at Peshawur, and to Captain James Abbott for the gallant stand he has made in the hills at Huzara.

Lieut. Taylor has earned the full approbation of the Government by his judicious and persevering efforts which regained and have held the province of Bunnoo.

The sustained defence of the Fort at Attock, which was made by Lieut. Herbert, under circumstances of great difficulty, has been viewed by the Government of India with admiration, and entitled him to their warmest praise.

Mr. John Lawrence, Commissioner of the Trans-Sutlej Province, has received the thanks of the Governor-General. Well seconded by his assistants in the district, he has greatly contributed by his promptitude, energy, and firmness to the maintenance of the general tranquillity which has prevailed in these newly acquired territories.

The Governor-General especially wishes to record his marked approbation of the manner in which Major Mackeson, C.B., as his agent with the army, has discharged the duties which were entrusted to him. In the important political matters in which he has been engaged, Major Mackeson's proceedings have been distinguished by ability, judgement discretion and firmness; and the Governor-General begs to convey to him the expression of his unqualified satisfaction.

The Governor-General concludes by tendering to the officers of the Government in his camp, sincere thanks for the assistance he has at all times received from them.

He particularly desires to express his obligation to Mr. Henry Elliot, Secretary to the Government of India, for his very able, laborious, and most valuable aid in the important affairs which occupied the Governor-General's attention:—and to Colonel Stuart, C.B., Military Secretary to the Government of India, and to Lieutenant-Colonel Benson, C.B., Member of the Military Board with the Governor-General, for the great assistance he has derived from their experience and judgment in the affairs of their respective departments.

While thus congratulating the army and British subjects in India on the triumphant success which has been achieved, the Governor-General desires humbly to acknowledge the Hand by which alone all victory is given.

He has accordingly intimated to the Lord Bishop his wish that, on the first Sunday in May, thanksgivings shall be offered to Almighty God, for the successful termination of the war in which we have been engaged, and for the restoration to the people of the blessings of peace.

By order of the Right Honourable the Governor-General of India.

(Signed) H. M. ELLIOT,
Secretary to the Government of India,
with the Governor-General.

(Copies.)

From H. E. the Commander-in-Chief, to the Right Hon. the Governor-General of India.

Head-Quarters, Camp, Army of the Punjaub,
Wuzeerabad, March 25, 1849.

My Lord,—I have sincere satisfaction in forwarding to your Lordship a copy of a despatch received this day from Major-General Sir Walter R. Gilbert, K.C.B., commanding the advanced force of this army, No. 291, of the 21st instant, announcing the occupation of Peshawur by the British troops, the precipitate retreat of the Ameer Dost Mahomed Khan and his followers beyond the Khyber Pass, and the consequent dissolution of the Affghan confederacy. These brilliant results have been obtained, your Lordship will observe, without a single shot being fired by our troops since the victory of Goojerat on the 21st ultimo.

It is almost superfluous for me to repeat to your Lordship how very highly I estimate the unwearied and zealous exertions in these subsequent movements of that most energetic and able officer Major-General Gilbert, and the excellent troops under his command.

In soliciting your Lordship's particular attention to Major-General Gilbert's commendation of Major F. Mackeson, C.B., your Lordship's agent with the force, I beg to repeat the high sense I entertain of that officer's merits and the excellent service he has rendered throughout the campaign.

The Sikh rebellion and Affghan confederacy having been now effectually put down and overthrown, I beg to be favoured with your Lordship's instructions for breaking up the army of the Punjaub, which has, I trust, merited the approbation of your Lordship and the country.

I have, &c.

(Signed) Gough, General,
Commander-in-Chief in India.

No. 291.

From Major-General Sir W. R. Gilbert, K.C.B., Commanding Field Force on Special Service, to the Adjutant-General of the Army.

Camp Peshawur, March 21, 1849.

Sir,—I advanced this morning from Nowshyra to Peshawur with the Bengal division of my force, and have much satisfaction in reporting, for the information of his Excellency the Right Honourable the Commander-in-Chief, that I am in possession of the city of Peshawur and its Balla Hissar.

The Affghan army under command of Ameer Dost Mahomed Khan retreated from Peshawur on the 19th instant, and is to-day reported to have reached Dakka, on the western side of the Khyber Pass. The city I found untouched by the Affghans, the Ameer having directed the gates to be closed against his troops; but most of the garden houses in its neighbourhood have been burnt or otherwise rendered uninhabitable, and the Sikh Cantonment at Alli Mardan Khan's Bagh, has been burnt to the ground; the fort of Jumrood is also reported to be destroyed.

By the expulsion from the province of Peshawur of the Ameer and his army, I have carried to a successful conclusion the whole of the instructions of the Right Honourable the Governor-General of India, conveyed to me through his Excellency the Commander-in-Chief, with your letter of the 3rd March instant.

The Sikhs have been humbled and their power crushed; the British prisoners released from an irksome captivity; and the rich province of Peshawur freed from its Mahomedan invaders. To my troops I am indebted, under Providence, for these glorious results. Since the 1st of the month they have marched from the Jhelum to the Indus and Peshawur, crossing both rivers under many disadvantages, and overcoming all the obstacles of the road, which are naturally great, and were much enhanced by our large train of stores and baggage—the necessary incumbrances of a force like this. To both officers and men I am deeply indebted for their cheerful endurance of the fatigues and privations to which all have been exposed.

I cannot permit myself to conclude this report of my arrival at Peshawur, without expressing to his Lordship my sense of the valuable services rendered me by Major F. Mackeson, C.B., who accompanies the force as agent of the Governor-General. I am particularly indebted to him for his ready assistance, and for the unwearied and unremitting zeal with which he has performed the important duties of his office. To his cool judgment and unswerving decision of purpose, I owe much of the success that has attended the progress of my force.

From my staff, generally, I have received every assistance.

(True Copy.)

(Signed) P. Grant, Lieut.-Col.,
Adjutant-General of the Army.

(True Copies.)

(Signed) H. M. Elliot,
Secretary to the Government of India,
with the Governor-General.

NOTIFICATION.

Foreign Department, Camp Ferozepore, Marcn 30.

The Governor-General is pleased to direct that the accompanying proclamation, by which the Punjaub is declared to be a portion of the British Empire in India, be published for general information, and that a royal salute be fired at every principal station of the army on the receipt thereof.

By order of the Right Honourable the Governor-General of India.

(Signed) P. MELVILL,
Under-Secretary to the Government of India,
with the Governor-General.

PROCLAMATION.

For many years in the time of Maharajah Runjeet Sing, peace and friendship prevailed between the British nation and the Sikhs.

When Runjeet Sing was dead, and his wisdom no longer guided the counsels of the state, the Sirdars and the Khalsa army without provocation and without cause, suddenly invaded the British territories. Their army was again and again defeated; they were driven with slaughter and in shame from the country they had invaded, and at the gates of Lahore the Maharajah Duleep Sing tendered to the Governor-General the submission of himself and his chiefs, and solicited the clemency of the British Government.

The Governor-General extended the clemency of his government to the state of Lahore. He generously spared the kingdom which he had acquired a just right to subvert; and the Maharajah having been placed on the throne, treaties of friendship were formed between the states.

The British have faithfully kept their word, and have scrupulously observed every obligation which the treaties imposed upon them.

But the Sikh people and their chiefs have, on their part, grossly and faithlessly violated the promises by which they were bound.

Of their annual tribute no portion whatever has at any time been paid, and large loans advanced to them by the Government of India have never been repaid.

The control of the British Government, to which they voluntarily submitted themselves, has been resisted by arms.

Peace has been cast aside. British officers have been murdered when acting for the State. Others engaged in the like employment have treacherously been thrown into captivity. Finally, the army of the State and the whole Sikh people, joined by many of the Sirdars in the Punjaub who signed the treaties, and led by a member of the regency itself, have risen in arms against us, and have waged a fierce and bloody war for the proclaimed purpose of destroying the British and their power.

The Government of India formerly declared that it desired no further conquest; and it proved by its acts the sincerity of its professions.

The Government of India has no desire for conquest now: but it is bound in its duty to provide fully for its own security, and to guard the interests of those committed to its charge.

To that end, and as the only sure mode of protecting the State from the perpetual recurrence of unprovoked and wasting wars, the Governor-General is compelled to resolve upon the entire subjection of a people, whom their own Government has long been unable to control—and whom (as events have now shown) no punishment can deter from violence, no acts of friendship can conciliate to peace.

Wherefore, the Governor-General of India has declared, and hereby proclaims, that the kingdom of the Punjaub is at an end: and that all the territories of Maharajah Duleep Sing are now and henceforth a portion of the British Empire in India.

His Highness the Maharajah, shall be treated with consideration and with honour.

The few Chiefs who have not engaged in hostilities against the British, shall retain their property and their rank.

The British Government will leave to all the people, whether Mussalmen. Hindoo, or Sikh, the free exercise of their own religions: but it will not permit any man to interfere with others in the observance of such forms and customs as their respective religions may either enjoin or permit.

The Jagheers and all the property of Sirdars or others, who have been in arms against the British, shall be confiscated to the State.

The defences of every fortified place in the Punjaub which is not occupied by British troops shall be totally destroyed: and effectual measures shall be taken to deprive the people of the means of renewing either tumult or war.

The Governor-General calls upon all the inhabitants of the Punjaub—Sirdars and people—to submit themselves peaceably to the authority of the British Government which has hereby been proclaimed.

Over those who shall live as obedient and peaceful subjects of the State, the British Government will rule with mildness and beneficence.

But if resistance to constituted authority shall again be attempted; if violence and turbulence shall be renewed the Governor-General warns the people of the Punjaub that the time for leniency will then have passed away, and that their offence will be punished with prompt and most rigorous severity.

By order of the Right Honourable the Governor-General of India.

(Signed) H. M. Elliot,
Secretary to the Government of India,
with the Governor-General.

Head-Quarters, Camp Ferozepore, March 29, 1849.

The Battle of Chillianwallah.

A List of Non-commissioned Officers and Privates killed in action at Chillianwallah, on 13th January, 1849, or who subsequently died of their wounds; also a list of those missing.

3rd Light Dragoons.

Killed.—Serg. D. Thompson; Privates, A. Barry, N. Brett, J. Collins, J. Coomber, W. D. Digges, R. Griffiths, J. Hart, J. S. Hamilton, H. Hale, J. Hunt, E. Johnston, W. Langston, J. Markey, E. Marshall, R. McEnermy, G. Milligan, E. Norton, W. Pilbeam, R. Reed, O. Regan, J. Slade, W. Swan, J. Thyer.

9th Lancers.

Killed.—Lance-Serg. R. Calcutt; Privates R. Dalton, J. J. Cunniam, A. Matthews.

14th Light Dragoons.

Killed.—Privates G. Atkins, D. Evans, G. Tookey.

24th Foot.

Killed.—Serg. Maj. J. Coffee, Colour-Serg. W. Davies, Sergs. T. Lear, J. Webster; Corps. G. Eames, J. Sherriff; Privates W. Allsworth, J. Amos, J. Bowman, J. Burgess, J. Butcher, T. Byrne, T. Carpenter, S. Carter, W. Cuthbert, G. Dean, P. Fowlk, G. George, G. Hardman, J. Henshaw.

J. Horsfall, T. Hughes, J. Intin, T. Joblin, W. Lakin, C. Lander, P. McColey, J. McReary, T. Merchant, T. Pocock, R. Porter, W. Selby, J. Sharp, P. Westneat, D. Wheeler, W. Willis (1st), S. Andrews, J. Bailey, G. Bird, J. Byers, R. Campbell, D. Clifford, R. John Coates, R. Cockerton, W. Coult, T. J. O'Donoghue, G. Eagan, J. Fergusson, W. Fletcher, G. Harrison, W. Hobson, D. Houlston, E. Indle, T. Mackey, B. Magill, C. Mayo, C. Mitchell, J. O'Connor, N. Pulling, T. Regan, C. Rochford, W. Ryder, G. Saunders, J. Wakefield, J. Warren (2nd), W. Welton, J. Williams, R. Windle, J. Armett, W. H. Bailey, W. Barnett, E. Barr, C. Barnes, R. Burchett, W. Bone, J. Brewer, H. Cork, E. Everest, M. Green, J. Hanlon, J. Haston, S. Smith, W. Sladen, J. Tebble, J. Slattery, W. Walsh, H. Wrightman; Corps. W. Pattenden, W. Runchey; Privates P. Dales, J. Delmage, T. Ellice, W. Giles, J. Goodchild, T. Grandy, R. Harding, W. Hopkins, J. Kelly, J. McMullin, J. Mohan, M. Moore, T. Morrish, J. Newman, W. Oakley, T. Osborne, T. Parker, P. Quirk, J. Roxberry, J. Saunders, W. Seirs, J. Somersgill, J. Townend, C. Whitehead, T. Biddle, S. Bingham, J. Connelly, J. Dudley, J. Kenning, O. Loyd, T. List, J. Walker, F. Battlestone, J. Eginton, J. Elliott, S. English, H. Farner, C. Green, W. Gardner, T. Hanscombe, C. Lawrence, W. Pearson, T. Priest, W. Rampling, T. Robinson, T. Savage, J. Morton, J. Lake, T. Rostert, E. Shea, G. Smith, J. Tyers; Corp. J. Wilkes; Drum. E. Doughty; Privates T. Atkinson, J. Burton, J. McCullock, H. Meeds, J. Pratt, J. Terry, J. Tulley; Corp. H. Webb; Privates W. S. Duffan, J. Edwards, W. Francis, G. Harris, J. Hicks, W. Jervis, E. Johnson, T. Kelson, J. King, J. Pittman, D. Shea, C. Simson, J. Twigg, W. Smith, J. Welch, A. Whittell, W. Tobyn; Corp. F. Howell; Privates R. Edmonds, W. Ebeniely, J. Enright, J. Flinn, P. Flinn, G. Gibson, J. Hill, T. S. Hall, W. Hucker, B. John-

17

son, J. Lamb, J. Murphy, J. Overton, J. Patience, R. Pratt, J. Riddle, J. Shaw, W. Grover Simmonds, W. Thompson.

Died of Wounds.— Corp. W. Bugden; Privates J. Hawkins, J. Morris, J. Attwell.

Missing.—Privates G. Barrington, J. Barry, J. Bradbrook, G. Evans, E. Fry, C. Lancaster, W. H. Medlam, M. Whealan, R. Sandford, J. Wood, T. Chapple, W. Nevard, W. Nicols, J. Carrier, J. Clarke, W. Cross, B. Henry, F. Lang, R. Lang, E. Meade, J. Phillips, J. Sovatian, G. Worley, J. Bentley, M. Betson, T. Cleenen, P. Devaney, J. Killeen, P. Murphy, R. Smith, T. Cresswell, P. Managan, T. Murphy, A. Weldon, J. Hunter, T. Lancaster.

29th Regiment.

Killed.—Serg. P. Carey, R. Long; Privates T. Bunting, R. Beech, C. Buckley, J. Campbell, E. Cooney, P. Cotter, P. Dempsey, B. Dailey, J. Donovan, J. Darmon, H. Dawkins, J. Fidler, J. Farnol, E. Guest, J. Gostiler, W. Giles, M. Hopkins, J. Hussey, G. Haggitt, W. Jenkins, T. Marriott, D. McDermott, C. McGlaughlin, T. Mullin, J. Mayo, W. Naylor, W. Pratt, J. Shenton, J. Twamblay, J. Taylor, T. Walsh, J. Wildbore, S. Walker.

Died of Wounds.—Corp. G. Taylor; Privates A. Brown, G. Cathey, A. Dunn, R. Hodder, J. Hooper, M. Hadfield, T. Kennell, H. Souter, H. Smart.

Missing.—Privates T. Taylor, T. Vornem.

61st Regiment.

Killed.—Corp. G. Handlon; Privates W. Foster, J. Mason, R. Sherwood, T. Tuckwell, J. White, J. Humes, W. Jones, W. Gray, D. Tuckley, H. Johnson.

Died of Wounds.—Private E. Egan.

LORD GOUGH'S "FAREWELL."

General Order of the Commander-in-Chief.

Head-Quarters, Camp Skahdera, near Lahore.
March 31, 1849.

The Commander-in-Chief in India announces his farewell and adieu to the Army of the Punjaub.

The troops which, since October, have been in arms under his command, are dispersed to their respective cantonments, and on this, the last occasion of addressing them, Lord Gough desires to place on record his sense of the great services and exertions through which the sway of British India has been now extended over the broad plains and classic rivers and cities of this kingdom. The tide of conquest, which heretofore rolled on the Punjaub from the west, has at length reached and overcome it from the east; and that which Alexander attempted the British Indian army has accomplished. It is with no common pride that the Commander-in-Chief applauds the conduct and the valour which have led to so glorious a result.

The favour and approbation of the country and Government will, without doubt, mark enduringly the estimate entertained of its desert; and no time will efface from the memory of this army, and every true soldier in the field, the high sense of triumph and of the glory with which this campaign has terminated. Undismayed by stern opposition, untired by the procrastinations and delays which circumstances forcibly imposed, or by the great labours and exposure which have been borne so manfully, the army has emerged with a fame and a brightness only the more marked by the trying nature of its previous toils and endurances. The mere battle-day, when every glowing feeling of the soldier and gentleman is called into action, will ever be encountered nobly where British arms are engaged; but it is in the privations, the difficulties, and endless toils of war that the trial of an army consists; and it is these which denote its metal and show of what material it is formed.

Since the day when at Ramnugger the too hasty ardour and enthusiasm of the troops first gave signal of the determined character of the war, and of the fierceness with which a mistaken but brave enemy were bent to oppose the progress of our arms, till now that a crushing and overwhelming victory has prostrated at the feet of our ruler and his government an independent, a proud, and a warlike people, Lord Gough, relying upon British courage and endurance, has never for one moment entertained a doubt of the result, nor yielded, even to adverse chances and circumstances, a lurking fear of the successful issue, which true constancy and firmness never fail to attain. The rule which, despite the signal clemency and considerate mercy of the Government, it has nevertheless been found at length necessary to impose upon the Sikhs and their country, has not been thrust upon a defenceless or unresisting people; their valour, their numbers, their means, and preparation, and the desperate energy with which, in error and deceived, the Khalsa and Sikh nation mustered and rallied for the struggle, have been conspicuously apparent; and the army which, in virtue of a most persistive constancy, has reduced such a race and such troops to submission and obedience, merits well the highest eulogium which Lord Gough can bestow.

The Commander-in-Chief lingers upon the severance of those ties which may have bound him to that army, the last which in the field it was his duty and his pride to command. Long practice and experience of war and its trying vicissitudes have enabled him to form a just estimate of the conduct and merit of the troops now being dispersed; and the ardour, the vigilance, the endurance, the closing and triumphant bravery and discipline, which have marked their path in the Punjaub, will often recur to him in that retirement he is about to seek; and in which the cares, the earnest exertions, and grave anxieties inseparable from the duties of high military command, will be richly recompensed and rewarded by the sense of duty performed, and the consciousness of unwearied and uncompromising devotion to that sovereign and country which, in common with the British Indian army, it will ever be his boast and his pride to have so successfully served.

To every general, to every individual officer and soldier, European and native, of the army of the Punjaub, Lord Gough finally repeats his cordial and affectionate farewell. Their persons and services are engraven in his heart and affections; and to those among them who may hereafter, within the brief span of life yet before him, revisit their native country, he tenders the unaffected renewal of that intercourse and friendship which mutual esteem and regard, and mutual dangers and exertions, have produced and established.

(Signed) PAT. GRANT, Lieutenant-Colonel,
Adjutant-General of the Army.